H. G. WELLS AND THE MODERN NOVEL

Also by J. R. Hammond

A GEORGE ORWELL COMPANION
AN EDGAR ALLAN POE COMPANION
A ROBERT LOUIS STEVENSON COMPANION
AN H. G. WELLS COMPANION
H. G. WELLS: An Annotated Bibliography of his Works
H.G. WELLS: Interviews and Recollections (*editor*)
THE MAN WITH A NOSE AND OTHER UNCOLLECTED SHORT
STORIES OF H. G. WELLS (*editor*)

H. G. Wells and the Modern Novel

J. R. Hammond

St. Martin's Press   New York

First published in the United States of America in 1988

Printed in Hong Kong

ISBN 0–312–01627–1

Library of Congress Cataloging-in-Publication Data
Hammond, J. R. (John R.), 1933–
H.G. Wells and the modern novel / J. R. Hammond.
    p.   cm.
Bibliography: p.
Includes index.
ISBN 0–312–01627–1: / $35.00 (est.)
1. Wells, H. G. (Herbert George), 1866–1946—Criticism and
interpretation.   2. Modernism (Literature)   I. Title.
PR5777.H29 1988
823'.912—dc19   88–33
                                                                       C

For Jean, who made it possible

Contents

viii   *Contents*

Preface

David Lodge in *The Novelist at the Crossroads* observed that 'The centenary in 1966 of the birth of H. G. Wells found the literary and intellectual world still divided and perplexed as to how to assess his importance.' The years since then have seen the publication of a number of important critical, biographical and bibliographical studies resulting in a wider understanding of Wells's methods of working and his approach to the art of fiction. Despite these significant advances in Wells studies he remains an extraordinarily difficult writer to assess dispassionately and one about whom critical opinion is still deeply divided. The prevalent conception of him is of a writer who made a permanent mark on English literature through his contribution to science fiction and the short story but whose novels in the realist tradition are no longer relevant to the twentieth century.

The present study begins by questioning whether Wells was a novelist in the realist tradition at all. An introductory chapter giving an overview of his approach to fiction is followed by a reassessment of his debate with Henry James and an examination of his distinctive contribution to the modern novel. These chapters are followed by a close study of ten of his novels, beginning with his first full-length work of fiction, *The Time Machine*, and culminating in his last, *You Can't Be Too Careful*. The central thesis I hope to demonstrate is that Wells's work has far more in common with Kafka and Conrad than with Bennett and Galsworthy, and that he can properly be regarded as a transitional figure between realism and modernism.

In writing this book I have acquired many debts. My principal debt is to the members of the H. G. Wells Society for allowing me to share with them my discoveries about Wells and for the stimulus of many helpful discussions. I am particularly grateful to their Secretary, Mr Christopher Rolfe, who first drew my attention to the extensive use of mythological imagery in *The History of Mr Polly*. I am also indebted to Dr Patrick Parrinder of the University of Reading and Professor David Smith of the University of Maine who, by their untiring enthusiasm for Wells, have helped me in ways they may not fully appreciate.

I should like to make it clear that the interpretations of Wells's novels outlined in the following chapters are offered as possible readings without any sense of finality. His fiction is so rich in hermeneutic potential that it would be presumptuous to claim that any one reading could be definitive. I have tried throughout to bear in mind David Daiches's observation that literary criticism 'is not an end in itself, but a means to greater understanding and appreciation of literary works'. If this book encourages more readers to return to Wells's novels and to read them with heightened insight and enjoyment then my end will have been served.

J. R. H.

Author's Note

The text used for the extracts from the works of H. G. Wells is that of the first English edition in each case.

As the novels are available in a wide variety of editions quotations from his works are identified by chapter and section in each case, rather than page number.

Acknowledgements

The extracts from the works of H. G. Wells are reproduced by permission of the Literary Executors of the Estate of H. G. Wells and the following copyright holders:

Chatto and Windus and The Hogarth Press, for the extracts from *Apropos of Dolores*, *The Autocracy of Mr Parham*, *The Bulpington of Blup*, *The Food of the Gods*, *Marriage*, *Mr Blettsworthy on Rampole Island*, *Mr Britling Sees It Through*, *The Wife of Sir Isaac Harman*.

Faber and Faber Ltd and Little, Brown and Co., for the extracts from *Experiment in Autobiography* and *H. G. Wells in Love*.

A. P. Watt Ltd. for all other works by H. G. Wells.

The author and publishers wish to thank the following who have kindly given permission for the use of other copyright material:

George Allen and Unwin Publishers Ltd, for the extract from *Tristram Shandy* (Unwin Critical Library) by Max Byrd.

Basil Blackwell Ltd, for the extract from *The Social Context of Modern English Literature* by Malcolm Bradbury.

Century-Hutchinson Ltd, for the extract from *Editor: A Volume of Autobiography* by Kingsley Martin.

Chatto and Windus Ltd, for the extracts from *The Living Novel* by V. S. Pritchett and *The Long Revolution* by Raymond Williams.

William Collins, Sons and Co. Ltd, for the extract from *Four Portraits* by Peter Quennell.

Eyre and Spottiswoode (Publishers) Ltd, for the extract from *Principles and Persuasions* by Anthony West.

The Folio Society Ltd, for the extract from *A Survey of English Literature* by Gilbert Phelps.

Grafton Books, a division of the Collins Publishing Group, for the extract from *Henry James and H. G. Wells* by Leon Edel and Gordon N. Ray.

Harcourt Brace Jovanovich Inc., for the extract from *Theory of Literature* by Réne Wellek and Austin Warren.

Manchester University Press, for the extract from *The Early H. G. Wells* by Bernard Bergonzi.

Methuen and Co. Ltd, for the extract from *Games Authors Play* by Peter Hutchinson.

University of Nebraska Press, for the extract from *Anatomies of Egotism* by Robert Bloom.

Oliver and Boyd, for the extract from *Approaches to the Novel* by John Colmer.

Curtis Brown, London, for the extract from *Possibilities: Essays on the State of the Novel* by Malcolm Bradbury, © Malcolm Bradbury 1973.

Routledge and Kegan Paul Ltd, for the extract from *Language of Fiction* by David Lodge.

The Estate of the late Sonia Brownell Orwell and Secker and Warburg Ltd, for the extract from *Inside the Whale* by George Orwell.

Part One

Overview

1
Wells and the Novel

My conviction is that Wells the novelist, not merely Wells the scientific romancer, or Wells the prophet, or Wells the educator, or Wells the anti-utopian utopian, or Wells the thinker, or Wells the saviour, will have his day. If it be not now, yet it will come.

(Robert Bloom, *Anatomies of Egotism*)

Circumstances have made me think a good deal at different times about the business of writing novels, and what it means, and is, and may be; and I was a professional critic of novels long before I wrote them.

(H. G. Wells, *The Contemporary Novel*)

In his influential essay 'Technique as Discovery' Mark Schorer observes: 'as James grows for us . . . Wells disappears'.[1] This assessment is based on current critical attitudes towards Wells as a novelist. During his lifetime his novels enjoyed wide popularity but since his death, while his science fiction and short stories continue to be widely read, his reputation as a *novelist* has been almost totally eclipsed. He himself had no illusions concerning the transitory nature of his fame:

So far as I am concerned I find that thinking about the qualities of my work and my place in the literary world, or the world at large, an unwholesome and unprofitable employment. I have been keenly interested in the discussion of a number of questions, I have been a haphazard and pampered prophet, I have found it amusing and profitable to write stories and – save for an incidental lapse or so – I have never taken any very great pains about

3

writing. I am outside the hierarchy of conscious and deliberate writers altogether. I am the absolute antithesis of Mr James Joyce.[2]

This was written by H. G. Wells in 1930. By that time he had become a world figure, known and respected throughout the English-speaking community as a prophet, historian, educationalist and seer. As a novelist he had long ceased to command a world audience, his most ambitious effort in that direction – *The World of William Clissold* (1926) – having, in his own words, marked 'the collapse of an inflated reputation'. His heyday as a novelist had been during the years 1900–14 when, with *Kipps*, *Tono-Bungay*, *The History of Mr Polly*, *Ann Veronica* and *The New Machiavelli* he had fascinated and entertained an audience of millions. After the First World War there was no longer a world readership for his fiction. He was still very widely read – *The Outline of History* and *A Short History of the World* sold more than two million copies and were translated into many languages – but as a *novelist* his influence on the reading public had virtually evaporated. The commanding position he had once shared with Bennett and Galsworthy was now occupied by a new generation of literary idols – Joyce, Lawrence, Aldous Huxley and Virginia Woolf. At the end of his life he commented wryly that the novels he wrote in the 1930s did no more 'than make his decline and fall unmistakable'.[3]

Since his death there has been considerable critical interest in his science fiction and short stories but the prevailing attitude towards his novels is one of faint embarrassment. Today he is regarded as a somewhat old-fashioned figure, a writer who continued to repeat until well into the twentieth century the conventions and techniques of the Victorian realist tradition, a novelist who cannot be regarded as in any sense experimental and whose works are in a totally different category to those of Lawrence, Conrad and Joyce. Thus Bernard Bergonzi in his otherwise excellent study *The Early H. G. Wells* (Manchester University Press, 1961) states: 'I am assuming as axiomatic that the bulk of Wells's published output has lost whatever *literary* interest it might have had, and is not likely to regain it in the foreseeable future, whatever value it may possess for the social historian or the historian of ideas.' And Robert Barnard in his *A Short History of English Literature* (Basil Blackwell, 1984) writes disparagingly of Wells 'whose bouncy, punchy fiction in the realistic tradition has aged badly. With his incurable curiosity about life and his active social conscience he ought to be enjoyable still.' The thesis

I wish to argue in the present work is essentially twofold: first, that despite superficial indications to the contrary, his work has more affinity with the modernists than the realists – that is to say, he was much more consciously experimental in his work than is generally acknowledged and, secondly, that his novels are much more complex and diverse than a first reading would indicate. But first it will be useful to 'set the scene' by offering a concise summary of his novelistic career.

Wells graduated to writing novels after a long apprenticeship of producing short stories, essays and miscellaneous journalism. His first real breakthrough came in 1895, when he was 28, with the publication of *The Time Machine*. This was quickly followed by a series of 'scientific romances' including *The Invisible Man* (1897), *The War of the Worlds* (1898), *When the Sleeper Wakes* (1899), *The First Men in the Moon* (1901) and *The Food of the Gods* (1904). In these he made skilful use of the teeming possibilities of science to create a series of mythopoeic visions and speculations concerning man and his place in the universe. His first realistic novel – as distinct from the romance – was *The Wheels of Chance* (1896), a bicycling idyll notable for its evident nostalgia for the rural peace and beauty he had known as a young man. This was followed by a number of novels in which Wells discussed topical sociological themes – *Love and Mr Lewisham* (1900), *Kipps* (1905), *Tono-Bungay* (1909), *Ann Veronica* (1909) and *The New Machiavelli* (1911). These novels both fascinated and exasperated Henry James who, while admiring their abundant energy and craftsmanship, felt that they offended against his canons of artistry. 'You must at moments make dear old Dickens turn – for envy of the eye and the ear and the nose and the mouth of you – in his grave', he wrote, 'you are a very swagger performer indeed.'[4] Throughout this phase of his work Wells was still feeling his way as a literary artist, uncertain as yet of his direction or his true *métier*, deliberately trying over a range of styles and themes. Then followed a phase he described as the 'Prig Novels' – novels in which a solipsistic hero (usually the narrator) comments extensively on political, social and moral questions and in which the quest for a purpose in life is a predominant element. *Marriage* (1912), *The Passionate Friends* (1913), *The Wife of Sir Isaac Harman* (1914) and *The Research Magnificent* (1915) belong to this phase. They remain readable and interesting today, though inevitably with the passage of time the discussion of contemporary social problems has dated. The finest of this group is probably *Marriage*, if only because it is written with such evident care and because its central character, Marjorie Pope, is one of his most vital and convincing heroines. During the middle period of his life – the years from 1916 to 1930 – he experimented with a number of novels on topical issues of the day including *Mr Britling Sees It Through* (1916), *The Secret Places of the Heart* (1922), *Christina Alberta's Father* (1925) and *Meanwhile* (1927), stories which, *Mr Britling* excepted, did little to enhance his literary reputation and confirmed many critics in their judgement that he had severed himself from literature. In his final decade he embarked on a series of promising experiments – including *The Croquet Player* (1936), *Brynhild* (1937), *The Brothers* (1938) and *Apropos of Dolores* (1938) – in which he deployed allegory, satire and irony to ventilate his growing pessimism concerning the human condition and his continuing interest in problems of personality and character. He continued to write fiction until the end of his life, his last novels, *Babes in the Darkling Wood* (1940), *All Aboard for Ararat* (1940) and *You Can't Be Too Careful* (1941), revealing an abiding concern for humanity and a refreshing willingness – in a writer in his seventies – to experiment with new styles and themes. Critical opinion is sharply divided on the merits of the fiction of his final decade. To some it is simply additional evidence of his abdication of any major role in English literature and further proof of his steadily declining powers. To others the novels of his last period offer extraordinary riches of characterisation and insight and reveal a masterly writer completing 'the great imaginative work of a lifetime'.[5]

So much is familiar. What is not so familiar is the seriousness with which Wells himself regarded his novels. Despite his statement that 'I am outside the hierarchy of conscious and deliberate writers altogether' and the disingenuous aside in his autobiography that 'the larger part of my fiction was written lightly and with a certain haste',[6] the fact is that he regarded his novels with great seriousness and took immense pains over their writing. In a letter to his friend Arnold Bennett in 1901 (Bennett had published a study of popular novelists, *Fame and Fiction*, which omitted reference to Wells) he complained: 'For me you are part of the Great Public, I perceive. I am doomed to write "scientific" romances and short stories for you creatures of the mob, and my novels must be my private dissipation.' And to Frederick Macmillan in 1908 he wrote: 'As I told you long ago I want to specialise as a novelist. I think now my opportunity is ripe, and that if new novel follows novel without anything to distract people's attention – any other sort of work by me, I mean – it will be possible to consolidate the large confused reputation I have at the present time.' What distracted him from his laudable ambition to 'specialise as a novelist' was the First World War and the immense social, moral and intellectual ferment this engendered. But it is significant that during the last 30 years of his life when he was increasingly obsessed with the need for world unification and for fundamental changes in educational and political ideas he continued to write fiction, producing no fewer than 15 major novels between 1916 and 1946 in addition to novellas, sketches and short stories. The writing of fiction remained one of his primary concerns throughout his literary career and almost his last work, 'The Betterave Papers', was an ironic review of his literary achievement in which he looked back with whimsical detachment on his entire corpus as a novelist.

The evidence provided by his manuscripts and letters suggests that, far from having been written 'lightly and with a certain haste', his fiction was written and revised with great care. Much more is now known of his creative methods than was apparent during his lifetime. We know from the evidence of posthumously published works and from his correspondence with James, Gissing and Bennett that the writing of his novels involved a lengthy process of revision during which each work underwent a series of drafts until he was satisfied. In 1960, for example, a critical edition of *The History of Mr Polly* was published containing a reproduction of several pages of the original manuscript. In 1969 a hitherto unpublished novel, *The Wealth of Mr Waddy* (an early version of *Kipps*) was published in a scholarly edition containing much new material on Wells's methods of composition. From these and other sources it is abundantly clear that, whatever else he was, Wells was a painstaking and demanding artist who approached his work with thoroughness and care. Writing apropos *Love and Mr Lewisham* he observed: 'There is really more work in that book than there is in many a first class F. R. S. research, and stagnant days and desert journeys beyond describing.'[7] Wells's restlessness – his interest in a wide range of diverse subjects, his tendency to be working on several different projects at any one time, his ability to assume at will a style appropriate to the work in hand – has led to an assumption that he wrote hastily and with little attention to language or aesthetic considerations. It is becoming increasingly clear that this assumption is based on a superficial reading of his work and that the more closely his novels are studied the narrower the gap between

Wells and Joyce becomes. A number of recent studies have demonstrated convincingly that as a novelist Wells devoted the closest attention to language and imagery and that he is very far from being the careless writer he is so often held to be. Robert Bloom in *Anatomies of Egotism: A Reading of the Last Novels of H. G. Wells* (University of Nebraska Press, 1977) closely examines the novels of his final period and finds in them no diminution of his powers as a creative artist. David Lodge in *Language of Fiction* (Routledge and Kegan Paul, 1966) discusses in considerable detail the language of *Tono-Bungay* and concludes that it is a coherent and much underestimated work of art. Frank D. McConnell in *The Science Fiction of H. G. Wells* (Oxford University Press, 1981) examines the scientific romances and finds ample testimony to their literary and imaginative qualities. The evidence provided by Wells's own writings, then – including his manuscripts, drafts and letters – belies the view that his works were produced carelessly and suggests on the contrary that most were written with considerable (and in some cases meticulous) attention to language.

In the light of this testimony to his conscientiousness as a writer some explanation must be found for the widespread critical ambivalence towards Wells and for his perfunctory treatment in so many reference works on the English novel. There are, I suggest, four principal reasons which account for his comparative neglect in modern literary studies. First, he has been taken too readily on his own estimation, that is, his claim to be 'the absolute antithesis of Mr James Joyce' has been taken at face value. Second, his prolific work in other fields, what he termed in his letter to Macmillan his 'large confused reputation', has militated against his acceptance as a serious novelist. Third, the fact that he lived to be almost 80 and wrote some 50 full-length works of fiction has inevitably weakened his stature as a man of letters. In a word, he lived for too long and wrote too much to be retained readily in critical focus. Fourth, and most significantly, he is still widely regarded as a realistic novelist in the vein of Arnold Bennett, and as a writer whose novels have little relevance to the needs and concerns of the latter part of the twentieth century.

His own published estimation of his standing and attitudes has been accepted for many years as the definitive statement of his position. Because he insisted again and again that 'I had rather be called a journalist than an artist'[8] this has been taken to be a statement of the truth – instead of what it so patently was: a piece of exaggerated false modesty forced from him as a result of his quarrel with Henry James. When involved in an argument it is a natural human tendency to adopt an extreme position, to assume a defensive posture in the sharpest possible contrast to that adopted by one's opponent. Faced with James's claim that the novel had to conform to standards of excellence and purity as defined by himself, Wells felt he had no alternative but to assert the opposite view: that the novel could be whatever the author chose to make it, and that he (Wells) was making no claim that his own novels were fully harmonious works of art. Wells, then, has become a victim of his own protestations. Because he adopted as his critical stance the view that all art is essentially anarchic and discounted any claim that his fiction was of enduring literary merit this has come to be accepted as the received attitude to his work. By insisting that his fiction was of transitory interest ('I wave the striving immortals onward, and step aside') he unwittingly did himself a disservice, for whereas the novels of Joyce, Lawrence, Conrad and James have received sustained critical attention, only a small proportion of his own fiction has received serious study. During the past two decades his scientific romances have been the subject of increasing scholarly attention and there is now wide recognition of their literary and artistic importance. The same recognition has yet to be accorded to his *novels*.

A second reason why he has received comparatively little critical attention as a novelist is the fact that he diversified (some would say dissipated) his literary talents over so many different fields. He was not simply a novelist, nor was he content to express himself solely in the form of fiction. He was simultaneously a sociologist and prophet, in works such as *Anticipations, A Modern Utopia* and *The Shape of Things to Come*; a popular educator, in *The Outline of History* and *The Science of Life*; a prolific journalist and commentator on world affairs; and a world figure in his own right, a man who interviewed Lenin, Stalin and Roosevelt and who, at the height of his fame, commanded an audience of millions. Angus Ross in his article on Wells in the *Penguin Companion to Literature* writes: 'Wells's writings suffer from the restlessness which kept his astonishing talents from being completely and satisfactorily effective in any one direction.' Thus he is now paying the price for having been so immensely popular during his lifetime, for having diversified his skills over so many different areas of intellectual life. He *was* a novelist, certainly. But he was at the same time an educator, a popular historian, a writer on social problems, a pioneer of women's emancipation and a host of other things. It is precisely this diffusion of his talents which makes it so difficult to appraise him. Indeed, he was such a prolific writer and interested himself in so many aspects of human affairs that it is only now, 40 years after his death, that his achievement can be assessed dispassionately and the wheat separated from the chaff.

Wells is now paying the penalty for having written too much and too unevenly over a long period of time. His literary career spanned exactly half a century, 1895–1945, and throughout that time he poured out a seemingly endless flow of novels, short stories, romances, speculations, pamphlets and forecasts in addition to a very considerable amount of journalism (it has been estimated that he wrote at least 3000 unreprinted articles). Inevitably in such a vast body of work there are considerable variations in quality. Whereas at the height of his powers he was producing work of the calibre of *Tono-Bungay* and *The History of Mr Polly* he was also capable of writing mediocre novels such as *The Soul of a Bishop*, *The Wife of Sir Isaac Harman* and *The Secret Places of the Heart*. This very unevenness, coupled with the repetitive nature of some of the later fiction and journalism, has done grave damage to his literary reputation. His contemporaries Joyce and Conrad were content to write a comparatively small quantity of fiction of a consistently high standard. Wells was constitutionally incapable of this. Restless and mercurial by nature, he was always eager to be working on the next project, the next idea. New themes, ideas, plans and speculations poured from him in a never-ending flood – so much so that quite early in his career W. E. Henley warned him of the dangers of overproduction:

> You have a unique talent; and – you have produced three books, at least, within the year, and are up to the elbows in a fourth! It is magnificent, of course: but it can't be literature.[9]

Had he possessed the patience and determination to concentrate instead on producing a smaller number of novels of a more uniform standard his literary standing today would probably be considerably higher. *The Times Literary Supplement* said of Joyce: 'James Joyce was and remains almost unique among novelists in that he published nothing but masterpieces.' It is difficult to resist the conclusion that the gravest disservice Wells rendered to himself was in over-production: in the continual flow of novels, some magnificent, some indifferent, which poured from his pen.

But perhaps the most important single factor militating against his acceptance as a serious and relevant novelist is the dominance of the received view that he belongs firmly with the naturalist school. In the great divide in English literature between 'realists' and 'modernists' Wells is felt to belong wholly with the realists, that is, with the realistic tradition of the novel as exemplified by Dickens, George Eliot and Arnold Bennett. The tenacity with which this view is held is surprising in the light of the wealth of evidence to the contrary. Since 1960 a number of influential studies have demonstrated that his scientific romances and short stories are extraordinarily rich in imagery – religious, psychological, mythological – and that many are capable of an allegorical interpretation. Yet the view persists that *as a novelist* he was writing in a firmly established nineteenth-century mode and continued to do so until the day of his death. The dominant attitude to Wells is that his novels are to be read at face value: that they possess a surface meaning and no more. The detailed textual, linguistic and analytical study devoted to such works as *Ulysses*, *Sons and Lovers* and *To the Lighthouse* has bypassed Wells altogether. He is simply not regarded as a fruitful field for academic scrutiny.

It is true that some of his early novels – *The Wheels of Chance, Love and Mr Lewisham, Kipps* – bear many of the hallmarks of the realist tradition, but simultaneously with these he was writing *The Time Machine, The Sea Lady* and *The Food of the Gods*: works which are dense in imagery and rich in allegorical overtones. From the outset his work was consciously experimental in tone and method. Wells was 21 in 1887. The formative years of his life coincided with the breakup of the old order in science and philosophy and the beginnings of modern psychology and sociology. The years of his literary apprenticeship, 1886–95, saw the discovery of X-rays, the publication of the first works on psychoanalysis, the first English edition of Marx's *Capital*, the internal combustion engine, the first electric power station and the first telephone switchboard. T. H. Huxley's *Agnosticism* appeared in 1889 and Frazer's *Golden Bough* in 1890. The year of the publication of *The Time Machine*, 1895, also saw the invention of wireless telegraphy and the cinematograph and the first electrified main-line railway. A new spirit of innovation, enquiry and experiment was abroad. As Malcolm Bradbury has observed: 'The communal universe of reality and culture on which nineteenth century art had depended was over.'[10] The intellectual climate of uncertainty and questioning – it should not be forgotten that the debate stimulated by the publication of Darwin's theory of evolution was raging throughout Wells's childhood and adolescence – is reflected in changes in literature and the arts. The beginnings of Wells's literary career coincided with the publication of innovative works by Conrad, Strindberg and Chekhov and, in other arts, by Gauguin, Munch and Mahler.

It would be remarkable indeed if this spirit of experiment was not evident in Wells's own writings. His earliest significant essay 'The Rediscovery of the Unique' (1891) drew attention to the uniqueness of all things, that no two objects of the same class are exactly alike. He was quick to perceive that a recognition of this fact has implications in the field of morality:

> We may, however, point out that beings are unique, circumstances are unique, and that therefore we cannot think of regulating our conduct by wholesale dicta. A strict regard for truth compels us to add that principles are wholesale dicta: they are substitutes of more than doubtful value for an individual study of cases.[11]

Years later he described this paper as his 'first quarrel with the accepted logic' and throughout his life he adhered to the view that logical processes and language shared 'the profoundly provisional character, the character of irregular limitation and adaptation that pervades the whole physical and animal being of man'.[12] From the outset his writings reflect this sense of doubt and provisionality, a deep awareness of the future. In place of a confident faith in social advance his early novels and stories are notable for their profound pessimism, their troubled sense of a society in process of fragmentation, a world which is no longer solid. In *The Time Machine*, *The Invisible Man* and *The Island of Doctor Moreau* he questioned the complacent assumption that human evolution would inevitably lead to progress, and in such short stories as 'The Remarkable Case of Davidson's Eyes', 'The Plattner Story' and 'The Story of the Late Mr Elvesham' implicitly cast doubt on the validity of the accepted framework of reality. In place of belief in a 'knowable world wholly accessible to reasoned and rational enquiry'[13] – which one would surely expect to find if Wells was indeed a realist writer – we find the reverse: a novelist obsessed with the unconscious, with imagery of death and corruption, with themes of alienation and violence.

Ambiguity is his hallmark rather than assurance. In the preface to a collected edition of his short stories he observed: 'I would discover I was peering into remote and mysterious worlds ruled by an order logical indeed but other than our common sanity.'[14] This preoccupation with states of mind and experience 'other than our common sanity' is characteristic of his work. His novels and stories are *disturbing*, not only in the sense that they explore themes of alienation, apocalypse and decay but in their representation of inward states of consciousness. Edward Prendick, the narrator of *The Island of Doctor Moreau*, is obsessed by the sense that he is not a rational creature 'but only an animal tormented with some strange disorder in its brain, that sent it to wander alone, like a sheep stricken with the gid'. The stress on anxiety and isolation we associate with such authors as Kafka and Camus is also characteristic of Wells. Even in the works which are generally regarded as comedies, there is a significant element of violence and disorder. One thinks of the dismissal of Parsons and the battles with Uncle Jim in *Mr Polly*, the 'Battle of Crayminster' in *Bealby*, and the spirited destruction that occurs in *The War of the Worlds* and *The War in the Air*. The reader has an impression of a world which has run amok, a society at odds with itself. Many of the novels contain a discordant element, a character who introduces an effect of imbalance into the narrative and deflects the tidy progression of the plot. Montgomery in *The Island of Doctor Moreau*, Marvel in *The Invisible Man*, Chaffery in *Love and Mr Lewisham*, Ramage in *Ann Veronica*, The Tramp in *Bealby* – each acts as an irritant, a dislocating force which compels the reader to acknowledge man's irrationality.

As Wells developed self-confidence as a novelist he became increasingly aware of the flexibility of his medium and began to experiment more and more openly with the conventions and assumptions of the nineteenth-century realist tradition. Throughout his life he was fascinated by the relationship between fiction and reality. His scientific training under T. H. Huxley had convinced him of the provisional nature of all forms of life, and in his early speculations such as 'The Possible Individuality of Atoms' and 'Another Basis for Life' he questioned the solidity of accepted notions of the physical world. Since his central philosophical belief was to assert 'the necessary untrustworthiness of all reasoning processes arising out of the fallacy of classification'[15] his scepticism is inevitably reflected in his approach to the novel. On entering a Wells novel – even those which on the surface appear to be realistic – one is continually aware of a blurring of the distinction between the fiction one is reading and the world beyond the text. The opening sentence of his earliest 'realistic' novel, *The Wheels of Chance*, contains the name of a drapery emporium followed by the words 'a perfectly fictitious "Co.", by the bye'. This reminder that what the reader has before him is a *novel* destroys the illusion of reality: an illusion which the author is at pains to erode at several points in the story.

In an early novel, *The Wealth of Mr Waddy* (1898–9), there is an interesting example of his indebtedness to Sterne:

> Allusion has been made to a Mr. Kipps during the course of this story. He has flitted in a transitory way into quite a number of scenes. . . .
>
> The manifest intention of the author has been to arouse interest and curiosity in this person, to provoke the reader to ask, What the devil has Kipps to do with it? I don't see how Kipps comes in. Who *is* this Kipps? Dammy, here's Kipps again! and so forth. Now, manifestly while Mr Waddy trundles with a steadily accelerated velocity down that steep place upon the Leas, there comes a pause of awful expectation. And in that pause there can be nothing more fitting than two or three intercalary chapters about this same intrusive Kipps. That mystery disposed of, the time will be ripe for us to return and look for the surviving fragments (if any) of Mr Waddy. (ch. 7)

The jocularity of the style disguises the fact that he is deliberately toying with the reader, arousing expectations which may or may not be fulfilled. The passage calls to mind the scene in *Tristram Shandy* (One, XXI) when Sterne interrupts the narrative with a digression and then continues: 'But I forget my Uncle Toby, whom all this while we have left knocking the ashes out of his tobacco pipe.' Similar instances of toying with the reader are scattered throughout his work. In the opening chapter of *Tono-Bungay* the narrator, George Ponderevo, refers at numerous points to his father, arousing anticipations that his father is to be a significant character in the story. In fact the father plays no part in George's adventures: a deliberate mocking of narrative conventions which is an important element in Wells's overall design. George's failure to discover his roots strengthens the theme of alienation which underlies much of the novel's imagery.

Wells was also testing out approaches in structure and method. *The Invisible Man* and *The History of Mr Polly* both have an unusual structure which on first reading appears to fracture the narrative but on subsequent readings can be seen to contribute in a material way to the unfolding of the story. In *The War of the Worlds* (1898) he employs the device of two narrators: a technique Stevenson had previously used with great effectiveness in *Treasure Island*. In *A Modern Utopia* (1905) he achieves a hybrid which is neither a realistic novel nor a romance but a fusion of the two, 'a sort of shot-silk texture between philosophical discussion on the one hand and imaginative narrative on the other'.[16] In *The Dream* (1924) the story begins in the distant future but then becomes a realistic novel with interjections from the standpoint of a future age. In *The World of William Clissold* (1926), which is significantly subtitled 'A Novel at a New Angle', he was seeking to break new ground in the English novel by elaborating a full-scale mental autobiography. Arnold Bennett wrote to him: 'This is an *original* novel. My novels never are.'[17]

Throughout his life he was an experimental writer, regarding each new novel as a fresh departure and consciously experimenting with a range of styles, themes, techniques and approaches. Indeed the closer one studies Wells the more one is aware of a depth of complexity which deserves careful attention. As B. Ifor Evans observes in *A Short History of English Literature*: 'Uneven as he is, the danger is always to underestimate him.'

In her influential essays 'Modern Fiction' (1919) and 'Mr Bennett and Mrs Brown' (1924) Virginia Woolf criticised Bennett and Wells for being 'materialists' who were more interested in describing external details than the inner lives of their characters. By using the term 'materialist', she explained, she meant that 'they write of unimportant things; that they spend immense skill and immense industry making the trivial and the transitory appear the true and the enduring'. In bracketing Wells and Bennett together she was unwittingly rendering Wells a disservice, for in doing so she was perpetuating a misconception which is still very widely held. Bennett was an heir to the French realists: a classic example of a writer whose novels are windows on reality. Wells, by contrast, was a novelist whose work implicitly challenges realist conventions. It is precisely because his novels *are* self-conscious and pessimistic, that they reject the cohesive world view of the Victorians and focus increasingly on the inner lives of their characters that he can be regarded, like Conrad, as a transitional figure between realism and modernism.

In looking at Wells as a novelist one is continually struck by a number of factors which mark out his work from that of his contemporaries: his skill in creating narrators of a wide range (wider than is commonly supposed) and in exploring their inner consciousness; his fertility in deploying myths and imagery drawn from a wide range of English and classical literature; and his creative use of ambiguity as a leitmotif.

It is commonplace in Wells studies to assume a close identification between author and narrator – to assume, for example, that the 'I' in such novels as *Tono-Bungay*, *The Dream* and *The World of William Clissold* is Wells himself. It will be demonstrated in the following chapters that such an identification is too simplistic, that with few exceptions his narrators are consciously *invented* personalities with idiosyncracies and attitudes appropriate to their character.

In his essay 'The Question of Poe's Narrators' James W. Gargano states:

> It goes without saying that Poe, like other creative men, is sometimes at the mercy of his own worst qualities. Yet the contention that he is fundamentally a bad or tawdry stylist appears to me to be rather facile and sophistical. It is based, ultimately, on the untenable and often unanalysed assumption that Poe and his narrators are identical literary twins.[18]

The same criticism is frequently levelled against Wells. George Ponderevo, William Clissold, Richard Remington and Stephen Stratton are held to be reincarnations of Wells himself, mere mouthpieces for the exposition of his own views. Few critics have acknowledged that in fact many of his narrators are more complex than a first reading would suggest, that in many cases he is at pains to distance himself from the narrator's views and attitudes. An examination of such short stories as 'The Diamond Maker', 'Aepyornis Island', 'The Story of the Late Mr Elvesham' and 'The Sad Story of a Dramatic Critic' reveals his gift for creating narrators of wide diversity and his ability to make startling shifts in attitude, style and tone. The same is true of the novels. Frobisher in *The Croquet Player*, Arnold Blettsworthy in *Mr Blettsworthy on Rampole Island* and Rowland Palace in *Brynhild* are manifestly remote from Wells in their attitudes and beliefs yet he succeeds in reaching *inside* each persona to present a rounded and convincing portrait. In other instances – *Tono-Bungay, The New Machiavelli, The World of William Clissold* – there is clearly a closer sympathy between author and narrator, but even here Wells is careful to draw a distinction between the two. It cannot be overemphasised that these are *novels* – they are not fictionalised autobiographies – and even in those cases where there is a close parallel between his personal life and the events being described, each remains a novel: with all that that involves in terms of characterisation, plot and incident.

Wells has, in fact, been consistently underrated as a novelist of *character*. E. M. Forster, in his well-known essay on 'flat' and 'round' characters, states: 'With the possible exceptions of Kipps and the aunt in *Tono-Bungay*, all Wells's characters are as flat as a photograph. But the photographs are agitated with such vigour that we forget their complexities lie on the surface and would disappear if it was scratched or curled up.'[19] Forster here is surely guilty of an oversimplification. If one thinks, for example, of George Ponderevo in *Tono-Bungay*, of Ann Veronica, Marjorie Pope in *Marriage*, of Lewisham, of Tewler in *You Can't Be Too Careful*, one is struck by their verisimilitude: each is an individuality, deliberately distanced from the author; each has solidity and depth.

An example illustrates the point. In the third chapter of *Love and Mr Lewisham* there is an illuminating reference to an aspect of Lewisham's personality:

> In those days much of Lewisham's mind was still an unknown land to him. He believed among other things that he was always the same consistent intelligent human being, whereas under certain stimuli he became no longer reasonable and disciplined but a purely imaginative and emotional person.

What is interesting about the passage is its twofold admission: first, that his mind was an unknown land *to himself*; and, second, that under certain stimuli he ceased to be a rational and ordered being and became instead an undisciplined personality swayed by emotion and imagination. The remainder of the novel is wholly consistent with this diagnosis. As the story unfolds and more and more facets of Lewisham's character become clear to the reader it is increasingly evident that he is very far from being 'as flat as a photograph'. His character is in fact a complex of emotions, drives and impulses – not always clear either to himself or his wife – and it *changes* as the novel proceeds: under the impact of time, stress, responsibility, circumstance. Lewisham at the end of the novel is a different person from the Lewisham of the opening chapters; he has different aspirations, different drives, different responses. He is not a *static* character. A similar process can be seen to be at work in the case of Arthur Kipps, Alfred Polly and George Ponderevo. Nor is this only true of the earlier novels. A careful reading of the later fiction – including *The Bulpington of Blup*, *Brynhild*, *Apropos of Dolores* and *You Can't Be Too Careful* – provides numerous instances of skilful characterisation. Theodore Bulpington, the central character of *The Bulpington of Blup*, is an extremely interesting example of Wells's ability to create a wholly credible personality completely alien in attitudes and temperament to himself. And even the lesser novels are not without interest from this perspective. Lady Charlotte Sydenham in *Joan and Peter* is an instance of his gift for creating a rounded, convincing character from the most unpromising material.

An aspect of Wells which is almost completely overlooked in modern academic criticism is his facility in making use of patterns, images and allusions drawn from an immense range of literature. In this tendency to enrich his novels with literary allusions and mythological imagery he almost rivals Joyce.

It is, of course, entirely possible for a writer to incorporate literary references in his work but to do so quite unconsciously. In Wells's case the tendency was undoubtedly deliberate, for he was aware from the outset of his indebtedness to the literature of an earlier age. In the preface to a collected edition of his scientific romances he wrote:

> These tales have been compared with the work of Jules Verne and there was a disposition on the part of literary journalists at one time to call me the English Jules Verne. . . . But these stories of mine collected here . . . are exercises of the imagination in a quite different field. They belong to a class of writing which includes the *Golden Ass* of Apuleius, the *True Histories* of Lucian, *Peter Schlemil* and the story of *Frankenstein*.[20]

As will be seen from the present study his works are extraordinarily rich in references to English, European and classical literature. This is evident not simply in the surface trappings of the novels – *The First Men in the Moon*, for example, bears on its title page a quotation from Lucian's *Icaromenippus*, the title page of *The War of the Worlds* carries a quotation by Kepler, *In the Days of the Comet* is prefaced by some lines from Shelley's *Hellas* – but in his predilection for modelling his works on earlier literary forms. Thus, *The Island of Doctor Moreau* clearly derives from Swift's *Gulliver's Travels*, *A Modern Utopia* is modelled on Plato's *Republic*, *Boon* on Mallock's *The New Republic*, *The Undying Fire* on the Book of Job, *Mr Blettsworthy on Rampole Island* on Voltaire's *Candide* and *The Anatomy of Frustration* on Burton's *Anatomy of Melancholy*. In using these earlier works as his models he does not simply emulate them but translates them into terms which are relevant to the twentieth century. In doing so he is consciously rendering in contemporary form a long-established literary tradition:

> The dialogue, written or staged, is one of the oldest forms of literary expression. Very early, men realised the impossibility of abstracting any philosophy of human behaviour from actual observable flesh and blood. . . . The Socratic Dialogue on the other hand produces character after character to state living views, to have them ransacked by an interlocutor who is also a character, subject to all the infirmities of the flesh.[21]

He is, then, an interesting example of a writer who is at once derivative in the sense that he makes extensive use of mythological and literary imagery, and experimental in the sense that he sought to widen the scope of the novel and enlarge its frame of reference.

His imagery ranges from Frazer's *Golden Bough* to Greek mythology, from the archetypes of Jungian psychology to the symbolism of primitive religion. Moreover it is evident in many aspects of his work, ranging from the use of principal leitmotifs in the novels and short stories – fire, water, drowning, dreams, gardens, caverns and so on – to such incidental details as the choice of surnames and names of locations. Thus, 'Montgomery', the name of Moreau's drunken, maudlin assistant in *The Island of Doctor Moreau* is a direct reference to the central character of *The Wide, Wide World*, a sentimental novel much loved by Wells's mother, Mrs Sarah Wells. The contrast between the emotional piety of the heroine and the dissolute weakness of Moreau's assistant could not be more marked and is the kind of literary pun which would have appealed irresistibly to Wells. His deliberate choice of the name is a further indication that he intended the story to be a satirical fantasia on religious and moral themes. In *Star Begotten* he names his central characters, the parents of a forthcoming child, Joseph and Mary Davis – a clear reference to Joseph and Mary in the story of the nativity. Job Huss in *The Undying Fire* is a modern rendering of Job of Uz in the Book of Job, while Dr Elihu Barrack in the same novel acts out the earlier role of Elihu the son of Barachel. And it can surely be no accident that the central figure in *The Invisible Man* is called 'Griffin', a peculiarly apposite name in each of its meanings: an imaginary creature, neither animal nor bird, and therefore an outcast from its kind; a newcomer; and a warning or portent. Numerous instances of this nature can be found in the novels, romances and short stories, showing that – contrary to the impression given in some modern criticism – his stories are usually prepared with care and that the names of the characters, including the minor ones, frequently bear a satirical or literary connotation. The names Wells chooses for his characters, then, serve to underpin his design and strengthen the web of didacticism and allegory which are so characteristic of his work.

The abiding impression of Wells's fiction is of its ambivalence. From *The Time Machine* to *You Can't Be Too Careful* it would be difficult to name any of his novels which ends on a note of resolution. The characteristic ending of a Wells novel is of a questioning, a deliberate ambiguity that is at once stimulating and disturbing. To compare the final paragraph of a novel by Austen, Trollope or Bennett with the ending of almost any Wells novel is to appreciate the contrast between realist fiction and what might be termed the novel of indeterminacy. It is rare in Wells's fiction to find a neat tidying up of loose ends. It is much more common to find an ending on a note of uncertainty or irresolution: Hoopdriver 'vanishes from our ken', George Ponderevo cleaves through the sea in a destroyer, Mr Polly ceases to admire the sunset and announces 'we can't sit here forever'. There is an apparent reluctance by the author to arrive at a point of fixity. In the place of a symmetrical conclusion one is left in a state of flux.

Consider, for example, the concluding sentences of *The New Machiavelli*. The closing paragraphs describe Remington and his mistress, Isabel Rivers, departing from London *en route* for exile in Italy. They are seated in a railway carriage, each lost in their own thoughts:

For a time I stared at her and was motionless, in a sort of still and weary amazement. Why had we done this injury to one another? Why? Then something stirred within me.

'Isabel!' I whispered.

She made no sign.

'Isabel!' I repeated, and then crossed over to her and crept closely to her, put my arm about her, and drew her wet cheek to mine.

This is by no means the conventional ending of a romantic novel. Remington does not know what Isabel is thinking. He only knows that she is silent and crying. What are her feelings? Is she glad at the prospect of exile from England or is she overwhelmed with regret at the destruction of his political career? He asks himself 'why had we done this injury to one another' and then repeats the question. When he speaks to her she makes no response: *She made no sign*. To the end we are left in doubt as to Isabel's thoughts and intentions.

Or consider the final paragraph of an apparently orthodox realistic novel, *Kipps*:

He still rested on his oars.

'I expect,' he said, 'I was thinking jest what a Rum Go everything is. I expect it was something like that.'

'Queer old Artie!'

'Ain't I? I don't suppose there ever was a chap quite like me before.'

He reflected for just another minute.

'Oo! – I dunno,' he said at last, and roused himself to pull.

To 'rest on one's oars' is to take things easily, to cease working. The question at issue here is whether Kipps can make a success of his new life with Ann. The wider question is whether he is exceptional in his attitudes and aspirations or typical of his time and background. Both questions remain unresolved. Kipps's final action, he 'roused himself to pull', brings his unspoken reflections to an end but leaves the conclusion indeterminate. For Kipps there can be no final solution, no tidy reconciliation of the tensions within his personality. For him, as for Ann, the riddle of life remains an enigma. Both are driven by forces beyond their comprehension and the novel terminates with the enigma unsolved: there is, as it were, a still photograph of the two caught in a moment of reflection.

Similar instances of ambiguity occur with surprising frequency in his fiction. An interesting example is the conclusion of *Mr Britling Sees it Through*, a novel describing the reaction of a representative Englishman to the First World War. Mr Britling has been writing in his study until dawn. He gets up from his desk and stands motionless at the window watching the sunrise:

> Wave after wave of warmth and light came sweeping before the sunrise across the world of Matching's Easy. It was as if there was nothing but morning and sunrise in the world.

> From away towards the church came the sound of some early worker whetting a scythe.

The scythe is a patently ambiguous image. It is a well-known symbol of death, shaped like the waning moon before extinction. Father Time is invariably depicted holding a scythe. On the other hand it is open to an opposite interpretation: that of life and renewal. The scythe is used to mow the old growth in order to make way for the new. It is open to argument which of these interpretations is intended here. Are we to infer that the war represents a new beginning, or is it on the contrary a harbinger of extinction? The drift of Wells's final chapter tends to the former, but the element of doubt remains.

On examination it can be seen that a number of his novels conclude with an ambiguous image – the scythe in *Mr Britling*, the destroyer in *Tono-Bungay*, the withered flower in *The Time Machine*, the fire in *The Wonderful Visit*. This deliberate ambivalence, a seeming reluctance to reach a point of finality, is characteristic of Wells's fiction. It stems from his attitude of mind and his refusal to admit that the world of physical reality is final and definite:

> I find most of the world that other people describe or take for granted much more hard and clear and definite than mine is. I am at once vaguer and more acutely critical. I don't believe so fully and unquestioningly in this 'common-sense' world in which we meet and exchange ideas, this world of fact, as most people seem to do. I have a feeling that this common-sense world is not *final*.[22]

This view of reality is crucial to an understanding of his approach to the novel. Because he rejected the realist world-view – the notion that the tangible world possesses a unifying logic – and because an awareness of man's provisional nature was central to his philosophy, his approach to literature and to all forms of art was inherently experimental. There could be no finality about man; man was 'finite and not final, a being of compromises and adaptations'.[23] It followed that all philosophy was provisional and tentative, all political thought, all psychology. The novel could be no more subject to rules and conventions than any other form of creative achievement. It must be provisional, an artefact to be perpetually renewed and reshaped. His sense of man's plasticity led him to write novel after novel in which a relatively stable environment is fractured by the introduction of a catalyst – the angel in *The Wonderful Visit*, Griffin in *The Invisible Man*, Chitterlow in *Kipps*, Trafford in *Marriage*. The arrival of this catalyst sets in motion a process akin to a chemical reaction in a laboratory experiment, with the characters reacting on one another in response to the disturbing agent. The process is analogous to the dropping of a stone into a tranquil pool. Each of the novels ends with the action still in a state of motion, while the water is in a state of agitation.

It is clear, then, that on balance Wells's fiction has more in common with that of Conrad and the twentieth-century modernists than is commonly acknowledged. It shares with their work an emphasis on flux rather than stasis, discursiveness rather than cohesion. As we shall see in the chapters that follow, it shares with them a richness of symbolism, imagery and metaphor and a relationship between author and text which is frequently more complex than appears on first reading. Above all, when studying Wells one is increasingly conscious of an oblique relationship between reader and narrator: the meaning does not reside only in the surface text but behind it. It is this which distinguishes his work most sharply from that of Bennett and Galsworthy.

The central question to which this study addresses itself is this: to what extent can Wells be considered a modernist writer? Or, to put the question in a different way, in what ways do his novels depart from the conventions and assumptions of realist fiction? These questions are implicit throughout. To answer them we need to clear the ground, first by examining the nature of his quarrel with Henry James and then by defining his distinctive contribution to the modern novel.

2

The Great Debate

The important point which I tried to argue with Henry James was that the novel of completely consistent characterisation arranged beautifully in a story and painted deep and round and solid, no more exhausts the possibilities of the novel than the art of Velasquez exhausts the possibilities of the painted picture.

(H. G. Wells, *Experiment in Autobiography*)

There is a peculiar agony in the paradox that truth has two forms, each of them indisputable, yet each antagonistic to the other.

(Edmund Gosse, *Father and Son*)

The debate between H. G. Wells and Henry James over the nature and purpose of fiction constitutes one of the most famous literary quarrels of the twentieth century. The quarrel has done immense harm to Wells's reputation, partly because James is widely assumed to have been the victor, and partly because in the course of the debate Wells was stung into making a series of disingenuous statements about his approach to art in order to distance himself from what he regarded as James's excessive pedantry. Yet the debate was much more than a personal dispute between two novelists. Underlying their argument was a polarisation of widely differing critical approaches to the novel and a profound divergence of attitudes to life and conduct.

Wells had hammered out his critical approach to fiction during a long and arduous literary apprenticeship extending over eight years (1887–94) and during his tenure as fiction critic for the *Saturday Review*. He was literary critic for the *Review*, then edited by Frank Harris, from March 1895 to April 1897 and during that time contributed some 92 essays containing 285 book reviews. These ranged from appraisals of potboilers by unknown novelists to reviews of works by Conrad, Hardy, Stevenson and Meredith.[24] His criticism for the *Saturday Review* coincided with a period of crucial importance in his own literary career, for this period saw the writing of *The Island of Doctor Moreau* and *The Wheels of Chance* and the beginning of work on *Love and Mr Lewisham*. Throughout this period he was gaining valuable experience in the expression of ideas and shaping his attitudes to life and art. Again and again when reading his book reviews one is struck by the prescience with which he singles out for praise the early Conrad, for example – his judicious review of *An Outcast of the Islands* is a skilful summary of Conrad's strengths and weaknesses as a novelist – and the perceptiveness of his appreciation of Stephen Crane and George Gissing, novelists who had at that time received little recognition. Praising writers as diverse as Bret Harte, Conan Doyle, Poe, Turgenev and Tolstoy he reveals the catholicity of his tastes in literature and his impatience with vacuous romanticism on the one hand and pretentious aestheticism on the other. The overriding impression one receives from a perusal of his literary criticism is of an unstinting admiration for craftsmanship and a lively appreciation of those novelists who succeed in illuminating aspects of life and behaviour. Literature, he argues, is 'the only possible countervailing force' to the inertia generated by the prevailing social order.[25] What is crucial to an understanding of his debate with James is that the most important formative influences upon him during these years – the years in which he was working out his fundamental attitudes to the practice and theory of fiction – were such discursive writers as Dickens, Sterne, Swift and Balzac. The whole thrust of his reading and appreciation was veering him away from restraint and classicism and towards the utmost freedom to experiment and digress.

His earliest sustained attempt to define his critical position appeared in the *Saturday Review* of 11 July 1896 under the title 'Certain Critical Opinions'. The immediate cause of Wells's essay was a review by Andrew Lang of Stevenson's *Weir of Hermiston* in which Lang had cavilled at another reviewer's alleged ignorance of Scottish dialect. Wells takes Lang to task for his obsession with the minutiae of philology and then widens his attack to embrace a critique of 'the peculiar standpoint of the Academic school':

> Put crudely, the system of this criticism is as follows: the entire works, good and bad together, of a series of men now dead are adopted as a canon of excellence in each department of literature; these works are studied philologically, passages of peculiar merit

are learnt by rote for purposes of allusion and quotation, the dates of publication, the private life of the author, any amusing anecdotes concerning him, and textual developments in successive editions, are 'got up' as if for examination purposes; and so the critic attains his 'pretensions to literature'.

Wells devotes the greater part of his essay to an attack on this school of criticism with its emphasis on academic pedantry and reference to supposed canons of excellence in the works of a select coterie of classical authors. In contrast to this, he maintains, the task of the critic is 'to appreciate essentials, to understand the bearing of structural expedients upon design, to get at an author through his workmanship, to analyse a work as though it stood alone in the world'. The significance of this essay lies in the fact that long before his encounter with Henry James, indeed before the two had met, the main outlines of their subsequent dispute are clearly apparent. Wells's dislike of pernicketiness, his refusal to concede the existence of absolute standards, his insistence that each novel was a unique work of art, are abundantly evident. Most telling of all is the final paragraph in which he draws attention to 'the perpetual conflict between pedant and maker, between past and future . . . of the intellectual world'. In identifying himself with all that is creative and forward-looking in contemporary criticism, by contrast with the sterile formality of academic scholarship, he foreshadows in unmistakeable terms the battle lines of his dispute with James.

Wells and James met in 1898 and began corresponding in the same year. Wells was then 32, a promising young writer who had produced a number of striking novels and romances and some engaging volumes of short stories. James was 55, the author of *Washington Square* and *The Portrait of a Lady* and already a famous, if perhaps not widely read, novelist. James had recently moved from London to Rye in Sussex and Wells was about to move to Sandgate in Kent, within cycling distance of Rye and, as he put it, 'in close conversational proximity to Henry James, Joseph Conrad and Mr Ford Madox [Ford]'.[26]

For some years their correspondence was genial and urbane. The two men commented favourably on one another's books, arranged meetings when they could continue their earnest literary discussions and engaged in polite badinage on the work of their contemporaries. For the first decade or so of their friendship James's attitude to Wells's work was that of a master heaping encouragement on the work of a promising pupil. Thus, *The Time Machine* was hailed as a 'masterpiece', *Tales of Space and Time* filled him 'with wonder and admiration', *Love and Mr Lewisham* was 'a bloody little chunk of life, of no small substance', *Kipps* was 'not so much a masterpiece as a mere born gem'. Mingled with this praise, however, was a note of reservation which became increasingly evident as the friendship proceeded. Having praised *The Time Machine*, for example, James added:

> I am beastly critical – but you are in a still higher degree wonderful. I rewrite you, much, as I read – which is the highest tribute my damned impertinence can pay an author.

And of *The First Men in the Moon* he wrote:

> It is only that my sole and single way of perusing the fiction of Another is to *write it over* – even when most immortal – as I go. Write it over, I mean, *re*-compose it, in the light of my own high sense of propriety and with immense refinements and embellishments.

James clearly felt that Wells was a gifted writer of great originality and potential but regarded it as his duty, as an older and more experienced novelist, to point out weaknesses in his style and approach. In their frequent meetings at Rye and Sandgate they continued their weighty discussions on each other's works and on literary topics of the day, James excessively polite and formal but always a fascinating talker, Wells respectful and eager, 'an inexhaustible source of ideas, of exposition, of wit and laughter'.[27] Their correspondence, copious as it is, is merely a footnote to their many conversations. Something of the flavour of these discussions can be derived from the conversations between the literary friends in *Boon*. In writing these chapters Wells reveals his profound intellectual and emotional antipathy to James and yet simultaneously displays his exasperated fascination with him. It is no accident that in his autobiography he records that throughout their quarrel he had 'a queer feeling that we were both incompatibly right'.[28]

With the publication of *The New Machiavelli* in January 1911 a new note becomes evident in their correspondence. For the first time James abandons his previously adopted tone of judicious appraisal and launches into a candid critique of Wells's methods:

I seem to feel that there can be no better proof of your great gift –
The N. M. makes me most particularly feel it – than that you
bedevil and coerce to the extent you do such a reader and victim as
I am; I mean one so engaged on the side of ways and attempts to
which yours are extremely alien and for whom the great interest
of the art we practice involves a lot of considerations and
preoccupations over which you more and more ride roughshod
and triumphant – when you don't, that is, with a strange and
brilliant impunity of your own, leave them to one side altogether
(which *is* indeed what you now apparently incline most to do.)

In this letter (dated 3 March 1911) can be discerned James's hesitant
attempt to express his profound disagreement with Wells's approach
to the art of fiction and his sense of the wide gulf of understanding
separating him from his younger rival. The trouble with Wells's
novels, he complains, is 'that you bedevil and coerce to the extent
you do'. He then goes on to describe himself as one who is 'engaged
on the side of ways and attempts to which yours are extremely alien
and for whom the great interest of the art we practice involves a lot
of considerations and preoccupations over which you more and
more ride roughshod and triumphant'. This was candour indeed.
Wells replied courteously but James's strictures must have rankled
deeply. *The New Machiavelli* was a novel on which he had toiled
conscientiously over a long period and which he regarded as a
companion volume to *Tono-Bungay*. Though undoubtedly uneven
it contains some of his finest work, particularly in the opening
chapters with their unforgettable description of his mother and
father and his childhood home. Significantly there is a remarkable
passage (One, 2, 5) which summarises the history of Bromstead
(Bromley, Wells's birthplace) between the years 1750–1900. The
description of the impact of social change on this little community –
the immense upheavals caused by the arrival of the railway and
mechanical power – and the accompanying disorder and confusion,
had its parallel in the changes taking place in fiction. Wells was
deeply conscious of the shifts in political thought, in morality, in
sociology and psychology, and felt strongly that the novel must take
account of these by permitting frank discussion of behaviour. In his
view it was the duty of the novelist to explore the mental and
emotional lives of his characters and to do so by presenting a range
of situations in which problems of human conduct could be
explored.

Throughout his life Wells never departed from the view that the novel was an instrument for the discussion of *conduct*, for the discussion of human problems. In his essay 'The Contemporary Novel', originally prepared in 1911 under the title 'The Scope of the Novel', he sets out his position in unmistakeable terms:

> You see now the scope of the claim I am making for the novel; it is to be the social mediator, the vehicle of understanding, the instrument of self-examination, the parade of morals and the exchange of manners, the factory of customs, the criticism of laws and institutions and of social dogmas and ideas. It is to be the home confessional, the initiator of knowledge, the seed of fruitful self-questioning. Let me be very clear here. I do not mean for a moment that the novelist is going to set up as a teacher, as a sort of priest with a pen, who will make men and women believe and do this and that. The novel is not a new sort of pulpit; humanity is passing out of the phase when men *sit under* preachers and dogmatic influences. But the novelist is going to be the most potent of artists, because he is going to present conduct, devise beautiful conduct, discuss conduct, analyse conduct, suggest conduct, illuminate it through and through. He will not teach, but discuss, point out, plead, and display.[29]

The novel, as Wells sees it, is to be a vehicle for 'the criticism of laws and institutions and social dogmas and ideas'. It is sometimes argued that this was a characteristic of the later Wells – the Wells who was writing after 1914 – but that the early Wells possesses no such didactic element. This is not so. The didactic intention was there from the beginning. Geoffrey West in his *H. G. Wells: A Sketch for a Portrait* observes:

> But he protested strongly against the inclination to see in (say) *Dr Moreau* only a 'festival of horrors'. Each of his books pointed a moral: *The Time Machine* was meant to suggest 'the responsibility of men to mankind'; *The Wonderful Visit* 'the littleness, the narrow horizon, of people's ordinary lives by bringing into sharp contrast with typical characters a being who is free from the ordinary human limitations'; *Dr Moreau* pointed to 'the bestial aspect of human life', while Graham, the sleeper, symbolized a humanitarianism which seemed to Wells to have been falling into an ever deeper slumber from the 'sixties to the 'nineties. *The Invisible Man*

and *The War of the Worlds* illustrated the dangers of power without moral control, the development of the intelligence at the expense of human sympathy.[30]

What Wells sought to achieve in his novels was a discussion of *ideas*, a discussion of the problems of human conduct, of the forces which had moulded the society of his time. In this he was profoundly influenced by Dickens. His admiration for Dickens and for the literary tradition he embodied found expression in his own novels – novels in which he criticised the institutions and conventions of his day. In *The Island of Doctor Moreau, Mr Blettsworthy on Rampole Island* and many others he satirised the prevailing social, political and religious ideologies and did so with biting wit and invective. In doing so he wanted to discuss the whole range of human life and behaviour, to discuss 'those deeply passionate needs and distresses from which half the storms of human life are brewed'.[31] It was this refusal to omit problems of human conduct which divided Wells most sharply from Henry James and Virginia Woolf.

Praising 'the lax freedom of form, the rambling discursiveness, the right to roam, of the earlier English novel, of *Tristram Shandy* and of *Tom Jones*', Wells goes on to draw a distinction between two types of novel:

> It is no new discovery that the novel, like the drama, is a powerful instrument of moral suggestion. But excepting Fielding and one or two other of those partial exceptions that always occur in the case of critical generalisations, there is a definable difference between the novel of the past and what I may call the modern novel. It is a difference that is reflected upon the novel from a difference in the general way of thinking. It lies in the fact that formerly there was a feeling of certitude about moral values and standards of conduct that is altogether absent today.

Throughout the years in which he knew James he was testing out these problems of conduct in a series of novels posing fundamental questions of morality and behaviour. What James objected to in these novels was Wells's use of the first person narrator – this he described as 'that accurst autobiographic form which puts a premium on the loose, the improvised, the cheap and the easy'[32] – and the consequent lack of detachment, the 'chemical transmutation for the aesthetic', which he regarded as an indispensable part of the novelist's craft. James held that for this reason *David Copperfield*, *Jane Eyre*, *Kidnapped* and *Robinson Crusoe* could not be regarded as novels because they lacked detachment, because 'the great stewpot or crucible of the imagination' had not played its part. Wells seems to have taken the criticism to heart, for he replied 'The only artistic "first-person" is the onlooker speculative "first-person", and God helping me, this shall be the last of my gushing Hari-Karis.' After *The Passionate Friends* he abandoned the first person method of narration for some years – he did not return to it until *The World of William Clissold* in 1926 – and the 'onlooker speculative first-person' is precisely the method he chose to adopt in *The Wife of Sir Isaac Harman* (1914). He might have replied, however, as with George Ponderevo, that 'I must sprawl and flounder, comment and theorise, if I am to get the thing out I have in mind', and that it was only through the device of the autobiographical narrator that he could fully express himself as prophet and critic. He was deeply conscious that the novels for which he had the greatest admiration, and which were the most powerful 'instruments of moral suggestion' – the works of Defoe, Fielding and Dickens – were precisely those which contained a strong autobiographical element and in which the novelist's freedom to comment and digress was integral to their achievement.

In March 1912 Wells was invited to become a member of the Academic Committee of the Royal Society of Literature. The Academic Committee at this time included – in addition to James – Conrad, Barrie, Galsworthy, Hardy and Shaw. When the invitation was conveyed to him by Edmund Gosse, Wells not surprisingly declined. Given his attitude to any suggestion of standards or objective criteria by which literature could be judged his refusal was perhaps inevitable. On hearing from Gosse of Wells's refusal, James wrote an eloquent letter pleading with him to change his mind. The Committee 'would be so fortified by your accession', he wrote, 'that a due consideration for the prestige of current English letters surely ought to move you'. Wells replied with characteristic truculence:

> I have an insurmountable objection to Literary or Artistic Academies as such, to any hierarchies, any suggestion of controls or fixed standards in these things. I feel it so strongly that indeed I would rather be outside the Academic Committee with Hall Caine, than in it with you and Gosse and Gilbert Murray and

Shaw. This world of ours, I mean the world of creative and representative work we do, is I am convinced best anarchic. (25 March 1912)

Reluctant to concede defeat James renewed his appeal, begging him 'for the general amenity and civility and unimportance of the thing' to give the Academic Committee the benefit of the doubt. Wells, however, remained immovable and went so far as to buttonhole James at his club the following day to let the Master see how implacable he was. Sensing that further remonstration would be useless James wrote to Gosse: 'He has cut loose from literature clearly – practically altogether; he will still do a lot of writing probably – but it won't be *that*.'

Despite this apparent breach in their relationship – a breach which Wells himself described as his 'disobedience' – the two continued to be good friends and resumed their debate with the publication of *Marriage* in September 1912. James responded to *Marriage* with a letter of ponderous complexity which reads almost like a parody of 'The Spoils of Mr Blandish' in *Boon*:

> Meanwhile if I've been deprived of you on one plane I've been living with you very hard on another; you may not have forgotten that you kindly sent me 'Marriage' (as you always so kindly render me that valued service;) which I've been able to give myself to at my less afflicted and ravaged hours. I have read you, as I always read you, and as I read no one else, with a complete abdication of all those 'principles of criticism,' canons of form, preconceptions of felicity, references to the idea of method or the sacred laws of composition, which I roam, which I totter, through the pages of others attended in some dim degree by the fond yet feeble theory of, but which I shake off, as I advance under your spell, with the most cynical inconsistency.   (18 October 1912)

Despite its superficial politeness it is apparent that James is being even more brutally candid than in his lecture on *The New Machiavelli*. To admit that the only way in which he can read a Wells novel is to abandon all his critical principles is tantamount to saying that Wells's novels are formless, that they cannot be regarded as works of art. His use of the phrase 'the sacred laws of composition' encapsulates all that divided the two men: Wells consistently declined to acknowledge the existence of such laws, believing, on the contrary, that the novel could not be subject to prescriptive criteria and that its only limitations were those of the writer's imagination. He continued to correspond genially, praising James's *A Small Boy and Others* and adding 'As I grow up to a kind of technical understanding I begin to understand just what your amazing skill in atmospheres amounts to.' In September 1913 Wells's novel *The Passionate Friends* was published and once again James received a complimentary copy. James's letter of thanks begins with the now customary bouquets: 'I am too impatient to let you know *how* wonderful I find this last. I bare my head before the immense ability of it.' After extolling the artistry of the chapters describing the narrator's sojourn in South Africa he then turns to a fault he finds in the book as a whole:

> Where I find myself doubting is where I gather that you yourself see your subject more particularly – and where I rather feel it escape me. That is, to put it simply . . . the hero's prodigiously clever, foreshortened, impressionising *report* of the heroine . . . doesn't affect me as the real vessel of truth about them; in short . . . I don't care a fig for the hero's report *as an account of the matter.*   (21 September 1913)

What he is drawing attention to here is a tendency in Wells's fiction which he felt was increasingly in evidence in the novels of 1900–14: that of *telling* rather than *showing*. Instead of permitting the heroine, Lady Mary Justin, to speak for herself or permitting her to be shown from the standpoint of other characters Wells chooses once again the first person method of narration. The result, James complains, is that she is seen solely from the point of view of the narrator, Stephen Stratton. There is some substance in this criticism though it is arguable that the character of Lady Mary is presented with rather more subtlety than James acknowledged – we will return to this point a little later. Once again Wells replied apologetically, likening his novels to 'premature births' and contrasting the 'unworthiness and rawness' of his own works with the accomplishment of James's.

James returned to the charge of lack of artistry in his essay 'The Younger Generation' which appeared in *The Times Literary Supplement* in March and April 1914. After remarking that Wells's work possesses 'a breadth with which it has been given no one of his fellow-craftsmen to enjoy anything' he lapses into what can only be described as damning with faint praise:

> Such things as 'The New Machiavelli,' 'Marriage,' 'The Passionate Friends,' are so very much more attestations of the presence of material than of interest in the use of it that we ask ourselves again and again why so fondly neglected a state of leakage comes not to be fatal to *any* provision of quantity, or even to stores more specially selected for the ordeal than Mr. Wells's always strike us as being. Is not the witnessed pang of waste, in fact, great just in proportion as we are touched by our author's fine offhandedness as to the value of the stores, about which he can for the time make us believe what he will?

Wells must have been deeply wounded to read that James – whom in his own way he genuinely admired and respected – regarded his novels as 'so very much more attestations of the presence of material than of an interest in the use of it', and to discover that his friend speculated 'again and again why so fondly neglected a state of leakage comes not to be fatal to *any* provision of quantity'. After drawing attention to what he regards as a serious structural defect in *Marriage* – a conversation between the two central characters in which they declare their love for one another is omitted completely – James concludes by questioning what *The Passionate Friends* 'is specifically about and where, for treatment of this interest, it undertakes to find its centre'.

Until this point Wells had never criticised James in public but now, in the light of these strictures, he felt free to do so. He took up *Boon*, a novel on which he had been working sporadically for many years, and added the now famous chapter 'Of Art, of Literature, of Mr Henry James', including a description of an imaginary conversation between James and a group of literary friends including George Moore. He must have realised that what would annoy James so much when he came to read it was not so much this, nor the lampooning of his elaborately ornate style in the short story 'The Spoils of Mr Blandish', but the comments *about* him by Wells's surrogate George Boon. Many critics have seized on the much-quoted comparison of James to 'a magnificent but painful hippopotamus resolved at any cost, even at the cost of its dignity, upon picking up a pea which has got into a corner of its den'. But much more significant is Boon's perceptive criticism of James's conception of the novel:

> But if the novel is to follow life it must be various and discursive. Life is diversity and entertainment, not completeness and satisfaction. All actions are half-hearted, shot delightfully with wandering thoughts – about something else. All true stories are a felt of irrelevances. But James sets out to make his novels with the presupposition that they can be made continuously relevant. And perceiving the discordant things, he tries to get rid of them. He sets himself to pick the straws out of the hair of Life before he paints her. But without the straws she is no longer the mad woman we love. He talks of 'selection' and of making all of a novel definitely *about* a theme. He objects to a 'saturation' that isn't oriented. And he objects, if you go into it, for no clear reason at all. Following up his conception of selection, see what in his own practice he omits. In practice James's selection becomes just omission and nothing more. He omits everything that demands digressive treatment or collateral statement. For example, he omits opinions. In all his novels you will find no people with defined political opinions, no people with religious opinions, none with clear partisanships or with lusts or whims, none definitely up to any specific impersonal thing. There are no poor people dominated by the imperatives of Saturday night and Monday morning, no dreaming types – and don't we all more or less live dreaming? And none are ever decently forgetful. All that much of humanity he clears out before he begins his story. It's like cleaning rabbits for the table.   (*Boon*, 4, 3)

When James had read the chapter (he confessed that he had not read the book as a whole) he wrote Wells a dignified, pained letter complaining that 'there has grown up the habit of taking some common meeting-ground between [us] for granted, and the falling away of this is like the collapse of a bridge which made communication possible'. Wells responded with an abject letter of apology in which he attempted once again to define their differences:

> There is of course a real and a very fundamental difference in our innate and developed attitudes towards life and literature. To you literature like painting is an end, to me literature like architecture is a means, it has a use. Your view was, I felt, altogether too

dominant in the world of criticism, and I assailed it in tones of harsh antagonism.   (8 July 1915)

But James would have none of it. Refusing to accept Wells's apology, he dictated a reply rejecting the distinction between painting and architecture as 'wholly null and void' and ending with the eloquent plea: 'It is art that *makes* life, makes interest, makes importance, for our consideration and application of these things, and I know of no substitute whatever for the force and beauty of its process.' Three days later Wells wrote again saying that he could only read sense into this 'by assuming you are using "art" for every conscious human activity. I use the word for a research and attainment that is technical and special.' Whether James replied to this is not known. He died less than a year later, in February 1916, having been in poor health for the last months of his life.

In reflecting on the troubled relationship between Henry James and H. G. Wells one is reminded inevitably of Remington's comments apropos the Baileys (Sidney and Beatrice Webb) in *The New Machiavelli*:

> It is not nearly so easy to define the profound antagonism of spirit that also held between us. There was a difference in texture, a difference in quality. How can I express it? The shapes of our thoughts were the same, but the substance quite different. It was as if they had made in china or cast iron what I had made in transparent living matter. (The comparison is manifestly from my point of view.)   (Two, 2, 4)

Wells surely touches here on the root of the problem. For their debate was not simply a philosophical argument about the means and ends of fiction but one aspect of a profound emotional antipathy. It is symptomatic of this that the novels Wells wrote during this period of their quarrel have as their theme disentanglement and rebellion. *The Wife of Sir Isaac Harman* describes the frustration of a woman unhappily married to a business magnate and her spirited attempt to lead an independent life. *Bealby* is the story of a servant boy who runs away from the constricting atmosphere of home to find happiness in the life of a gipsy. In both novels there is a sense of release, an implicit contrast between freedom and discipline. Both are essentially fantasias on the theme of escape from a limiting environment. What is so remarkable about *The Wife of Sir Isaac Harman* is Wells's sense of man's loneliness and insecurity. The novel was written in 1913, before European civilisation capsized in the holocaust of the First World War and at the apex of post-Edwardian confidence. After several chapters of conventional story-telling the narrator records, as it were *sotto voce*, this revealing aside:

> The warm lights that once rounded off our world so completely are betrayed for what they are, smoky and guttering candles. Beyond what once seemed a casket of dutiful security is now a limitless and indifferent universe. Ours is the wisdom or there is no wisdom; ours is the decision or there is no decision. That burden is upon each of us in the measure of our capacity. The talent has been given us and we may not bury it. (5, 6)

It is precisely this sense of uncertainty, of the precariousness of man's foothold on the universe, which differentiates James and Wells so sharply. On the one hand James's novels and letters posit a conception of the universe in which man's stability and security are axiomatic, in which there can be no argument concerning the function of literature or art. In contrast the whole thrust of Wells's writings was an implicit rejection of this world-view. For this reason it may be questioned whether either fully understood the other. Wells, for his part, had no sympathy with James's conception of the novel as a wholly cohesive and carefully elaborated edifice. James, on his side, could not understand Wells's anarchic approach to literature and was perplexed and hurt by what he regarded as Wells's rudeness in *Boon*. The fundamental issue dividing them was whether the novel as an art form could embrace approaches to fiction other than the beautifully constructed and rounded concept as exemplified by Jane Austen and James himself. It was this which lay at the root of their quarrel and which continued to exercise Wells throughout his life.

The damage done to his literary standing by his quarrel with Henry James has been incalculable. Not only did it deceive him into making unwise and misleading statements about himself – 'I have to admit that the larger part of my fiction was written lightly and with a certain haste'[33] – but it has contributed to the widely held view that he was indifferent to art and that his novels, whilst brimming with vitality, lack the artistic and imaginative qualities of his contemporaries Joyce and Conrad. Gilbert Phelps, in his *A Survey of English Literature*, expresses a by no means untypical judgement when he comments:

> In reading *Tono-Bungay* one has the feel that Wells *could* have achieved a convincing artistic pattern if he had wanted to, but that in vindication of his picture of himself as primarily a journalist, propagandist and teacher, he deliberately and wilfully refused to do so.[34]

Leon Edel and Gordon Ray make much the same point in their introduction to *Henry James and H. G. Wells*:

> Wells's mockery of James in *Boon* and in his 'Digression About Novels' is more than a failure in perception; it reveals that this remarkable man, whose imagination could soar through space and time and create tales of wonderful new worlds, was yet limited and earth-bound when it came to understanding the true nature of art.

This conception of Wells as a philistine who wilfully diluted the literary quality of his own work is one which has held sway for many years and has only come to be challenged since his death. During the past 20 years there has been increasing evidence of a shift in critical attitudes towards him and a slowly widening recognition of the artistic merit of his novels. Whilst Edel and Ray complain that he had no understanding of 'the *true* nature of art' (my italics) Wells would have denied the existence of such a concept. There could be no single, objective interpretation of literature or art nor any universally applicable criteria by which they could be judged. Running through the entire debate between the two novelists is James's unyielding adherence to a unitary concept of the novel and Wells's equally uncompromising insistence on the diversity of the novel as a means of expression.

Since their debate James's comment that Wells had 'cut loose from literature clearly – practically altogether' has come to be accepted as the received view. Later critics have followed James in assuming as axiomatic the substance of the charge. Joseph Warren Beach in *The Method of Henry James* (1918) wrote:

Authors like Thackeray, or Balzac, say, or H. G. Wells . . . are always *telling* the reader what happened instead of showing them the scene, telling them what to think of the characters rather than letting the reader judge for himself or letting the characters do the telling about one another. I like to distinguish between novelists that *tell* and those that *show*.

James could not have foreseen the artistry of the later novels such as *The Bulpington of Blup* and *Apropos of Dolores* but he was surely guilty of an oversimplification in complaining of Wells's lack of craftsmanship. There are numerous instances in the novels, including those he criticised most strongly, of scenes and conversations in which aspects of a character are revealed through a process of *showing*. Consider, for example, the scene in *The Passionate Friends* in which the naïve and idealistic Stephen Stratton begs the aristocratic Lady Mary to marry him:

'But, Mary,' I said looking at her colourless delicate face, 'don't you love me? Don't you want me?'

'You know I love you, Stevenage,' she said. 'You know.'

'But if two people love one another, they want to be always together, they want to belong to each other.'

She looked at me with her face very intent upon her meaning. 'Stevenage,' she said after one of those steadfast pauses of hers, 'I want to belong to myself.'

'Naturally,' I said with an air of disposing of an argument, and then paused.

'Why should one have to tie oneself always to one other human being?' she asked. 'Why must it be like that?'

I do not remember how I tried to meet this extraordinary idea. 'One loves,' I may have said. The subtle scepticisms of her mind went altogether beyond my habits of thinking; it had never occurred to me that there was any other way of living except in these voluntary and involuntary mutual servitudes in which men and women live and die. 'If you love me,' I urged, 'if you love me . . . I want nothing better in all my life but to love and serve and keep you and make you happy.'

She surveyed me and weighed my words against her own.

'I love meeting you,' she said. 'I love your going because it means that afterwards you will come again. I love this – this slipping out to you. But up there, there is a room in the house that is *my* place – me – my own. Nobody follows me there. I want to go on living, Stevenage, just as I am living now. I don't want to become someone's certain possession, to be just usual and familiar to anyone. No, not even to you.'

'But if you love,' I cried.

'To you least of all. Don't you see? – I want to be wonderful to you, Stevenage, more than to anyone. I want – I want always to make your heart beat faster. I want always to be coming to you with my own heart beating faster. Always and always I want it to be like that. Just as it has been on these mornings. It has been beautiful – altogether beautiful.'

'Yes,' I said, rather helplessly, and struggled with great issues I had never faced before.

'It isn't,' I said, 'how people live.'

'It is how I want to live,' said Mary.

'It isn't the way life goes.'

'I want it to be. Why shouldn't it be? Why at any rate shouldn't it be for me?'   (4, 3)

What is striking about this scene is that the obtuseness is all on Stephen's part and the comprehension on Mary's. Stephen has to admit that 'the subtle scepticisms of her mind went altogether beyond my habits of thinking'; when faced with questions he cannot answer he 'struggled with great issues [he] had never faced before'. While he falls back on vapid rhetorical statements it is Mary who sees through his posturing to ask the much more searching question 'Why should one have to tie oneself always to one other human being? Why must it be like that?' Stephen's intensely naïve romanticism contrasts sharply with Mary's practicality and understanding. Moreover her independence and spirit emerge clearly through their dialogue. Mary has no intention of becoming 'someone's certain possession, to be just usual and familiar to anyone'. She wishes to lead her own life, answerable only to herself. When he objects that 'It isn't how people live', she answers 'It is how I want to live.' When he persists with his objection she counters with 'I want it to be. . . . Why at any rate shouldn't it be for me?' It seems to me that much of Mary's personality is revealed through this conversation – more than James would readily admit – and that many facets of her character are disclosed through her conversations and letters. It is true that the novel as a whole presents her personality largely from the narrator's point of view rather than her own but it is equally apposite to remind ourselves that the story was written with much more care then James (or Wells) would admit.

In the year before his death Wells published a serene and memorable work, *The Happy Turning*, in which he described the dreams and reflections which haunted him during his terminal illness. In the moving final chapter, 'The Divine Timelessness of Beautiful Things', he describes an imaginary gathering of poets, artists and writers who talk about beauty. The gathering agrees that 'Beauty is eternal and final, a joy for ever' and discusses the 'immortal visitations' of beauty which have found expression in the work of Shakespeare, Wordsworth and Shelley. Wells then makes a last eloquent plea for the beauty of artistic expression:

> But when he turned to literature which does not pretend to beauty in the first place, but to interest of statement or narrative, we found something, that only verges, as it were, in a few incidental passages, and by accident, on poetic beauty. For the rest, literature, both the philosophical, the 'scientific', and the fictitious, is telling about what things are, what life is; about its excitements, its emotional effects, its expectations, its laughter and tears. . . . This literature of reality has not the permanence of beauty. It absorbs and reproduces the storytelling and statements of the past. . . . Yet every new realisation, every fresh discovery, has for those who make it, a quality of beauty, transitory indeed but otherwise as clear and pure as that enduring Beauty we cherish for ever, an ephemeral beauty for one man or for a group of mortals, sufficient to make a life's devotion to the service of truth worthwhile.[35]

At the close of his life Wells continued to hold that the function of literature was to tell 'about what things are, what life is'. He continued to deny that the writing of fiction – the literature of reality – possessed 'the permanence of beauty'. But in the grip of his final illness, having remained in London through the dark years of the war, he could still reflect that 'every fresh discovery, has for those who make it, a quality of beauty'. His attitude to art remained fundamentally antipathetic to that held by James. But in his own way he sought to make a contribution to the modern novel which, whilst profoundly different from James's, may yet prove to be no less enduring.

3

The Frame and the Picture

Throughout the broad smooth flow of nineteenth century life in Great Britain, the art of fiction floated on this same assumption of social fixity. The Novel in English was produced in an atmosphere of security for the entertainment of secure people who liked to feel established and safe for good. Its standards were established within that apparently permanent frame and the criticism of it began to be irritated and perplexed when, through a new instability, the splintering frame began to get into the picture. I suppose for a time I was the outstanding instance among writers of fiction in English of the frame getting into the picture.

(H. G. Wells, *Experiment in Autobiography*)

Moreover, literary language is far from merely referential. It has its expressive side; it conveys the tone and attitude of the speaker or writer. And it does not merely state and express what it says; it also wants to influence the attitude of the reader, persuade him, and ultimately change him.

(René Wellek and Austin Warren, *Theory of Literature*)

Wells's distinctive contribution to the modern novel was to widen the scope of fiction by changing the function of the descriptive frame. In making this contribution he was much more innovative than is commonly acknowledged.

Malcolm Bradbury, in *The Social Context of Modern English Literature* has observed:

There has been a marked tendency in modern criticism to *underplay* the creative innovation of writers of this type. H. G. Wells, for instance, was consciously concerned with the creation of a new type of novel based on 'life' and 'change', as opposed to

42

'artifice' and 'omission', a novel of deliberate contingency based on the fluidity of the autobiographical narrator.[36]

In his experiments to achieve a satisfactory form for the development of his theory of fiction Wells was greatly indebted to Sterne, Fielding and Dickens and, as we shall see in the following chapters, owed much to their discursive and innovative spirit. At the same time he was seeking to break new ground in his conscious use of 'the splintering frame'. David Lodge has drawn attention to the fact that 'the main vehicle of Wells's social analysis of the condition of England in *Tono-Bungay* is not the story or the characters, but the descriptive commentary which, in most novels, we regard as the frame'.[37] The same is true for a number of his novels including *The New Machiavelli, Joan and Peter* and *The World of William Clissold*, didactic fictions which are notable for their weight of descriptive apparatus and their tendency to digress. In such works he was experimenting with a new type of novel, one in which (to use his own phrase) 'the frame began to get into the picture'. It is important to understand that the early work – *The Time Machine, The Island of Doctor Moreau, When the Sleeper Wakes* – is as didactic in intent as *Babes in the Darkling Wood* and *You Can't Be Too Careful*. It is impossible to read with care *The Time Machine*, for example, or *The Island Of Doctor Moreau* or many of the short stories without being aware that these stories contain rich strands of imagery and that they draw freely upon mythology and archetypal symbols. He was not simply a story-teller: and he did not wish to be regarded as simply that. Writing to Arnold Bennett in 1902 he asserted:

> There is a quality in the worst of my so-called pseudo-scientific stuff which differentiates it from Jules Verne, just as Swift is differentiated from fantasia. . . . There is something other than either story writing or artistic merit which has emerged through the series of my books, something one might regard as a new system of ideas. It's in *Anticipations* and it's in my Royal Institution Lecture and it's also in *The First Men in the Moon* and *The Invisible Man* and Chaffery's chapter in *Love and Mr Lewisham*
> (8 February 1902).

From his student writings of the 1880s to the dream speculations of *The Happy Turning* (1945) he was seeking a satisfactory means of expression for his developing ideas concerning man and society.

After some years of experiment he arrived at this in the form which he termed 'the dialogue novel'. He acknowledged that his contributions to the genre of the dialogue novel 'may be infinitesmal, but that does not alter the fact that they follow in a great tradition, the tradition of discussing fundamental human problems in dialogue form'.[38] The attraction this tradition held for him can be traced to his reading Plato's *Republic* while still a boy at Up Park. The reading of this seminal work not only opened his eyes to the possibility that the rigid social order of Victorian England might be 'cast into the melting pot and made anew', but revealed to him the immense potentialities of fiction as a medium of social criticism. Long before he became a novelist in his own right he had studied Plato, Voltaire, Swift and Sterne: he had been fascinated by the fluidity of the novel and its widening scope for irony and satire. He set himself to explore ways in which the boundaries of fiction could be extended so that the novel would not simply mirror society but would comment upon it. In his hands the novel would be a potent instrument through which the problems of man in a disintegrating and unstable society could be explored.

In his important essay 'The Novel of Ideas' (the introduction to *Babes in the Darkling Wood*) Wells observed:

> I found myself, and I got to the dialogue novel, through a process of trial and error. The critical atmosphere was all against me. As I felt about rebelliously among the possibilities of fiction, I found certain of my characters were displaying an irresistible tendency to break out into dissertation. Many critical readers, trained to insist on a straight story, objected to these talkers; they said they were self-projections, author's exponents. But in many cases these obtrusive individuals were not saying things I thought, but, what is a very different thing, things I wanted to put into shape by having them said.

It is interesting to note that he prefaces his defence of the dialogue novel with the words: *as I felt about rebelliously among the possibilities of fiction*. His *opus* from beginning to end was consciously experimental, a continual attempt to examine human problems from fresh points of view. This willingness to experiment manifested itself in a testing out of differing approaches to the novel – in methods of narration, structure, form and perspective. He arrived at the dialogue novel, he confesses, 'through a process of trial and error'.

In the opening chapters of *The Time Machine*, 'Mr Chaffery at Home' in *Love and Mr Lewisham* and 'The Labyrinthodon' in *Kipps* can be discerned his early experiments in the dialogue form. One senses a hesitancy, as if the author is still uncertain of his sense of direction. He is still feeling his way, alternately testing and rejecting a series of approaches to fiction in a search for a form which would both accommodate social commentary and permit the maximum freedom to digress.

The dialogue novel in its matured form can be seen in *Boon, Joan and Peter, The Undying Fire*, and in most of the fiction of his final two decades. What these novels have in common is that each is a discussion, a *conversazione* in which contemporary social and moral problems are looked at from a number of different angles. Wells's remark that his characters say 'things I wanted to put into shape by having them said' is interesting and is a further reminder of his indebtedness to Plato and Socrates – a debt he acknowledges in 'The Novel of Ideas'. The conversation novel in which the characters 'state living views, to have them ransacked by an interlocutor who is also a character, subject to all the infirmities of the flesh' was a genre that held for him a vital attraction. In his hands it was a genre which, at the height of his powers, yielded works of the stature of *Boon* and *The Bulpington of Blup*, novels to which we still return for the vitality of their ideas and freshness of presentation. In these novels the reader is an unseen listener at a conversation, an observer looking into a transparent room in which the dialogue is conducted. This effect of looking in on a conversation that is going on in a different dimension – of peering into a magic crystal to adopt the simile used in *The World of William Clissold* – owes something to the conversations of the Shandy family in *Tristram Shandy*. There is an effect of timelessness, as if the interlocutors have been conducting their dialogue off stage before the book has been opened and will pursue it after the book has been put aside. Consider, for example, the conversations in 'The Garden by the Sea' in *Boon*, the dialogue on religious belief in *The Undying Fire* or the 'Sanguine Interlude' chapter in *Mr Blettsworthy on Rampole Island*. There is a sense of an audience, of being present at a *scene*. When the narrator of *A Modern Utopia* is introducing himself to the reader he uses the suggestive phrase 'The curtain rises upon him so.' This sense of a curtain rising, of being a participant in a series of dramatised tableaux, is an important element in the experience of reading a Wells novel. The reader is at once a participant and an observer, aware that language is being employed with a sense of a real or implied audience.

In emphasising Wells's creation of novels 'of deliberate contingency based on the fluidity of the autobiographical narrator' Malcolm Bradbury is drawing attention to an element of central importance in his novels: the freedom of the narrator to comment on the story as it unfolds and to enclose the action within a descriptive frame of reference, which is often more subtle than it appears. The striking analogy of the frame and the picture highlights the question of the relationship between the enclosing frame – the web of descriptive commentary in which the narrative is set – and the picture, that is the flow of scenes and incidents of which the novel is composed. In a Wells novel the balance between frame and picture is almost invariably less straightforward than it appears.

A question which is central to any discussion of Wells as a novelist is the nature of the relationship between the author and the text. Of his 54 full-length works of fiction (as distinct from short stories) 17 are written in the first person and 37 in the third person. This is not such a tidy distinction as it appears since the conventions of the respective forms are by no means followed consistently. If one looks closely at *A Modern Utopia*, for example, one is aware of a relationship between author and narrator which is decidedly unconventional:

> Throughout these papers sounds a note, a distinctive and personal note, a note that tends at times towards stridency. . . . Now, this voice, and this is the peculiarity of the matter, is not to be taken as the voice of the ostensible author who fathers these pages. (I, 1)

This separation between the 'distinctive and personal voice' of the narrator and the voice of the 'ostensible author' is one which Wells is careful to maintain in a number of his novels. In *Boon* the framework of the story is narrated by Reginald Bliss, the purported editor of Boon's posthumous papers, but his antipathy to many of Boon's ideas permits a degree of detachment which would not have been possible had Wells adopted a more conventional narrative device. In *The Dream* a first-person autobiographical narrative is enclosed within a frame cast in the third person. The device enables the characters within the 'frame' to comment upon the scenes and characters in the first person narrative: a perspective which adds a dimension of immediacy to the novel as a whole.

One of his most interesting experiments in narrative technique is *The Research Magnificent*, a novel written in 1914 when he was preoccupied with questions of conduct and intermittently at work on *Boon*. The posthumous papers of the central character, William Benham, are edited for publication by his friend White, a novelist and journalist. White weaves the disconnected fragments together to form a novel composed partly of Benham's manuscript and partly of the reminiscences of himself and others who had known Benham. The central figure is thus seen from a number of different angles. At times Benham is seen from the point of view of his mother, Lady Marayne, at times from White's point of view, and at others from that of his wife Amanda and his friend Prothero. What is unusual about this method of presentation is that the narrator is referred to throughout as 'he'. White himself is seen from the outside, speculating on Benham and his motives and thinking aloud on the form in which to present his material. White, in fact, serves the same function as the unnamed narrator in Conrad's *Heart of Darkness* – a narrator who is a participant in the story and yet deliberately distanced from it. He is simultaneously inside and outside the narrative. Though much of the novel is cast in conventional third-person form there are frequent shifts in perspective, as in this passage apropos Benham:

> Lady Marayne felt he had escaped her. The controversy that should have split these two young men apart had given them a new interest in each other. When afterwards she sounded her son, very delicately, to see if indeed he was aware of the clumsiness, the social ignorance and uneasiness, the complete unsuitability of his friend, she could get no more from him than that exasperating phrase, 'He has ideas!'
>
> What are ideas? England may yet be ruined by ideas. He ought never to have gone to Trinity, that monster packet of everything. He ought to have gone to some little *good* college, good all through. She ought to have asked some one who *knew*.
>
> (One, 10)

To whom is the statement beginning 'What are ideas?' to be attributed? Clearly not Benham, nor to White. The narrative voice here can only belong to Lady Marayne. Yet at other points in the novel the voice is that of Amanda or White or Benham himself. The

flexibility with which the narrative perspective is varied enhances
the totality of the reader's perception of Benham. Because he is not
seen from a static point of view he has a solidity that would have
been absent had the story been told in the first person.

The anonymous narrator of the third person novels occasionally
addresses the reader directly, as in *The History of Mr Polly*: 'I am
puzzled by his insensibility to Dickens, and I record it, as a good
historian should, with an admission of my perplexity.' Or again,
after Mr Polly has set fire to the shop and left his wife the narrator
comments: 'I wish from the bottom of my heart I could add that he
was properly sorry.' These direct asides have the effect of involving
the reader in the narrative process. The reader becomes a confidant,
one of a select number invited to share with the author in his
reflections. In other instances the narrative voice does not simply
appeal to the reader but enters into a kind of soliloquy in which the
narrator muses on the motivations or beliefs of his characters. The
opening paragraphs of *Marriage*, for example, begin conventionally
enough in third person form. An omniscient narrator describes 'an
extremely pretty girl', Marjorie Pope, seated in a train travelling
through the Kentish countryside. Without warning there is a
transition to this:

What a queer thing the invisible human being would appear if, by
some discovery as yet inconceivable, some spiritual X-ray photo-
graphy, we could flash it into sight! Long ago I read a book called
Soul Shapes that was full of ingenious ideas, but I doubt very much
if the thing so revealed would have any shape, any abiding solid
outline at all. It is something more fluctuating and discursive than
that – at any rate, for every one young enough not to have set and
hardened. Things come into it and become it, things drift out of it
and cease to be it, things turn upside down in it and change and
colour and dissolve, and grow and eddy about and blend into
each other. One might figure it, I suppose, as a preposterous
jumble animated by a will; a floundering disconnectedness
through which an old hump of impulse rises and thrusts
unaccountably; a river beast of purpose wallowing in a back eddy
of mud and weeds and floating objects and creatures drowned.
Now the sunshine of gladness makes it all vivid, now it is sombre
and grimly insistent under the sky of some darkling mood, now
an emotional gale sweeps across it and it is one confused
agitation. . . .

And surely these invisible selves of men were never so jumbled, so crowded, complicated, and stirred about as they are at the present time. Once again I am told they had a sort of order, were sphered in religious beliefs, crystal clear, were arranged in a cosmogony that fitted them as hand fits glove, were separated by definite standards of right and wrong which presented life as planned in all its essential aspects from the cradle to the grave. Things are so no longer. That sphere is broken for most of us; even if it is tied about and mended again, it is burst like a seed case; things have fallen out and things have fallen in. . . .

Can I convey in any measure how it was with Marjorie?

What was her religion?   (One, 1, 2)

Clearly something very odd is happening here. Since the novel is not told in the first person the 'I' can only be Wells himself. Here we have an instance of an author not simply commenting on his own characters (as happens occasionally in novels by George Eliot or Jane Austen) but entering into a metaphysical speculation on the nature of the unconscious self. Beginning with a series of vivid metaphors – 'a river beast of purpose wallowing in a back eddy of mud and weeds', 'sombre and grimly insistent under the sky of some darkling mood', 'an old hump of impulse rises and thrusts' – the narrative voice then goes on to speculate on the fragmentation which is endemic to the twentieth century: 'That sphere is broken for most of us . . . it is burst like a seed case.' This intimate aside to the reader, the reminder that characters both in fiction and reality have a mental self, is strangely disturbing. After this intervention the narrative voice resumes the story in a conventional novelistic manner and the reader is plunged into an entertaining account of the Pope family and their ménage. But the illusion of fictiveness has been momentarily destroyed by the aside. In *The New Machiavelli* the narrator, Remington, looks through his mother's papers after her death and finds a scrap of verse in her handwriting which amazes him because it implicitly questions her religious beliefs. He comments that the discovery of the verse 'affected me as if a stone deaf person had suddenly turned and joined in a whispered conversation'. This aside has precisely that effect. It is as if a hole has been rent in the text through which the reader peers into a different reality – neither the world of the novel nor the 'real' tangible world but a hybrid of the two. This deliberate breaking of fictional conventions was novel at the time (1912) and one would have to wait until John Fowles's *The French Lieutenant's Woman* (1969) before encountering a comparable effect. The famous Chapter 13 of the latter work in which the author speculates on the motivations of Sarah Woodruff – a speculation which leads into a discussion on the relation between fiction and reality – is an interesting modern example of the device adopted in *Marriage* and in many of the novels and short stories: a conscious questioning of the boundaries between the frame and the picture.

When reading a Wells novel one has to be constantly aware of the 'point of view', the perspective from which one is observing the action. In a memorable short story, 'Through a Window',[39] the central character, Bailey, is recuperating after breaking his leg. He lays on a couch before an open window, unable to settle to reading or writing. For a time the view from the window is his entire world. He spends hours watching the boats and people passing up and down the river, regarding the toing and froing on the water as 'an entertainment got up to while away his illness'. The passing scene suddenly erupts directly into his life when a Malay runs amok pursued by men with a gun. The climax of the story is reached when the cornered man climbs through the window into Bailey's room. As he does so he is shot and badly wounded by one of his pursuers, being finally overcome by a bottle thrown by the invalid. There are a number of indications to suggest that the story is open to both a literal and a symbolic interpretation. The dream-like texture of the narrative, the haunting landscape (the bend in the river marked by three poplars recurs in *The History of Mr Polly*), the mannered language, the richness of imagery, all suggest that Wells intended the story to be rather more than a diverting tale. One possible reading is that this rather slight sketch is an allegory on the deceptive nature of reality.

The view which Bailey admires through his window is seen originally as a picture, described in terms which recall a Constable landscape:

> In the foreground was the weltering silver of the river, never quiet and yet never tiresome. Beyond was the reedy bank, a broad stretch of meadow land, and then a dark line of trees ending in a group of poplars at the distant bend of the river, and, upstanding behind them, a square church tower.

This tranquil, idyllic scene is rudely shattered by the arrival of the Malay. What has hitherto been a picture, a passing scene enclosed in a frame, becomes peopled with movement and excitement as the pursuit gathers momentum. When the cornered man, wounded and dripping water, climbs over the window sill and enters the room the scene passes from one dimension to another. One experiences the same sensation when reading of Alice passing through the looking glass: the picture has suddenly melted. The landscape which has formed the substance of Bailey's thoughts and dreams abruptly enters physically into his life – frame and picture have become one. This transition from one level of experience to another – which 'became almost as exciting as any window show very well could be' – can be taken as a metaphor for the splintering frame, for Wells's sense of the illusory dividing line between life and art. The world of the solid and the real impinges with dramatic suddenness on the world of contemplation. When Benham in *The Research Magnificent* observes that 'The habitual life of man is breaking up all about us, and for the new life our minds, our imaginations, our habits and customs are all unprepared',[40] he is articulating this sense of fragmentation, the uneasy awareness of an age in which certainty and faith are being replaced by doubt and confusion.

To illustrate what is meant by 'the frame getting into the picture', let us look at three passages selected at random from his fiction. Here is a passage from *Marriage* which illustrates Wells in one of his most didactic phases:

And now, indeed, the Traffords were coming to the most difficult and fatal phase in marriage. They had had that taste of defiant adventure which is the crown of a spirited love affair, they had known the sweetness of a maiden passion for a maid, and they had felt all those rich and solemn emotions, those splendid fears and terrible hopes that weave themselves about the great partnership in parentage. And now, so far as sex was concerned, there might be much joy and delight still, but no more wonder, no fresh discoveries of incredible new worlds and unsuspected stars. Love, which had been a new garden, an unknown land, a sunlit sea to launch upon, was now a rich treasure-house of memories. And memories, although they afford a perpetually increasing enrichment to emotion, are not sufficient in themselves for the daily needs of life. (II, 3, 2)

It may be objected at once that this is an instance of *telling* rather than *showing*. Instead of allowing the reader to judge the Traffords for himself the author *tells* the reader what to think: a trait which James, for one, heartily deprecated. But look at the passage more closely. If it is recast as a poem its literary quality at once becomes apparent:

> There might be much joy and delight still
> But no more wonder
> No fresh discoveries of incredible new worlds
> And unsuspected stars.
> Love, which had been a new garden
> An unknown land
> A sunlit sea to launch upon, was now
> A rich treasure-house of memories

This is not in any way a conventional example of homiletic commentary. It is a highly stylised, self-conscious piece of writing, a reminder of the fact that for Wells language is an instrument for both defining and enlarging the scope of the novel. To observe that the Traffords 'had felt all those rich and solemn emotions, those splendid fears and terrible hopes that weave themselves about the great partnership in parentage' is to do more than simply intrude with an authorial intervention. It is to interweave the text with a web of connotative prose which both heightens and transforms the narrative. Where the novels are unsuccessful – as in *The Secret Places of the Heart* and *The Soul of a Bishop* – it is precisely because this literary and poetic quality is absent. In his finest work he is interweaving the narrative with a tracery which functions both as an imaginative and didactic frame.

As a second example of 'the splintering frame' consider a passage from *Joan and Peter*. In this paragraph Wells is describing the dingy room to which Mrs Pybus brings the kidnapped children:

Small as this room was there had been a strenuous and successful attempt to obliterate such floor space as it contained by an accumulation of useless furniture; there were flimsy things called what-nots in two of the corners, there was a bulky veneered mahogany chiffonier opposite the fireplace, and in the window two ferns and a rubber-plant in wool-adorned pots died slowly upon a rickety table of bamboo. The walls had been a basis for much decorative activity, partly it would seem to conceal or minimise a mysterious skin disease that affected the wall-paper, but partly also for a mere perverse impulse towards litter. There were weak fretwork brackets stuck up for their own sakes and more or less askew, and stouter brackets entrusted with the support of more 'ornaments', small bowls and a teapot that valiantly pretended they were things of beauty; there were crossed palm fans, there was a steel engraving of Queen Victoria giving the Bible to a dusky potentate as the secret of England's greatness; there was 'The Soul's Awakening,' two portraits of George and May, and a large but faded photograph of the sea front at Scarborough in an Oxford frame. A gas 'chandelier' descended into the midst of this apartment, betraying a confused ornate disposition in its lines, and the obliteration of the floor space was completed by a number of black horsehair chairs and a large table, now 'laid' with a worn and greyish-white cloth for a meal. Such were the homes that the Victorian age had evolved by the million in England, and to such nests did the common mind of the British resort when it wished to meditate upon the problems of its Imperial destiny. Joan and Peter surveyed it open-mouthed. (8, 3)

One notices, as with Dickens, the abundance of concrete detail (it is instructive to compare this with the description of Parload's room in *In the Days of the Comet* or the description of Mr Polly lovingly admiring the bar of the Potwell Inn). One is also aware of the cumulative effect of satirical polemic – the reiteration of 'useless', 'flimsy', 'litter', 'confused'. The ruling motif of the picture is disorder – the floor space is covered with needless furniture, there is a perverse impulse towards untidiness, the ornaments 'valiantly pretended they were things of beauty', the gas chandelier betrays 'a confused ornate disposition in its lines'. Over all broods an atmosphere of decay – the plants are slowly dying, the wallpaper is afflicted with 'a mysterious skin disease', the photograph is 'faded', the tablecloth is 'worn and greyish-white'. Here the descriptive frame ministers directly to his theme for an important subsidiary element in *Joan and Peter* is the decay of society in Victorian England and the faded gentility of its institutions. The themes of decay, disorder and outmodedness are powerfully reinforced in the description of the room and its owner (Mrs Pybus herself is described as 'a small, white-faced, anxious woman' wearing 'a greyish-black dress that ended in a dingy, stiff buff frilling at the neck and wrists') and in the account of Joan and Peter's education at the High Cross Preparatory School. The irony of Wells's concluding reflection, 'to such nests did the common mind of the British resort when it wished to meditate upon the problems of its Imperial destiny', will not be lost upon the reader. Indeed irony is present throughout the passage, not least in the reference to the 'steel engraving of Queen Victoria giving the Bible to a dusky potentate as the secret of England's greatness'. The language is charged with ironic and satirical force. As in many of his descriptions of rooms (and it may be remarked in passing how obsessed Wells is with domestic architecture) one is struck with the accumulation of detail and the tone of disbelief tinged with ridicule.

As a third example let us take the following passage from *Meanwhile*. A group of English people gather at a house party at an Italian villa. The hostess, Cynthia Rylands, decides to take an after-dinner stroll in the moonlight:

> After dinner there was a luminous peacefulness in the world outside and an unusual warmth, the rising moon had pervaded heaven with an intense blue and long slanting bars of dreamy light lifted themselves from the horizontal towards the vertical, slowly and indolently amidst the terraces and trees and bushes. At two or three in the morning when everyone was asleep they would stand erect like sentinel spears.
>
> 'I think I could walk a little,' said Mrs Rylands and they went outside upon the terrace and down the steps to the path that led through the close garden with the tombstone of Amoena Lucina to the broad way that ended at last in a tall jungle of subtly scented nocturnal white flowers. They were tall responsible looking flowers. The moonlight among their petals armed them with little scimitars and bucklers of silver. Among these flowers were moths, great white moths, so that it seemed as if ever and again a couple of blossoms became detached and pirouetted together. Hostess and guest – for Miss Fenimore, with her instinctive tact, did not join them – promenaded this broad dim path, to and fro, and Mr Plantagenet-Buchan spread his Epicurean philosophy unchallenged before Mrs Rylands' inquiring intelligence.   (2, 7)

The extensive use of symbolism is immediately apparent – 'the rising moon', bars of light standing erect 'like sentinel spears', 'nocturnal white flowers', 'bucklers of silver', 'great white moths', blossoms 'pirouetted together'. The contrasting use of masculine/ feminine – conscious/unconscious imagery is striking and powerfully underpins one of the main themes of the novel: the pursuit of sexual gratification. What is not so apparent is the continual presence of the narrative voice. Notice the use of such phrases as 'responsible looking flowers', 'it seemed as if ever and again', 'with her instinctive tact'. By inserting these phrases Wells imposes a distinctive authorial voice on the narrative. Though one is much more aware of the narrative voice in the early novels – in *Love and Mr Lewisham* and *Kipps* there are moments when the voice intrudes with much less subtlety – it is present in varying degrees of intensity throughout his work.

It is worth noting, then, that even in the novels which appear to follow an orthodox third person form – the device of the omniscient narrator – the reader is intermittently aware of the danger of accepting the narrative voice at face value. The dominant impression of a study of Wells's fiction is of the fluidity of the narrative and the manner in which language is employed to achieve extraliterary effects. A text which appears to be solid suddenly becomes translucent, a window looking out on a different level of experience. Consider the moment in *The Research Magnificent* when Benham is compelled to admit that his wife has been unfaithful to him:

> I insisted upon believing that she was as fastidious as myself and as faithful as myself, made indeed after my image, and I went on disregarding the most obvious intimations that she was not, until that still moment in the Indian Ocean, when silently, gently as a drowned body might rise out of the depths of a pool, that knowledge of love dead and honour gone for ever floated up into my consciousness. (5, 21)

The words *silently, gently as a drowned body might rise out of the depths of a pool* have an impact which is at once arresting and disturbing. The striking analogy of the slow awareness of the floating body with the 'knowledge of love dead and honour gone' is haunting in its impact. The image remains in the mind long after the novel has been read. Frequently in the chapters which follow we will look more closely at Wells's use of language, at his use of metaphor, imagery and psychological insight, and draw attention to the craftsmanship present in his novels.

In reflecting on Wells and on the strengths and weaknesses of his novels one is reminded inevitably of Orwell. Raymond Williams in his essay 'Realism and the Contemporary Novel' states:

> When I think of the realist tradition in fiction, I think of the kind of novel which creates and judges the quality of a whole way of life in terms of the qualities of persons . . . it offers a valuing of a whole way of life, a society that is larger than any of the individuals composing it, and at the same time valuing creations of human beings who, while belonging to and affected by and helping to define the way of life are also, in their own terms, absolute ends in themselves. . . . We attend with our whole senses to every aspect of the general life, yet the centre of value is always in the individual human person.[41]

Both Wells and Orwell excelled in the writing of this kind of novel. Whether one terms it the discussion novel, or the social novel, or the novel of ideas, it is a recognisable literary form. Orwell in such works as *Keep the Aspidistra Flying* and *Coming Up for Air*, and Wells in *Love and Mr Lewisham* and *Tono-Bungay*, were criticising the society of their time and doing so by illuminating the lives and motives and actions of individuals. Raymond Williams's phrase 'a novel which creates and judges the quality of a whole way of life' is interesting and significant. Orwell and Wells were both sociological novelists in that they possessed the gift of criticising society through the medium of their novels. This is sometimes achieved through dialogue, sometimes through description, sometimes through direct authorial comment:

> Lady Charlotte Sydenham was one of those large, ignorant, ruthless, low church, wealthy and well born ladies who did so much to make England what it was in the days before the Great War.[42]

As novelists both Wells and Orwell were following in a distinguished literary tradition, a tradition which can be traced back through Dickens to Defoe, Fielding, Swift and Sterne. It is significant that both men were profoundly influenced by Dickens. Both men read and reread Dickens over a period of many years. Frank Swinnerton recorded of Wells that 'a worn set of Dickens's works, in the fine red square "Charles Dickens Edition", filled always a handy place on his bookshelves, with *Bleak House* the best-worn of them all'.[43] Orwell discusses Dickens's great contribution as a radical novelist, a critic of nineteenth-century institutions:

> for even if Dickens was a bourgeois, he was certainly a subversive writer, a radical, one might truthfully say a rebel. Everyone who has read widely in his work has felt this. Gissing, for instance, the best of the writers on Dickens, was anything but a radical himself, and he disapproved of this strain in Dickens and wished it were not there, but it never occurred to him to deny it. In *Oliver Twist*, *Hard Times*, *Bleak House*, *Little Dorrit*, Dickens attacked English institutions with a ferocity that has never since been approached. Yet he managed to do it without making himself hated, and, more than this, the very people he attacked have swallowed him so completely that he has become a national institution himself.[44]

In such novels as *Little Dorrit* (consider, for example, the chapter entitled 'Containing the Whole Science of Government' with its description of the Circumlocution Office), *Bleak House*, *Dombey & Son* and *Great Expectations* Dickens employed a whole panoply of techniques in his critique of the English society of his time – satire, irony, symbolism, invective, prophecy. In his turn Wells employed similar techniques. He shared with Dickens a deep intellectual curiosity and a profound concern for human decency. They shared a belief that the novel could be an instrument for the discussion of ideas, that the problems confronting man could be illuminated most effectively through the fictional presentation of individual lives. *Above all they shared a conviction that fiction could both comment on life and change the readers' attitudes towards it.* It is in this belief – that the novel could not only illuminate society but question it and comment upon it – that both men made a permanent contribution to our literature.

4

Experiments with Time

Perhaps I am a man of exceptional moods. I do not know how far my experience is common. At times I suffer from the strangest sense of detachment from myself and the world about me; I seem to watch it all from the outside, from somewhere inconceivably remote, out of time, out of space, out of the stress and tragedy of it all.

(H. G. Wells, *The War of the Worlds*)

It was to have been a story of wandering about in the world that is; the story of the happy adventures of a well tempered mind in a well understood scheme of things. But Bobby was beginning to realise that there is not, and there never has been, a world that is; there is only a world that has been and a world that is to be.

(H. G. Wells, *Christina Alberta's Father*)

From his earliest speculations as a science student concerning the fourth dimension to the writings of his last years Wells was fascinated with time. One has only to glance at the titles of many of his novels and speculations to recognise an obsession with time, past, present and future: *The Time Machine, Tales of Space and Time, A Story of the Days to Come, The Discovery of the Future, What is Coming?, The Shape of Things to Come, The Conquest of Time.* Throughout his fiction he is consciously experimenting with time, playing with the idea of dislocations in time sequence, contrasting 'clock' time with that in dreams, or toying with the reader's notions of reality.

It is this fascination with time and chronology that accounts, I believe, for the unusual structure of so many of the novels. *The History of Mr Polly, The Invisible Man, The Island of Doctor Moreau, The World of William Clissold, Apropos of Dolores* and others contain sequences narrated in flashback or make use of shifts in time

58

sequence – sometimes what appear to be rather awkward shifts – which fracture accepted notions of reality and compel the reader to reconsider his conceptions of time. This oscillation between differing levels of time is a central motif in much of his fiction. From *The Time Machine* to *You Can't Be Too Careful* his abiding concern is the fluidity of duration: the fragility and provisionality of our notions of quotidian time and the liberating effects of release from the boundaries of the present. It is this which accounts for the sense of exhilaration which so many readers experience on reading a Wells novel: a sense of being on the wing, of being released from the constraints of time. The narrator of 'Under the Knife' has a dream while under an anaesthetic – a dream in which he has a dazzling moment of release from the limitations of time and space – and proclaims: 'I perceived, suddenly, that the dull melancholy of half a year was lifted from my mind.' Mr Polly, freed from the stifling inertia of Fishbourne, 'felt as the etiolated grass and daisies must do when you move the garden roller away to a new place'. Stephen Wilbeck, at the conclusion of *Apropos of Dolores*, confides to the reader he is in a state 'of hope and elation'. Again and again when reading Wells's fiction one is aware of this sense of release: a recognition that the boundaries of daily existence are not immutable, that perspectives can be opened on to new and different worlds.

Few writers of this century have had a stronger sense of evolutionary time than Wells. An awareness of man as a product of vast aeons of adaptation, a creature of infinite plasticity, permeates all his work. In his first book, *Textbook of Biology* (1893), he expressed his conviction that 'the world is not made and dead like a cardboard model or a child's toy, but a living equilibrium; and every day and every hour, every living thing is being weighed in the balance and found sufficient or wanting'.[45] This sense of the past, of the mutability of all living things in the vast conspectus of time, haunts his work from beginning to end. It animates the haunting apocalyptic vision of *The Time Machine* and *The War of the Worlds*, a brooding sense of man as a creature of adaptations and compromises striving to overcome his animal legacy.

This sense of the novelist as a God-like figure observing with detachment the foibles of humanity can be seen in the 'Prologue in Heaven' chapter in *The Undying Fire*, the 'Elemental Powers' sequence in the film scenario *Man Who Could Work Miracles* and in the conversations between God and Noah Lammock in *All Aboard* for Ararat. It is as if author and reader are beyond time, observing life and behaviour with stoical compassion from the perspective of an extrafictional dimension.

Christina Alberta's Father is a novel obsessed with an awareness of the past. In its closing pages Mr Preemby muses on his vision of evolutionary time:

> You – you perhaps are still unawakened – but you are Sargon too. His blood is in our veins. We are co-heirs. . . . We are all descended from Sargon, just as we are all descended from Caesar – just as nearly all English and Americans are descended from William the Conqueror. . . . Long before the Christian era the blood of Sargon was diffused throughout all mankind. His traditions still more so. We all inherit.　(III, 3, 4)

This awareness of a past that is all around us, of an ancestry that is in our veins, is juxtaposed with an acute awareness of contemporary issues and mores. It is a novel of refreshing vitality.

In Christina Alberta's Father Wells sets in motion a series of expectations which are not fulfilled, as if he is deliberately toying with conventional notions of time. The novel begins in an ostensibly straightforward manner:

> This is the story of a certain Mr Preemby, a retired laundryman and widower, who abandoned his active interest in the Limpid Stream Laundry, in the parish of Saint Simon Unawares, near Woodford Wells, upon the death of his wife in the year of grace 1920.

The title of the novel would suggest, then, that Mr Preemby is to be the central character. As the story proceeds, however, Christina Alberta herself increasingly assumes a central role. Matters are complicated by her discovery, midway through the narrative, that her father is not Preemby at all but a Wilfred Devizes. Is the novel intended to be the story of Christina Alberta, or Preemby, or Devizes? To the end the reader is left in doubt. The reader is also in doubt as to what kind of novel he is reading. Mr Preemby believes himself to be the reincarnation of Sargon, King of Kings, and much of the story is taken up with an account of his dreams of grandeur and quest for disciples. The narrative implicitly poses the question: what is reality? Is Preemby, with his vision of restoring the reign of

Sargon, really mad? Is the account of his attempt to set up the new reign merely a dream? Does each individual consist of more than one self? The questioning of our notions of personality intensifies as the story proceeds and is continued through the reflections of the various characters. At times Preemby/Sargon is seen from the *outside*, from the perspective of Christina Alberta, or Devizes, or Paul Lambone. At other moments he is seen from the *inside*, as an inoffensive little man consumed and perplexed by his conviction that he is in reality a great ruler sent back to earth to heal the world's disorders. This dual perspective has an odd effect, as if Preemby is simultaneously both the observer and the observed.

The novel is disturbing on a different level. Half way through the story a character named Robert Roothing is seen at work writing a novel. He has written the title, *Ups and Downs*, and the title of the opening chapter, 'Which Introduces Our Hero'. At the end of *Christina Alberta's Father* Roothing is seen in his study, poised once again before these opening words: 'It was nearly two years now since he had first begun his novel in this fashion', we are told, 'and he was still quite uncertain about the details of his hero's introduction.' He falls into a day-dream about his projected novel and about Christina Alberta, with whom he is in love. He changes the title of the novel to *New Country* and alters the subtitle from 'A Pedestrian Novel' to 'The History of an Explorer'. Distracted by the sound of a bird outside the study window he steps into the garden:

> Presently a little breeze blew into the study through the open glass door and lifted the sheet of paper which was to introduce our hero, and wafted it softly and suggestively on to the unlit wood fire upon the hearth. There it lay for a long time. (III, 4, 7)

On this enigmatic note the novel ends. *Christina Alberta's Father* has ended but Roothing's novel *New Country*, 'The History of an Explorer', is still unwritten. It is strongly implied that he is to be the hero of his own novel. Each individual, Wells suggests, is potentially the central character in a novel of his own making. But the implication is wider than this. *Christina Alberta's Father*, in common with much of Wells's fiction, is a novel about the nature of reality. Or, to express it in a different way, it is a novel about the nature of fiction, about the process of creating imaginary worlds. The process of reading it can be likened to that of entering a room on several different levels. On one level is the surface narrative, the story of Mr

Preemby and Christina Alberta and their unremarkable adventures in Tunbridge Wells and Chelsea. On another level is the story of Mr Preemby's apparent reincarnation and his grandiose attempts to assert his Kingship. Beyond these and linked to them is a third level, the relationship between Christina and her friend Paul Lambone, and between them both and Devizes, and their separate and mutual attempts to understand Preemby and the workings of his mind. The three levels are welded together with considerable skill, but one is left with a series of tantalising speculations concerning the nature of the self. The impact of the past upon the present is clearly a dominant theme. Equally important is the relationship between fictiveness and actuality: to what extent are we deluded in our conceptions of the 'real'? Roothing's unwritten novel becomes a metaphor for the creative process, for the infinite plasticity of life: as he sits with the manuscript of his novel before him he can make of it what he will. *Christina Alberta's Father* is by no means alone in creating a sense in the mind of the reader that he or she is also a participant in the creative process – that the reader is being invited by the writer to peer into his workshop, to join with him in the shaping of mind and behaviour.

A recurring theme in Wells's fiction is the thin dividing line between illusion and reality, between time in the mental world, the world of dreams, and in actuality. In *A Modern Utopia*, for example, there is an abrupt transition from Utopia to Trafalgar Square, a transition which occurs in a chapter entitled significantly 'The Bubble Bursts'. The metamorphosis occurs without warning, literally in mid sentence:

> He does not need to finish his sentence, he waves an unteachable destructive arm.
>
> My Utopia rocks about me.
>
> For a moment the vision of that great courtyard hangs real. There the Utopians live real about me, going to and fro, and the great archway blazes with sunlight from the green gardens by the riverside. . . .
>
> And then –
>
> 'Scars of the past! Scars of the past! These fanciful, useless dreams!'
>
> There is no jerk, no sound, no hint of material shock. We are in London, and clothed in the fashion of the town. The sullen roar of London fills our ears. . . . For a moment we stand there, and my

dream of Utopia runs off me like water from an oiled slab.

(11, 1 and 2)

The transformation from the mountain passes of Utopia to the grime and noise of London is instantaneous, as if the ideal world of the narrator's dream has simply melted away. 'I forget', he remarks, 'that a Utopia is a thing of the imagination that becomes more fragile with every added circumstance, that, like a soap bubble, it is most brilliantly and variously coloured at the very instant of its dissolution.' The metaphor of a bubble of quotidian time from which reader and narrator can be released is suggestive and Wells toys with the idea in a number of novels and short stories. In *The Time Machine*, *When the Sleeper Wakes* and such stories as 'The New Accelerator' and 'The Queer Story of Brownlow's Newspaper' he is continually playing with the idea of time, challenging conventional notions of duration through a deliberate process of displacement.

A similar moment of transition from reverie to actuality occurs in *Mr Blettsworthy on Rampole Island*. Blettsworthy is being pursued by savages intent on his life and, together with the girl he loves, flees to the haven of a cave. At the climax of the chase there is a moment in which time seems to stand still:

> We paddle swiftly for a time and then we are held up by a swirling rapid, we hang motionless and then thrust forward again. That struggle goes on for immense periods.   (3, 10)

The use of the present tense throughout the pursuit sequence heightens the sense of immediacy, the sense that what is being narrated is taking place *now*. The pursuit has the clarity of a vivid dream, a nightmare from Kafka or Poe. Abruptly the scene changes: 'It is daylight and the cave is less like a cave than a commodious, pleasant room.' Blettsworthy awakens from his reverie to find himself in New York. The narrative then continues in the past tense of novelistic convention. But that instant when the bubble of time has been pierced remains in the memory, a disturbing vision.

Wells's most sustained attempt to juxtapose dream and reality is *The Autocracy of Mr Parham* (1930), the story of an Oxford don who, after attending a seance, has a series of visions in which he becomes Lord Paramount of England. In this capacity he assumes the role of a dictator and embarks on a grand tour of Europe, allying himself with Mussolini and other rulers. His aggressive policies eventually lead to conflict – there is a spirited account of a world war fought with battleships and bombing aeroplanes – and to growing opposition to his rule. Fearing defeat, he resolves to use poison gas as a weapon against his adversaries. In an armed confrontation in the gas-factory there is a massive explosion in which Parham imagines himself to be killed. He awakens to find himself at the seance, having dreamt the entire sequence of events.

As a story *The Autocracy of Mr Parham* is undistinguished – it is composed of materials Wells had employed previously and was to use again – but it is notable for its skilful handling of the relationship between the real and the imaginary. At the instant of the explosion there is a moment in which time seems to be arrested:

> The world and all things in it vanished in a flash of blinding light. The word 'extinction' sang like a flying spark through the disintegrating brain of Mr Parham. Darkness should have swallowed up that flying spark, but instead it gave place to other sparks, brighter and larger. . . . With a sort of amazement Mr Parham realised that experience was not at an end for him. He was still something, something that felt and thought.   (5, VIII)

The narrator reminds the reader that 'A dream, as everyone knows, can happen with incredible rapidity. It may all have happened in a second.' It is with a sense of surprise, almost disbelief, that the reader grasps the assertion that Mr Parham's highly circumstantial adventures as the Lord Paramount, which occupy the substance of the novel, are not real at all but the figment of his imagination. Wells deliberately destroys the illusion, returning firmly to earth:

> It seemed to Mr Parham that all reality had deserted him. Not only had Sir Bussy gone off with all his dearest hopes, but it was as if his own substance had gone from him also. Within, the late Lord Paramount was nothing now but a vacuum, a cavernous nothingness craving for reassurance.   (5, IX)

The phrase 'all reality had deserted him' is interesting. What Wells does in this story is to postulate a series of versions of reality, all of which prove to be illusory. Mr Parham's dreams of empire, his secret yearning to edit a weekly newspaper, his conception of an unfolding purpose in history, his longing for feminine companionship, his desire to dominate the world, each proves to be a chimera. He is revealed to be not one integrated personality but a series of masks, 'a cavernous nothingness craving for reassurance'. Wells destroys the illusion twice: once at the moment of the explosion, and again on the last page of the novel:

> And so, showing a weary back to us, with his evening hat on the back of his head, our deflated publicist recedes up Pontingale Street, recedes with all his vanities, his stores of erudition. . . . *and his author, who has come to feel a curious unreasonable affection for him*, must needs bid him a reluctant farewell.
>
> (5, IX, my italics)

Again we notice the shift from the past tense to the present, as if time is being arrested. The use of the words 'us' and 'our' involves the reader as a participant, as if he is being invited into the author's confidence. But this is more than the conventional 'our hero' of a popular novel. There is something pathetic in this last image of Parham's receding back, a moment of sentiment – 'weary' and 'deflated' somehow engage the reader's sympathy. But the concluding phrase 'his author . . . must needs bid him a reluctant farewell' calculatedly destroys the image. For it is not simply Parham as Lord Paramount which is a fiction but Parham himself: in the last sentence Wells intervenes *in propria persona* to remind us that all we have read is a product of his imagination.

Immediately before the final paragraph the narrator remarks, as in an aside, 'there is an element of revelation in every dream'. What is revealed by Mr Parham's dream is the elusive nature of reality, the narrow frontier between fiction and truth. In creating the elaborate fantasia of Mr Parham's 'remarkable adventures in this changing world' and then destroying it, admitting that both the fantasia and the mind that dreamt it is a fiction, Wells implicitly questions established notions of reality.

The idea of transcending the limitations of earthly time was one which haunted Wells from 'The Chronic Argonauts' of 1888 (an early version of *The Time Machine*) to the sombre writings of his last years. The central character of 'The Chronic Argonauts', Dr Nebogipfel, describes himself as 'a man born out of my time – a man thinking the thoughts of a wiser age'. Before departing on his time machine he announces to his incredulous onlooker:

> Thirty years of unremitting toil and deepest thought among the hidden things of matter and form and life, and then *that*, the Chronic Argo, *the ship that sails through time*, and now I go to join my generation, to journey through the ages till my time has come.

What is so striking about Wells's novels and stories is not so much the literal idea of 'sailing through time' as exemplified in *The Time Machine* but the notion of release from earthly chronology, a shaking off of the constraints of time as measured by the clock. A particularly striking instance of this occurs in 'Under the Knife' when the narrator experiences a moment of transcendence in which he is freed from the limitations of earthly time:

> Presently it dawned upon me that my sense of duration had changed: that my mind was moving not faster but infinitely slower, that between each separate impression there was a period of many days. The moon spun once round the earth as I noted this; and I perceived clearly the motion of Mars in his orbit. Moreover, it appeared as if the time between thought and thought grew steadily greater, until at last a thousand years was but a moment in my perception.[46]

This feeling of detachment, of observing life from a standpoint in which 'a thousand years was but a moment in my perception', is a powerful element in Wells's vision, enabling him to observe man from a perspective beyond contemporary time.

A comparable moment of transcendental vision occurs in *The Bulpington of Blup*. One summer evening Theodore Bulpington, then a dreamy youth of 16, is admiring the sunset across the English Channel. It is a particularly beautiful sunset, creating memorable effects of light and radiance among the cirrus clouds. As he watches he has a transitory sensation of timelessness:

> The sunset was there still, but suddenly it was transfigured. The weedy rocks below him, the flaming pools and runlets, the wide bay of the estuary shining responsive to the sky, were transfigured. The universe was transfigured – as though it smiled, as though it opened itself out to him, as though it took him into

complete communion with itself. The scene was no longer a scene. It was a Being. It was as if it had become alive, quite still, but altogether living, an immense living thing englobing himself. He was at the very centre of the sphere of Being. He was one with it.

Time ceased. He felt a silence beneath all sounds; he apprehended a beauty that transcends experience.

He saw his universe clear as crystal and altogether significant and splendid. Everything was utterly lucid, and all was wonder. Wonder was in Theodore's innermost being and everywhere about him. The sunset and the sky and the visible world and Theodore and Theodore's mind, were One. . . .

If time was still passing, it passed unperceived, until Theodore found himself thinking like a faint rivulet on the melting edge of Heaven. This he realised quite clearly was the world when the veil of events and purposes was drawn aside, *this was the timeless world in which everything is different and lovely and right. This was Reality.* (III, 3, my italics)

This idea that the familiar world of everyday is not the only reality, that there are other realities in different dimensions of time and space, was always with Wells. It permeates the short stories and scientific romances and is implicit in many of the novels: a disturbing sense that there can be no final truth, that 'when the veil of events and purposes was drawn aside' a different reality, no less tangible than our own, would be revealed. What is so unusual and stimulating in his work is this awareness that the bubble of time in which we live and move could be punctured; that time, which for so many is a prison, can be deflected. After the fire in *The History of Mr Polly* there is a revealing moment when the retailers on the High Street, realising that they are all insured, are inwardly congratulating themselves on their good fortune. The narrator comments: 'Not one of those excellent men but was already realising that a great door had opened . . . in the opaque fabric of destiny.'

It is this detachment from quotidian time which gives such a powerful distancing effect to so many of the novels. One thinks, for example, of the opening chapters of *Tono-Bungay* and *The New Machiavelli*, 'The Man Who Wrote in the Tower' in *In the Days of the Comet*, the beginning of *The Dream* or 'View from a Window in Provence' in *The World of William Clissold*. Each is viewed from a perspective remote in space and time, as if the narrator is looking back on scenes and events in the distant past. This ability to distance himself from chronological time, to view life and behaviour from the perspective of an unseen time traveller, is one of his most fruitful contributions to the modern novel.

Wells's preoccupation with time is never far from the surface of his novels. In the memorable concluding chapter of Tono-Bungay, 'Night and the Open Sea', there is a particularly interesting example of the way in which he fuses together his concern for the past and the future and weaves them into his overall design. Time, a central element in the novel, permeates the narrative with increasing force until at last, with George Ponderevo's triumphant journey down the Thames, it is woven into the very texture of its language.

The frequent changes of tense from past to present heighten the sense of immediacy as the journey hastens to its sombre climax. As the destroyer rushes out to sea the narration reaches a note of lyricism:

> The old facade of the Hospital was just warming to the sunset as we went by, and after that, right and left, the river opened, the sense of the sea increased and prevailed reach after reach from Northfleet to the Nore.
>
> And out you come at last with the sun behind you into the eastern sea. You speed up and tear the oily water louder and faster, sirroo, sirroo – swish – sirroo, and the hills of Kent – over which I once fled from the Christian teachings of Nicodemus Frapp – fall away on the right hand and Essex on the left. They fall away and vanish into blue haze and the tall slow ships behind the tugs, scarce moving ships and wallowing sturdy tugs, are all wrought of wet gold as one goes frothing by. They stand out bound on strange missions of life and death, to the killing of men in unfamiliar lands. And now behind us is blue mystery and the phantom flash of unseen lights, and presently even these are gone, and I and my destroyer tear out to the unknown across a great grey space. We tear into the great spaces of the future and the turbines fall to talking in unfamiliar tongues.   (IV, 3, 2)

This is a linguistically complex passage in which metaphor, tense and mood coalesce to achieve a word picture rich in imagery of time and movement. 'And out you come at last' immediately creates an effect of anticipation: a sense that all that has been described before is the prelude to a climax. This is immediately followed by a relapse into past tense – 'over which I once fled' – as George reminds himself and the reader of unpleasant experiences in the distant past. These memories are erased in the exultant journey of the destroyer out to the open sea. The effect of rapid movement is achieved by a deliberate contrast of pace. The 'scarce moving' ships and 'wallowing' tugs are contrasted with the 'frothing' destroyer and the 'flash' of lights. There is a proliferation of active verbs – 'speed', 'tear', 'fall', 'vanish'. The vivid use of metaphor – the ships 'wrought of wet gold' and the turbines 'talking in unfamiliar tongues' enhances the sense of movement and impresses the scene on the imagination. But despite the mood of urgency and activity there is a marked sense of doubt – 'blue haze', 'strange missions', 'unfamiliar lands', 'blue mystery', 'the unknown'. *Tono-Bungay* no less than *The Time Machine* ends on a note of ambiguity. When George tears 'into the great spaces of the future' he is haunted by doubt; by a sombre recognition that he is embarking on a journey into the unknown. For Wells, as for his Time Traveller, there could be no final certainty regarding the future of mankind. His attitude to human progress remained one of stoical agnosticism for, as he expressed it in *Apropos of Dolores*: 'There were no biological precedents to guide us to a prophecy of the outcome, because man's limited but incessant intelligence makes his case unique.'[47] His concerns as a novelist were to arouse the reader's sense of wonder, to cause him to look afresh at human potentialities and failings, to open up new dimensions of living – but to do so with no certainty or claim to be offering final truths.

One of the dominant motifs of his fiction is a continual questioning of ostensible reality. Whether his theme is the fluidity of time, the relationship between the real and the imaginary, the significance of dreams or the nature of the self, a recurring theme in his work is a lack of assurance concerning the fundamentals of existence. Stephen Stratton, the narrator of *The Passionate Friends*, expresses his uncertainty in these terms:

We idealists are not jolly people, not honest simple people; the strain tells upon us; even to ourselves we are unappetising. Aren't the burly, bellowing fellows after all righter . . .? Good fellows! While we others, lost in filmy speculations, in moon and star snaring and the chase of dreams, stumble where even they walk upright.   (XI, 1)

From this standpoint each of his novels can be regarded as a speculation, as a provisional statement in which the narrator engages in 'the chase of dreams', in a continual quest for beauty and experience. 'All art', he wrote, 'all science, and still more certainly all writing are experiments in statement.'[48] Each of his novels is a window upon reality, questioning received ideas of time or opening up fresh perspectives of living.

In this sense each of his novels is a time machine, an argosy which permits the reader to escape from the tyranny of quotidian time into a world rich in possibilities of transcendence and wonder. By compelling the reader to define and redefine reality, to admit that the world of the 'solid' and the 'real' is not necessarily final or concrete, Wells opens a door onto wider possibilities of perception. In so doing he widens the scope of the novel in an essentially creative and modernist way.

Part Two

Case Studies

5

The Time Machine: the Riddle of the Sphinx

Without question The Time Machine *is the best piece of writing. It will take its place among the great stories of our language. Like all excellent works it has meanings within its meaning.*

(V. S. Pritchett, *The Living Novel*)

Indeed, I would claim that Wells's early fiction is closer to the symbolic romances of Hawthorne or Melville, or to a complex fantasy like Dr Jekyll and Mr Hyde, *or even to the fables of Kafka, than it is to the more strictly scientific speculations of Verne.*

(Bernard Bergonzi, *The Time Machine: An Ironic Myth*)

The Time Machine is of literary significance as Wells's first full-length work of fiction. It was published in book form in May 1895 after serialisation in W. E. Henley's *New Review* between January and May of that year. All the evidence suggests that it was most carefully written and revised, passing through at least eight different versions from its first publication under the title 'The Chronic Argonauts' in 1888. Between 1889 and 1894 Wells worked away on successive versions of the story, refining, collating and improving on the various drafts. It is clear from this meticulous process of revision that he attached considerable importance to the story and recognised that it would make or break his literary reputation. Writing to his friend Elizabeth Healey in December 1894 he confided:

You may be interested to know that our ancient 'Chronic Argonauts' of the *Science Schools Journal* has at last become a complete story and will appear as a serial in the *New Review* for

January. It's my trump card and if it does not come off very much I shall know my place for the rest of my career.

In the event Wells's hopes for it were amply justified. Favourable notices of it appeared in a number of influential journals including the *Review of Reviews* and the *Spectator*, while Israel Zangwill in the *Pall Mall Magazine* hailed it as a 'brilliant little romance'.[1]

The first novel of a writer who subsequently achieves literary renown is always of intrinsic interest since almost invariably the author in his earliest work expresses much of his personality and attitude to life. In Wells's case an examination of *The Time Machine* is particularly rewarding for, as Bergonzi has remarked, 'the book not only embodies the tensions and dilemmas of its time, but others peculiar to Wells himself'.[2] The writing of *The Time Machine*, occupying as it did a period of seven years, represents not simply his literary apprenticeship – the process through which he transformed himself from an unknown schoolmaster to an imaginative writer – but his first attempt to embody in fictional form his deeply felt convictions concerning the nature of man. It is of seminal interest to the student of his work, first as an example of an allegorical myth – a genre to which he returned many times – and second as a significant departure from the nineteenth-century realist tradition and an important anticipation of the work of Conrad and Kafka. In the discussion which follows I will examine some of its satirical and allegorical elements before turning to a summary of its significance as a modernist text.

The Time Machine has been described as 'one of the most desolating myths in modern literature'.[3] When it was published Wells was a rising young author of 28. He had turned to authorship after abandoning a teaching career on grounds of ill-health and from the outset his work had attracted attention for its originality and austere scientific vision. As a student of biology under T. H. Huxley he had absorbed an evolutionary approach to life and history, a vision of the universe as a single biological process which dominated his beliefs and writings throughout his career. In his first full-length work, *Text Book of Biology* (1893), he acknowledged the central importance of this conception:

In the book of nature there are written, for instance, the triumphs of survival, the tragedy of death and extinction, the tragi-comedy of degradation and inheritance, the gruesome lesson of parasitism, and the political satire of colonial organisms. Zoology is, indeed, a philosophy and a literature to those who can read its symbols. (vol. I, 131)

Nowhere is his preoccupation with 'the tragi-comedy of degradation and inheritance' more evident than in *The Time Machine* (and its successor, *The Island of Doctor Moreau*): written at a time when Wells was deeply influenced by Swift and determined to challenge the complacent assumptions of evolutionary theory. Its indebtedness to Swift, especially the final book of *Gulliver's Travels*, is clear. As a boy Wells had read an unexpurgated edition of *Gulliver's Travels* and had a lifelong admiration for Swift's satirical genius. He openly acknowledged this influence on his work, and in a preface to the 1931 edition of *The Time Machine* observed:

In his [Wells] adolescence Swift had exercised a tremendous fascination upon him and the naive pessimism of this picture of the human future is, like the kindred *Island of Doctor Moreau*, a clumsy tribute to a master to whom he owes an enormous debt.

As an allegory it needs to be seen against the context of his other pessimistic writings of the same period. In such short stories as 'The Sea Raiders' and 'The Empire of the Ants' and in such essays as 'The Extinction of Man' and 'Zoological Retrogression' he repeatedly challenged the notion that evolution must inevitably lead to progress. In contrast to the facile optimism of so much contemporary writing he repeatedly advanced the idea that 'the growing pile of civilisation' may be 'only a foolish heaping that must inevitably fall back upon and destroy its makers in the end'.[4] In the place of the euphoria of such Utopian works as William Morris's *News from Nowhere* he advanced the opposite notion: that civilisation may not lead to a social paradise but to a society in a state of chronic imbalance. Indeed, *News from Nowhere* is openly satirised in an early chapter of the novel:

Social triumphs too, had been effected. I saw mankind housed in splendid shelters, gloriously clothed, and as yet I had found them engaged in no toil. There were no signs of struggle, neither social nor economical struggle. The shop, the advertisement, traffic, all that commerce which constitutes the body of our world, was gone. It was natural on that golden evening that I should jump at the idea of a social paradise.   (ch. VI)

The first impressions of the Time Traveller, with his confident assumption that he has arrived in the golden age, are soon followed by disillusionment. One realisation after another compels him to accept the fact that the society into which he has fallen is not a Utopia at all but a world dominated by cruelty and fear, a world in which the aristocratic and indolent Eloi are preyed upon by the malign subterranean Morlocks. His disillusionment reaches a climax in a stark vision of man's destiny:

> I grieved to think how brief the dream of the human intellect had been. It had committed suicide. It had set itself steadfastly towards comfort and ease, a balanced society with security and permanency as its watchword, it had attained its hopes – to come to this at last.   (ch. XIII)

This is followed by 'The Further Vision', a chapter of extraordinary poetic intensity, in which the Time Traveller journeys 30 million years hence to find that man is apparently extinct in a frozen, dark, inhospitable world. The reader shares with the Time Traveller his fascination with 'the mystery of the earth's fate', his stoical acceptance of man's degradation and ultimate decline. The notion of man as heir to all the ages – a concept implicit in the Darwinian vision of the universe – gives way to a much less complacent idea: that man is simply one of many species and is subject to the same immutable laws governing all forms of life.

The Time Machine is not only an assault on the idea of Utopia but can also be read as a parody of the 'upstairs, downstairs' world in which Wells had lived all his life up to that time. He had spent much of his childhood in an underground kitchen beneath his parents' crockery shop on Bromley High Street and during his years as a shop apprentice had spent much of his time in underground dormitories and stockrooms.[5] During the years in which his mother, Sarah Wells, was housekeeper at Up Park (1880–93) he had spent many hours in the housekeeper's underground room and had been fascinated and repelled by the network of subterranean tunnels linking the kitchens and service areas with the great house. His son, Anthony West, has described *The Time Machine* as a 'violent gut reaction' to the elitist society of Up Park,[6] and indeed it is not difficult to see in the world of the Eloi and Morlocks a description of Up Park writ large. This rigid, stratified world – which he was to describe in great detail in *Tono-Bungay* – was one in which

> every human being had a 'place.' It belonged to you from your birth like the colour of your eyes, it was inextricably your destiny. Above you were your betters, below you were your inferiors.
> (*Tono-Bungay*, I, 1, 3)

It was this ossified society which Wells sought to parody in his satirical vision of England in the year 802,701. It is interesting to note that before embarking on his journey into the future the Time Traveller constructs a miniature version of the time machine, a model which is in every respect a copy of the full-size version. In the same way Up Park can be seen as a microcosm for the Eloi and the Morlocks – what Wells has done is to extrapolate from the country house and estate he knew so well as a child to a picture of the whole world divided into above and below stairs. But already he senses that Up Park and all it represents is in decline. It is a world slowly crumbling, slowly but surely giving way to a new order of things. In 'The Extinction of Man' he had written:

> In the case of every other predominant animal the world has ever seen, I repeat, the hour of its complete ascendancy has been the eve of its entire overthrow.

The careful reader is struck by the repeated references to decay. The sphinx is described as 'greatly weather-worn' and imparting 'an unpleasant suggestion of disease'. The dilapidated building in which the Eloi eat and sleep has broken windows 'and the curtains that hung across the lower end were thick with dust'. The derelict museum is 'deserted and falling into ruin. Only ragged vestiges of glass remained in its windows, and great sheets of the green facing had fallen away from the corroded metallic framework.' The world described by the Time Traveller is a civilisation in decline, a society in which on every hand are signs of corrosion and decay. This emphasis on decline was unusual for a work published at the climax of the Victorian age but wholly characteristic of Wells and consistent with his training and beliefs. Its implicit pessimism was in marked contrast to the facile optimism of the period. Herbert Spencer's *Man versus the State* had been published in 1884, Edward Bellamy's

Looking Backward in 1888 and William Morris's *News from Nowhere* in 1891. In place of the assumption that evolution would inevitably lead to progress Wells posited a very different thesis: that there was no reason whatever to believe that nature was biased in favour of man. Nature was, at best, indifferent; at worst, hostile.

In this connection Wells's repeated stress on the word 'white' is interesting: 'white stone', 'white figure', 'white marble'. The image of the white sphinx, diseased and weather-worn, is a potent symbol of the decline of white imperialism – a remarkably prescient image in a book written at the apogee of the Victorian age.

> But, clearly, the old order was already in part reversed. The Nemesis of the delicate ones was creeping on apace. Ages ago, thousands of generations ago, man had thrust his brother man out of the ease and the sunshine. And now that brother was coming back – changed!   (ch. X)

Whether one sees this as an anticipation of the end of empire or the end of the old order exemplified by the country house it remains a remarkably accurate forecast, and a recurring theme throughout his fiction and sociological writings.

The pessimism of *The Time Machine*, then, is quite deliberate. It was a pessimism to which he returned not only in the early romances and short stories but in much of the later work including *Mr Blettsworthy on Rampole Island* (1928), *The Croquet Player* (1936) and *The Camford Visitation* (1937). In his 1931 preface he refers to this pessimism as 'naive', but Anthony West has argued convincingly that stoical realism was Wells's fundamental stance and that in the optimistic writings of his middle years he was frequently engaged in shouting down his own better judgement.[7] Throughout his life he did not depart from the view that man is inherently animal, that 'there is no reason whatever to believe that the order of nature has any greater bias in favour of man than it had in favour of the icthyosaur or the pterodactyl'.[8]

A further allegorical strand interwoven with the narrative is a complex substructure of religious imagery. The description of the Time Traveller's arrival in a beautiful garden can be read as a parody of the biblical account of paradise: 'The air was free from gnats, the earth from weeds or fungi; everywhere were fruits and sweet and delightful flowers; brilliant butterflies flew hither and thither.' Almost his first act on reaching the world of 802,701 is to eat a meal of fruit, a reflection of the biblical story of the Garden of Eden and the Fall of Man. The vivid account of the Morlocks in their underground cavern (ch. IX) closely resembles the picture of hell and its demons Wells had seen as a child in his mother's copy of Sturm's *Reflections*. (As a boy his mother had done her utmost to instil into him her rigid theology with its literal belief in the devil and the nether world. The Morlocks, 'these unpleasant creatures from below, these whitened Lemurs', can be seen as a personification of these childhood terrors.) The 'faint halitus of freshly-shed blood' in the Morlocks cavern is clearly a reflection of the Christian emphasis on a blood sacrifice, while the 'little table of white metal, laid with what seemed a meal' is a grotesque parody of the Last Supper. Most striking of all is the unforgettable description of the forest fire ('In the Darkness') with its vivid evocation of hell:

> And now I was to see the most weird and horrible thing, I think, of all that I beheld in that future age. This whole space was as bright as day with the reflection on the fire. . . . For the most part of that night I was persuaded it was a nightmare. I bit myself and screamed in a passionate desire to awake. . . . Then I would fall to rubbing my eyes and calling upon God to let me awake. Thrice I saw Morlocks put their heads down in a kind of agony and rush into the flames. (ch. XII)

Demonic and paradisal imagery forms a significant element within the story and is a further reminder of Wells's lifelong debt to Swift. In writing his first novel he was expressing in the form of a myth his deepest intuitions concerning man and simultaneously creating a secular version of Eden.

In his preface to the definitive edition of *The Time Machine* (the Atlantic Edition of 1924) Wells remarked that 'a cleansing course of Swift and Sterne intervened' between his early attempts to write a novel and his first published journalism. The reference to Sterne as a formative influence on the writing of *The Time Machine* is interesting for several reasons. Peter Quennell, in his study *Four Portraits*, has remarked that 'Sterne, mined by disease and haunted by the idea of death, was consequently obsessed by the idea of time . . . at his back Sterne heard always the rush of the time-stream, carrying himself

and his personages towards extinction.' A number of recent critical
studies have demonstrated that *Tristram Shandy* can fairly claim to
be the first 'modern' novel and that in its shifts in time sequence and
use of stylistic devices it anticipates such twentieth-century writers
as Joyce and Virginia Woolf.[9] Moreover *Tristram Shandy* is a classic
example of a novel in which there is no narrator whom the reader
can trust (unlike the realist tradition which held sway almost
throughout the nineteenth century): the ostensible narrator is
continually playing tricks on the reader. This device, as we shall see,
is one which Wells employs to the full in *The Time Machine*. And it
can surely be no accident that the Time Traveller describes the
experience of journeying through time as 'a kind of hysterical
exhilaration' – an extremely apposite phrase with which to describe
the experience of entering a Sterne novel. In entering *The Time
Machine* or *Tristram Shandy* the reader is embarking on an imaginative quest in which nothing is as it seems – in each case what appears
to be a solid, reliable narrative proves, on examination, to be a
labyrinth capable of many different interpretations.

The first clue that the narrative is not as straightforward as it
appears is contained in the novel's subtitle: 'An Invention'. This
clearly refers to both the time machine itself as an artefact and the
story as a fictional creation. At a number of points in the story the
reader's attention is drawn to an element of unreality in the
appearances of things:

> 'This little affair', said the Time Traveller, resting his elbows upon
> the table and pressing his hands together above the apparatus, 'is
> only a model. It is my plan for a machine to travel through time.
> You will notice that it looks singularly askew, and that there is an
> odd twinkling appearance about this bar, as though it was in some
> way unreal.'   (ch. II)

> I stared for a moment at the Time Machine and put out my hand
> and touched the lever. At that the squat substantial-looking mass
> swayed like a bough shaken by the wind.   (ch. XVI)

> I seemed to see a ghostly, indistinct figure sitting in a whirling
> mass of black and brass for a moment – a figure so transparent that
> the bench behind with its sheets of drawings was absolutely
> distinct; but this phantasm vanished as I rubbed my eyes.
> (ch. XVI)

These references to an apparently solid world that was 'in some way unreal', to a figure who is so transparent that he is referred to as a 'phantasm', should alert the reader to the fact that it is not simply the time machine which is insubstantial but the narrative itself; one is invited continually to look both at it and through it.

The story is dominated by the image of the sphinx. This is almost the first object the Time Traveller sees on reaching the year 802,701:

My sensations would be hard to describe. As the columns of hail grew thinner, I saw the white figure more distinctly. It was very large, for a silver birch tree touched its shoulder. It was of white marble, in shape something like a winged sphinx, but the wings, instead of being carried vertically at the sides, were spread so that it seemed to hover. The pedestal, it appeared to me, was of bronze, and was thick with verdigris. It chanced that the face was towards me; the sightless eyes seemed to watch me; there was the faint shadow of a smile on its lips. It was greatly weather-worn, and that imparted an unpleasant suggestion of disease. I stood looking at it for a little space – half a minute, perhaps, or half an hour. It seemed to advance and to recede as the hail drove before it denser and thinner. At last I tore my eyes from it for a moment, and saw that the hail curtain had worn threadbare, and that the sky was lightening with the promise of the sun.

I looked up again at the crouching white shape, and the full temerity of my voyage came suddenly upon me. (ch. IV)

This figure seems to watch him through all his subsequent explorations:

and so I was led past the sphinx of white marble, which had seemed to watch me all the while with a smile at my astonishment, towards a vast grey edifice of fretted stone. (ch. V)

Above me towered the sphinx upon the bronze pedestal, white, shining, leprous, in the light of the rising moon. It seemed to smile in mockery of my dismay. (ch. VII)

The narrator senses instinctively that the sphinx with its watching eyes and 'faint shadow of a smile on its lips' contains the clue to this strange world. It seems to mock him, to challenge him with the unspoken riddle: what does this world mean? He expresses his dilemma in these terms:

> I felt I lacked a clue. I felt – how shall I put it? Suppose you found
> an inscription, with sentences here and there in excellent plain
> English, and, interpolated therewith, others made up of words, of
> letters even, absolutely unknown to you?   (ch. VIII)

The whole of his sojourn in 802,701 is an effort to read the palimpsest, to solve the riddle posed by the inscrutable white figure of the sphinx. Not only does the sphinx lie at the centre of the story in the sense that the narrator cannot travel very far from it – 'a certain feeling, you may understand, tethered me in a circle of a few miles around the point of my arrival' – but it quite literally holds the key to his future for, unknown to him, the time machine lies imprisoned within it. (Wells here echoes the Greek legend of a sphinx which waylaid travellers and tormented them with a riddle: if they could not answer it devoured them.) The sphinx, then, is an implicit challenge to both the narrator and the reader. What, it seems to ask, is the meaning of the story? And behind this lies a larger question: what is the meaning of the riddle of life?

The narrator stresses that the eyes of the sphinx are 'sightless'. It poses many questions but it cannot itself offer any solution to the mystery. However, though the sphinx is silent the reader can share vicariously with the Time Traveller in the unravelling of the riddle; he can journey on through time, offering tantalising glimpses of the future of mankind. But in place of confident assumptions of material and moral progress Wells offers a vision of man as a doomed species, a race driven by fear and internecine hatreds. *The Time Machine* is characteristic of modernist texts in that none of the reader's assumptions are fulfilled: society is not based on harmony but on conflict, Weena is destroyed not by the Morlocks but in the fire lit by the Time Traveller himself, the Traveller disappears at the end of the story never to return. In each case the expectations so carefully built up by the narrator are overturned.

At intervals throughout the story one has the sense that the author is gently toying with the reader. There is a deliberate mocking of the interpretative process, as if the narrator is offering solutions to the riddle of the sphinx only to discard them one by one. The Time Traveller's own interpretations of the riddle are initially wholly erroneous. The first solution offered to the reader ('The

Sunset of Mankind') is a vision of humanity on the wane. The narrator elaborates a picture of a world 'of perfect comfort and security', a society in which men live in Utopian harmony in a state of ease and balance. Having developed this theory at length and convinced himself that he has 'mastered the whole secret of these delicious people' the narrator warns the reader that it is false: 'Very simple was my explanation, and plausible enough – as most wrong theories are!' In the following chapter ('Explanation') he puts forward the theory that mankind has differentiated into two distinct species, the Eloi above ground and the Morlocks below ground, and that the two live in a state of equilibrium. Humanity has become 'a real aristocracy, armed with a perfected science and working to a logical conclusion the industrial system of today'. But again the reader is warned that the interpretation may be mistaken:

> This, I must warn you, was my theory at the time. I had no convenient cicerone in the pattern of the Utopian books. My explanation may be absolutely wrong.   (ch. VIII)

Having descended into the subterranean world of the Morlocks the story-teller modifies his hypothesis yet again. Now he is convinced that it is the Morlocks who are the dominant species and that they are simply biding their time before returning to the surface and claiming their birthright. Later still comes the chilling realisation that the truth is even more horrible, that the Eloi are merely cattle for the carnivorous Morlocks and that the decadent aristocracy with which the Time Traveller has identified himself live in terror of their loathsome persecutors. Even at this stage a note of doubt is introduced: 'It may be as wrong an explanation as mortal wit could invent. It is how the thing shaped itself to me, and as that I give it to you.'

The device employed by the Time Traveller, then, is one of continually teasing the reader: expectations are built up only to be demolished. This pose is maintained to the end. At the conclusion of the story he turns to his audience and exclaims:

> No. I cannot expect you to believe it. Take it as a lie – or a prophecy. Say I dreamed it in the workshop. Consider I have been speculating upon the destinies of our race, until I have hatched this fiction. Treat my assertion of its truth as a mere stroke of art to

enhance its interest. And taking it as a story, what do you think of
it?   (ch. XVI)

To the very end the reader is left in a state of uncertainty. Is the
story to be read *as a story*, as a surface narrative with no deeper
meaning? Is it to be regarded as an ingenious speculation on human
destiny? Or is it parable, a myth containing profound implications
for the future of mankind? On this note of ambiguity the story ends.

It can be seen, then, that in a number of significant respects *The Time
Machine* marks a watershed in the coming of modernism. It pre-
dates Conrad's *Heart of Darkness* (1899), an equally seminal text
which owes much to Wells's sombre vision, and anticipates many of
the literary devices employed by twentieth-century modernists.
Whilst the opening chapters appear to place it in the tradition of 'an
imaginative romance stamped with many characteristics of the
Stevenson and early Kipling period in which it was written',[10] it soon
becomes apparent that it marks a major departure from the
conventions of the late Victorian romance. In its deliberate toying
with the expectations of the reader, its absence of authorial
omniscience, its extensive use of symbolism and ambiguous ending
it consciously rejects the norms of its time and looks ahead to such
writers as Kafka and Golding. And in implicitly questioning man's
domination the novel not only flies in the face of the Utopian
speculations of the age but is an important precursor of a new genre
of 'dystopias' including his own *When the Sleeper Wakes* (1899). In
his first novel Wells created a potent myth imbued with the
dilemmas and uncertainties of the modern age.

6

Tono-Bungay:
the Divided Self

> *One of the most important assumptions in modern thinking about
> the novel is the notion, prevalent among novelists and critics
> alike, that sometime in the concluding years of the last century or
> the early years of this one, at a point which is not exactly
> sensitive but is nonetheless there to be felt, there occurred a
> change, a redirection, a re-emphasis or a 'turn' of the novel.*
>
> > (Malcolm Bradbury, *Possibilities: Essays
> > on the State of the Novel*)

> *It is, I see now that I have it all before me, a story of activity and
> urgency and sterility. I have called it* Tono-Bungay, *but I had far
> better have called it* Waste.
>
> > (H. G. Wells, *Tono-Bungay*)

In any discussion of Wells in relation to the modern novel *Tono-
Bungay* must occupy a central place. Not only was it in his own
words 'his finest and most finished novel upon the accepted lines',[11]
but it is clearly a work in which he invested great pains and high
ambitions. In his autobiography he remarks that

> presently I was finishing *Kipps* and making notes for what I meant
> to be a real full-length novel at last, *Tono-Bungay*, a novel, as I
> imagined it, on Dickens–Thackeray lines. . . . It was planned as a
> social panorama in the vein of Balzac.[12]

It is apparent from these references and from indications in the
novel itself that in writing *Tono-Bungay* Wells intended a formal
imitation of the conventions of the Victorian novel. There is the
division of the narrative into compartments – 'Book the First, Book

the Second' and so on – corresponding to the formal divisions in *Middlemarch* or the 'stages' in *Great Expectations*. There is the use of chapter titles strongly reminiscent of Dickens – 'Of Bladesover House, and my mother; and the Constitution of Society' or 'The Dawn comes, and my Uncle appears in a New Silk Hat'. There is the carefully written opening paragraph which succeeds both in conveying a sense of portentousness and in alerting the reader to the fact that he is about to embark on a novel containing discussion of society as well as individual character:

> Most people in this world seem to live 'in character;' they have a beginning, a middle and an end, and the three are congruous one with another and true to the rules of their type. You can speak of them as being of this sort of people or that. They are, as theatrical people say, no more (and no less) than 'character actors'. They have a class, they have a place, they know what is becoming in them and what is due to them, and their proper size of tombstone tells at last how properly they have played the part. But there is also another kind of life that is not so much living as a miscellaneous tasting of life. One gets hit by some unusual transverse force, one is jerked out of one's stratum and lives crosswise for the rest of the time, and, as it were, in a succession of samples. That has been my lot, and that is what has set me at last writing something in the nature of a novel.

There is the chronological method of narration, reminiscent again of *Great Expectations* and *David Copperfield*, beginning with George Ponderevo as a child and telling the story of his life through adolescence and manhood. There is, finally, the deliberate attempt to render a personal vision, a *Weltanschauung* which will make his narrative comprehensible and complete – a very characteristic ambition of nineteenth-century fiction:

> I suppose what I'm really trying to render is nothing more nor less than Life – as one man has found it. I want to tell – *myself*, and my impressions of the thing as a whole.   (I, 1, 2)

Outwardly, then, *Tono-Bungay* appears to conform to many of the conventions of the realist tradition. This superficial conformity has meant that it has been largely bypassed by modern literary criticism – on the premise that it is a 'loose baggy monster' on a par with *The*

Old Wives' Tale, a novel firmly ground in the realist tradition from which it seems to derive. Closer examination reveals, however, that *Tono-Bungay* is not at all what a first reading might suggest and that in a number of fundamental respects it marks an important departure from the conventions of the realist novel. In its fluid method of narration, its self-awareness, its extensive use of metaphor and imagery and, above all, in its divided narrative voice can be recognised many of the hallmarks of the modern novel.

Wells is anxious to make it clear from the outset that his novel will be much more in the vein of Sterne than James:

> I warn you this book is going to be something of an agglomeration. I want to trace my social trajectory (and my uncle's) as the main line of my story, but as this is my first novel and almost certainly my last, I want to get in too all sorts of things that struck me, things that amused me and impressions I got – even although they don't minister directly to my narrative at all.   (I, 1, 1)

It is thus established from the beginning that the book will offend against the canons of the novel as defined by James, that it will be diffuse rather than austere – 'it isn't a constructed tale I have to tell but unmanageable realities' – and that the narrator reserves his freedom to digress and philosophise in telling his story. He then adds another disclaimer in even more unambiguous terms:

> I've read an average share of novels and made some starts before this beginning, and I've found the restraints and rules of the art (as I made them out) impossible for me. I like to write, I am keenly interested in writing, but it is not my technique. I'm an engineer with a patent or two and a set of ideas; most of whatever artist there is in me has been given to turbine machines and boat-building and the problem of flying, and do what I will I fail to see how I can be other than a lax, undisciplined story-teller. I must sprawl and flounder, comment and theorise, if I am to get the thing out I have in mind.   (I, 1, 2)

It has to be remembered that these words were written at a time when Wells and James had been corresponding for eight years and the younger novelist must have been aware that in deliberately distancing himself from the novel as a symmetrical, beautifully constructed work of art he was flying in the face of much advice from James and his circle. But the significance of Wells's disclaimer does not end here. Its effect is to alert the reader to the fact that he intends to 'sprawl and flounder, comment and theorise', and that his novel, by its very nature, cannot have the cohesion and unity of *Middlemarch* or *Mansfield Park*.

The reader is thus warned what *kind* of novel *Tono-Bungay* is to be – 'I warn you this book is going to be something of an agglomeration' – with the corollary that expectations of a neatly constructed novel of character and nuance will not be fulfilled. What Wells is setting out to do is to render in fictional form 'Life – as one man has found it' and in consciously attempting a novel of contingency and fluidity he was breaking new ground. For Wells, as for his *alter ego* George Ponderevo, all is provisional; the one enduring reality he finds is scientific truth. Beyond this all is uncertain – his attitudes, his beliefs, his actions, his method of narration all minister to the central fact of life's haphazardness, to the overriding presence of change in all things. When George stands contemplating the despoiled countryside caused by the erection of his uncle's vast house, Crest Hill, and reflects that 'all his world lay open and defenceless, conquered and surrendered, doomed so far as he could see, root and branch, scale and form alike, to change',[13] his observation has relevance not simply to the physical transformation around him but to his attitudes to literature and to the specific work he is writing. The overwhelming impression one derives from a reading of *Tono-Bungay* is one of fluidity, of the transitoriness of life and society, the instability of a world which is 'all one spectacle of forces running to waste, of people who use and do not replace, the story of a country hectic with a wasting aimless fever of trade and money-making and pleasure-seeking'.[14] The fluidity of Wells's theme is reflected in the apparently artless method of narration he chooses to adopt, a method characterised by frequent digressions and excursions into sociological comment. In fact the method is by no means as random as may appear. What seems on first reading to be a chaotic approach to his material has clearly been deliberately employed as commensurate with his theme. Only a novel 'based on the fluidity of the autobiographical narrator',[15] Wells feels, will be appropriate to the panorama of change, decay, waste and confusion he sees before him. For Wells the great issues of the twentieth century demanded a new kind of novel, one which would seek to convey the essential precariousness of life and the provisionality of man's attempts to interpret it.

Malcolm Bradbury has observed that 'an essential feature of the twentieth-century novel is the presence of a new kind of self-awareness, an introversion of the novel to a degree unprecedented in its fortunes'.[16] At a number of points in the narrative Wells specifically reminds the reader that he is reading a *novel*:

> I've reached the criticising, novel-writing age, and here I am writing mine – my one novel.   (I, 1, 2)

> I am trying to tell of all the things that happened to me. It's hard enough simply to get it put down in the remotest degree right. But this is a novel, not a treatise.   (II, 4, 10)

> All this writing is gray now and dead and trite and unmeaning to me; some of it I know by heart. I am the last person to judge it.   (IV, 3, 1)

By referring to his story as a piece of writing, an artificial creation – even at one stage describing the book in the process of composition ('Concurrently with writing the last chapter of this book I have been much engaged by the affairs of a new destroyer we have completed') – he distances himself from the narrative, as it were stepping outside the fictional frame and drawing attention to the world of reality beyond it – a technique occasionally employed by nineteenth-century writers but one much more typical of the modernists. The reader is not to lose sight of the fact that he is reading a *novel*, an artifice, one man's vision of life and experience. There is no pretence that the author is not present, that the novel has in some way written itself: *Tono-Bungay* is a world removed from the omniscient narrator of George Eliot or Trollope. The author is at once obtrusive and detached, both within and beyond the printed page. In insisting that his book 'is a novel, not a treatise' Wells calls attention to its fictionality and does so in a manner which Bennett, for example, would have found unthinkable.

Tono-Bungay is characteristically modernist in its extensive use of metaphor and imagery. Throughout the novel there is a dense cross-weaving of symbolism based on themes of decay, disease and the coming of change. At an early stage in the narrative, for example, there is a vivid comparison of the imminence of change with the onset of a sudden frost:

> The great houses stand in the parks still, the cottages cluster respectfully on their borders, touching their eaves with their creepers, the English countryside – you can range through Kent from Bladesover northward and see – persists obstinately in looking what it was. It is like an early day in a fine October. The hand of change rests on it all, unfelt, unseen; resting for awhile, as it were half reluctantly, before it grips and ends the thing for ever. One frost and the whole face of things will be bare, links snap, patience end, our fine foliage of pretences lie glowing in the mire.   (I, 1, 3)

Later in the novel Wells returns to the metaphor of the frost and remarks 'That I still feel was a good image.' What is impressive about it is not simply its literal appositeness but the ambivalent language with which the metaphor is described: 'The hand of change rests on it all, *unfelt, unseen*; resting for awhile, *as it were half reluctantly*, before it grips and ends the thing for ever.' His ambivalence towards the changes he is foreshadowing is clearly evident in this and other passages so that Wells's own attitude towards the passing of the Victorian age is uncertain.

The choice of Ponderevo as the name of his central character is peculiarly apposite since the name means literally 'to consider the age' (ponder = to weigh, to consider; ev = age, time). The novel as a whole is a reflection on the age, a confessional in which Wells expresses his deepest fears and uncertainties for the twentieth century. These are expressed in part through the story of George's life and adventures and in part through the web of imagery suggestive of ebb and change. The rise and fall of Edward Ponderevo's financial empire, the abortive attempt to steal the radioactive quap from Mordet Island, the death of Edward, George's unhappy love-affairs, his final voyage along the Thames out to the open sea – all these are metaphors linked to the author's overriding themes of waste and disintegration. It is worth examining one of these episodes in detail to see how Wells makes creative use of the technique.

The quap episode, much criticised by some commentators on the grounds that it is too disparate in theme to form a unified part of the novel, is an integral part of the overall design. Through its emphasis on language and imagery linked to cancer and decay the episode reinforces the dominant theme underlying the book of 'the broad slow decay of the great social organism of England' and makes explicit the analogy between the two.

But its significance lies deeper than this. Time and again when reading this chapter one is reminded of themes and images recalling Conrad's *Heart of Darkness* – a seminal modernist text – and Wells's own allegorical fable, *The Island of Doctor Moreau*. Long before the commencement of the quap chapter the reader has been prepared by a sense of foreboding:

> He gave a sense of heat and a perpetual reek of vegetable decay, and told how at last comes a break among these things, an arena fringed with bone-white dead trees, a sight of the hard blue sea-line beyond the dazzling surf and a wide desolation of dirty shingle and mud, bleached and scarred. (III, 1, 4)

This sense of a literal and metaphorical journey towards an impenetrable 'heart of darkness' is reinforced by the description of the voyage to Mordet Island aboard the brig *Maud Mary*. As the ship approaches nearer and nearer to the radioactive substance the veneer of civilisation falls away and the crew become noisy, argumentative and brutal. In a passage which vividly recalls Edward Prendick's sojourn aboard ship in *The Island of Doctor Moreau* George describes the miserable journey to Africa in a cramped brig in which 'the crew lived lives very much after the fashion of ours, more crowded, more cramped and dirty, wetter, steamier, more verminous. . . . And as we pitched and floundered southward they gambled and fought, were brutal to one another, argued and wrangled loudly, until we protested at the uproar'.[17] George contrasts the wretched life on the ship with the civilisation he has known in England, but the irony of this passage will not be lost on the reader. The 'civilisation' he has known is one based on greed, falsity, deceit and the relentless accumulation of material possessions. The implied contrast between the values of this society and the aggressiveness of the crew throws into sharp relief the shallowness of Edwardian London and its inherent artificiality.

At the centre of the quap chapter is a lengthy account of George's murder of an African native – an incident which is largely ignored in criticism of the novel yet is crucial to an understanding of the work from a modernist standpoint. The encounter between the two is described in terms which irresistably call to mind the confrontation between Crusoe and Man Friday:

> He wasn't by any means a pretty figure. He was very black and naked except for a dirty loin-cloth, his legs were ill-shaped and his toes spread wide, and the upper edge of his cloth and a girdle of string cut his clumsy abdomen into folds. His forehead was low, his nose very flat, and his lower lip swollen and purplish red. His hair was short and fuzzy, and about his neck was a string and a little purse of skin. He carried a musket, and a powder flask was stuck in his girdle. It was a curious confrontation. There opposed to him stood I, a little soiled perhaps, but still a rather elaborately civilised human-being born, bred and trained in a vague tradition. In my hand was an unaccustomed gun. And each of us was essentially a teeming vivid brain, tensely excited by the encounter, quite unaware of the other's mental content or what to do with him.　(III, 4, 6)

But whereas the encounter in *Robinson Crusoe* leads to friendship and affection, this confrontation leads directly to murder. Afraid that the savage will alert his countrymen to the presence of intruders George unceremoniously shoots him, killing him instantly. Mordet Island (Mordet = more death) now becomes not only a physical presence but a miasmatic force permeating the novel. In a nightmare the memory of the dead man is linked with an anticipation of his uncle's death:

> I lay after that wide awake, staring at my memories. . . .The black body which I saw now damaged and partly buried, but which, nevertheless, I no longer felt was dead but acutely alive and perceiving, I mixed up with the ochreous slash under my uncle's face. I tried to dismiss this horrible obsession from my mind, but it prevailed over all my efforts.　(III, 4, 6)

The image of a resurrected body 'acutely alive and perceiving' and reaching out to affect the living is not simply an echo of Wells's short story 'Pollock and the Porrah Man'[18] but a powerful metaphor for what follows. The corrupting influence of the island reaches out to affect all who come into contact with it.

George succeeds in retrieving the quap only to see the *Maud Mary* disappear into the sea, her timbers rotted away by radioactive emanations. His failure to bring the precious cargo back to England means that he is too late to save his uncle from bankruptcy and ruin. This in turn leads directly to his uncle's death, who dies despite George's well-intentioned but misguided attempt to avoid arrest by his pursuers. The death of Edward Ponderevo is followed by the death of his hopes to marry Beatrice and the crushing of his spirit. For a time George experiences the aboulia of black despair:

And then indeed I tasted the ultimate bitterness of life. For the first time I felt utter futility, and was wrung by emotion that begot no action, by shame and pity beyond words. . . . But the pain I felt then I have felt a hundred times; it is with me as I write. It haunts this book, I see, that is what haunts this book, from end to end. (IV, 2, 4)

His despair gives way to stoicism in the beautifully written final scene ('Night and the Open Sea') in which he rhapsodises on the death of the England he has known and the passing of an age:

Out to the open we go, to windy freedom and trackless ways. Light after light goes down. England and the Kingdom, Britain and the Empire, the old prides and the old devotions, glide abeam, astern, sink down upon the horizon, pass – pass. The river passes – London passes, England passes. . . . (IV, 3, 2)

'The End of an Age' was one of the titles Wells considered for the book before settling on *Tono-Bungay*[19] and it is evident that death is a leading strand in the novel's web of imagery – physical death in the case of George's mother, his uncle and the native; symbolic death in the sense that the old England he has known as a child has passed away. In a striking passage Wells draws an explicit comparison between radioactive decay and the gradual decline of the Victorian age:

But there is something – the only word that comes near it is *cancerous* – and that is not very near, about the whole of quap, something that creeps and lives as a disease lives by destroying; an elemental stirring and disarrangement, incalculably malefi-cient and strange. This is no imaginative comparison of mine. . . . It is in matter exactly what the decay of our old culture is in

society, a loss of traditions and distinctions and assured reactions. (III, 4, 5)

The killing of the savage is thus capable of both a literal and an
allegorical interpretation. Literally, as George suggests, the murder
is simply a meaningless incident, one more indication of the
selfishness and violence which lie at the heart of society. The
deliberate resemblance to *Robinson Crusoe* arouses the readers'
expectations only to have them overturned. Symbolically the
episode can be seen as a vivid reiteration of the death and decay
motif which permeates the narrative. The book is indeed a moving
account of the end of an age, and a remarkably prescient forecast of
the terminal cancer affecting the old order.

The novel is not only redolent of images of change and decay but
also of *a sense of loss*: 'Everybody who is not actually in the shadow
of a Bladesover is as it were perpetually seeking after lost
orientations.'[20] This sense of loss forms a powerful undercurrent in
the narrative and at one point leads him to repeat an image from
'The Door in the Wall', a short story published while *Tono-Bungay*
was still in draft.

> There stretches away south of us long garden slopes and white
> gravestones and the wide expanse of London, and somewhere in
> the picture is a red old wall, sunwarmed, and a great blaze of
> Michaelmas daisies set off with late golden sunflowers and a drift
> of mottled, blood-red, fallen leaves. It was with me that day as
> though I had lifted my head suddenly out of dull and immediate
> things and looked at life altogether. (II, 1, 3)

'The Door in the Wall' is the story of a prominent politician, Lionel
Wallace, who is haunted by a childhood memory of a door leading to
an enchanted garden and a dream-like experience of happiness.
Wallace places great emphasis on the fact that on the pavement
outside the door were fallen horse-chestnut leaves, from which he
deduces that his childhood adventure must have taken place during
October. All his life he is tormented by the memory of the door and
his lost happiness, a torment which ends when he steps through a
door over a deep excavation (in the mistaken belief that this will lead
to the enchanted garden) and falls to his death. Wells echoes the
image of the wall and the fallen leaves in *Tono-Bungay* and in the
picture of the 'red old wall, sun-warmed, and a great blaze of
Michaelmas daisies set off with late golden sunflowers and a drift of

mottled, blood-red, fallen leaves' brings together a cluster of imagery suggestive of autumn and loss. The wall symbolises the idea of a barrier and the narrator's failure to attain the contentment he seeks. George seeks his fulfilment in *Tono-Bungay*, in his love for Marion, in his experiments with flying machines, his love for Beatrice and finally in the manufacture of destroyers. Each of these proves to be illusory; the happiness he aspires to continually eludes him. In the symbolism of dreams the leaf is traditionally interpreted as an allegory of happiness[21] and through his emphasis on the mottled, fallen leaves Wells symbolises George's loss. Each path to fulfilment is closed to him: each satisfies for a time and then shrivels away. Moreover the leaves are *red*, symbolising passion or animality. Neither in his marriage nor outside it does George achieve a satisfactory love relationship and the story of his emotional life is one of frustration and disappointment. Always he is mocked by his impossible ideal.

As if to underline the significance of his reference to the wall Wells concludes the paragraph with the sentence: 'It was with me that day as though I had lifted my head suddenly out of dull and immediate things and looked at life altogether.' From the context the 'It' here can be taken as referring to the conversations on life and philosophy with his friend Ewart which immediately precede the paragraph but the deliberate echoing of the language and imagery of 'The Door in the Wall' – a story saturated with the idea of loss – leaves little doubt that the short story was uppermost in Wells's mind.[22] October, Michaelmas daisies, late golden sunflowers, blood-red leaves – all are suggestive of autumn and the decay and decline associated with the season. *Tono-Bungay* is in one sense a fantasia on the theme of England in decline, the decline of the age of certainty and its replacement by an age of confusion.

Tono-Bungay was published in 1909, and Lawrence's *Sons and Lovers* in 1913. Superficially the connection between the two novels may seem slight, yet on examination it can be seen that there are scenes in *Tono-Bungay* which anticipate many of the themes Lawrence was later to make his own. Lawrence had certainly read *Tono-Bungay* and praised it enthusiastically to his friends.[23] What impresses the modern reader on reassessing the novel is the extent to which Wells foresees the sterility of love and passion in an age devoted to the pursuit of ugliness, and the striking manner in which the tone and language of Lawrence's fiction are so clearly adumbrated.

It is widely accepted that as a novelist Wells was least successful in describing love relationships between men and women. There is a stilted quality about many of his love scenes, an artificial note – as if this most passionate of men was incapable of expressing in fiction the full beauty of adult love. Yet in the account of the affair between George Ponderevo and Beatrice Normandy ('Love among the Wreckage') Wells probably came closest to a wholly convincing description of a love-affair – and does so in a manner which is remarkably frank by the standards of the time. It has to be remembered that the novel appeared only nine months before the furore surrounding the publication of Wells's *Ann Veronica*, yet, despite its sexual frankness, it aroused none of the controversy associated with the latter work. One has only to read the encounter with Beatrice in the pavilion (Book 4, ch. 2, 1) to be aware that it is charged with sexual energy in a manner which strikingly anticipates the scenes between Paul Morel and Clara Dawes in *Sons and Lovers*.

Most striking of all is the language employed by Wells in describing the futility of love in the modern age:

> Love, like everything else in this immense process of social disorganisation in which we live, *is a thing adrift, a fruitless thing broken away from its connections*. . . . Once more this mighty passion, *that our aimless civilisation has fettered and maimed and sterilised and debased*, gripped me and filled me with passionate delights and solemn joys – that were all, you know, *futile and purposeless*.   (my italics)

Lawrence was to develop this theme much more fully in *Women in Love* and again in *Lady Chatterley's Lover*, but the germ of the idea can be clearly discerned in *Tono-Bungay*. What so concerned Wells was the corrupting influence of wealth, the falsity of an age in which beauty and naturalness were debased, the insidious corrosion of ugliness and waste. These are themes to which he returned many times in his later fiction but perhaps never again with such passionate intensity.

Modern academic criticism has tended to concentrate on the language and structure of *Tono-Bungay*, but what has so far received comparatively little attention is the perspective from which George Ponderevo views his world: the narrative voice. What impresses the reader at once about this voice is its uncertainty, its lack of any clear philosophical base from which to interpret his bewildering experiences. Patrick Parrinder has observed that the mixture of pragmatism and doubt with which the narrator surveys his life 'is utterly different from the calm narrative authority exercised in such representative Edwardian novels as *The Man of Property*, *The Old Wives' Tale*, *Howards End* and *Kipps*'.[24] The self-assurance of most Edwardian fiction is replaced by a much less confident note: 'a note of crumbling and confusion, of change and seemingly aimless swelling, of a bubbling up and medley of futile loves and sorrows'. At the outset of the book when George attempts to define the scope of the novel he is about to write he states that he wishes

> to say things I have come to feel intensely of the laws, traditions, usages and ideas we call society, and how we poor individuals get driven and lured and stranded among these windy, perplexing shoals and channels. (I, 1, 2)

The analogy between life and 'shoals and channels' is interesting but Wells's use of *windy* and *perplexing* is highly suggestive when viewed in the context of the novel as a whole. George is quite simply *perplexed* by his experiences, in the sharpest contrast to the narrators created by Bennett and Galsworthy. The novel is a journey not simply in the sense that George and his uncle and aunt are constantly moving onward in their social progression, but also in that George is ever seeking a satisfying personal faith, a rationale which will embody and unify the competing strands in his make-up.

In the long chapter entitled 'Marion' – a chapter which is in some senses the heart of the novel – George confides his uncertainty to the reader, making it plain that he has no solution to offer to the riddle of life.

> Don't imagine that I am coming presently to any sort of solution of my difficulties. Here among my drawings and hammerings *now*, I still question unanswering problems. All my life has been at bottom, *seeking*, disbelieving always, dissatisfied always with the thing seen and the thing believed, seeking something in toil, in force, in danger, something whose name and nature I do not clearly understand, something beautiful, worshipful, enduring, mine profoundly and fundamentally, and the utter redemption of myself; I don't know, – all I can tell is that it is something I have ever failed to find. (II, 4, 10)

The narrative voice employed in *Tono-Bungay* is, then, predominantly uncertain – a voice characterised by doubt and confusion, one far more reminiscent of Conrad than Bennett. But the most significant fact about it is that it is not only uncertain, but *divided*: there is in a sense not one narrator but two, corresponding to a division within Wells's own personality – that between romantic and classical elements – which dominated his life. Throughout his intellectual career Wells was torn between imaginative and romantic drives on the one hand, and sceptical and dispassionate inclinations on the other. This conflict can be seen in many aspects of his work. It is evident, for example, in his desire to establish a reputation for himself as the author of fantastic romances in such works as *The War of the Worlds* and *The First Men in the Moon* and, at the same time, his wish to write serious educational works such as *The Outline of History* and *The Science of Life*. It is evident in his admission that 'my disposition is diametrically opposed to my philosophy',[25] in his continual search for a satisfying emotional relationship, and in the co-existence within his personality of nostalgia and radicalism. George Ponderevo is a characteristically Wellsian hero in that he embodies these tensions within himself. On the one hand is the engineer: practical, impartial, sceptical, experimenting with flying machines and destroyers and devoted to the life of scientific research. On the other hand is the dreamer: romantic, imaginative, questing, passionate, falling in love with Marion and Beatrice and haunted by a vision of unattainable beauty. The conflict is well expressed by the narrator himself in a revealing passage:

> I stumble and flounder, but I know that over all these merry immediate things, there are other things that are great and serene, very high, beautiful things – the reality. I haven't got it, but it's there nevertheless. I'm a spiritual guttersnipe in love with unimaginable goddesses. (II, 4, 10)

The interaction between the two aspects – between the 'spiritual guttersnipe' with his doubting, pragmatic temperament, and the romantic yearning for 'unimaginable goddesses' – provides the novel with much of its interest and power.

The conflict makes itself felt at an early stage in the narrative when George describes his boyhood 'in the shadow of Bladesover House'. There is a lengthy (and decidedly unawed) description of the great house in which the narrator is brought up by his mother, the housekeeper, and spends so much of his childhood – a description notable for its tone of scepticism and detachment. The dominant tone is one of irony, almost mockery. George deflates the falsity and pretentiousness of the gentry, commenting on their shallowness and slavish adherence to outmoded conventions. This analytical section is followed by a brilliant and wholly Dickensian account of afternoon tea in the housekeeper's room, and this in turn is succeeded by a description of the park surrounding the house:

> About that park there were some elements of a liberal education; there was a great space of greensward not given over to manure and food grubbing; there was mystery, there was matter for the imagination. . . . There were corners that gave a gleam of meaning to the word forest, glimpses of unstudied natural splendour. There was a slope of bluebells in the broken sunlight under the newly green beeches in the west wood that is now precious sapphire in my memory; it was the first time that I knowingly met Beauty. (I, 1, 5)

Already in this short passage occur a number of key romantic terms: mystery, imagination, natural splendour, beauty. It is difficult to square this sensitive response with the outwardly sceptical persona maintained by the narrator (one might also add that it is difficult to reconcile it with the received view of Wells as a writer who was indifferent to beauty). In describing Bladesover House and its surrounding parkland Wells is drawing on his memories of Up Park, Sussex (now the property of the National Trust) where his mother was housekeeper for 13 years. The experience of seeing Up Park, of living there and being free to wander about its gracious park clearly made an immense impact on a boy who had spent the first 14 years of his life in Bromley. Not only does he confess in *Tono-Bungay* that 'when I was a little boy I took the place with the entirest faith as a complete authentic microcosm' and then go on to describe it in great detail, but the house also figures prominently in *The Passionate Friends* (as Burnmore Park), in *The World of William Clissold* (as Mowbray) and in *Experiment in Autobiography* where Wells is at pains to stress the crucial import-ance of the house in the development of his imagination.[26] The house and the park might almost be taken as a symbol of the ambivalence in his nature. Up Park is classical, severe, symmetrical, chaste; the park is romantic, wild, beautiful, untamed. In stating that Bladesover is 'the clue to all England'[27] George is undoubtedly highlighting an important truth – yet it is also the clue to his own personality. In all his subsequent adventures the dichotomy between scientific truth and the quest for romance never leaves him.

As a science student, first at Wimblehurst and later in London, George makes a determined effort to apply himself to a life of diligent research. But again and again his resolution 'to serve and do and make – with some nobility' is deflected: first by Marion, then by his uncle, then by Beatrice. Marion, whom he idealises and surrounds with a halo of romantic imagery – 'I saw her in dreams released, as it were, from herself, beautiful, worshipful, glowing' – distracts him more and more from his studies until at last his academic career is in ruins. Alternately attracted and exasperated by her he cannot apply his mind to 'the militant ideals of unflinching study' he had brought with him from Wimblehurst. She becomes, quite simply, his obsession. 'My work got more and more spiritless, my behaviour degenerated', George ruefully confesses. 'Such supplies of moral energy as I still had at command shaped now in the direction of serving Marion rather than science.' It is at this crucial point in his life that his uncle, Edward Ponderevo, offers him a partnership in a lucrative, but fraudulent, patent medicine enterprise. George has serious doubts about accepting this offer and holds out for a week while he debates his prospects. It is clear from his discussions with his uncle that he still hankers after scientific research or teaching – possibilities Edward dismisses contemptuously. George confides to his narrative his strong feeling that 'somewhere, a little overgrown perhaps, but still traceable, lay a neglected, wasted path of use and honour for me'.[28] After much hesitation he reluctantly accepts his uncle's offer and for some years devotes himself to the adventure of building up the Tono-Bungay enterprise. When this fails to satisfy his restless temperament he assuages his craving for the life of research by applying himself to ambitious experiments in aerial navigation. His experiments with navigable balloons consume more and more of his energy and distract his mind from Tono-Bungay but again he is deflected – this time by his childhood heroine Beatrice Normandy. His overpowering love for Beatrice betrays him into abandoning his steady application to science. At last he is compelled to admit that 'I cut down the toil of research in my eagerness and her eagerness for fine flourishes in the air, flights that would tell. I shirked the longer road.'[29] At each of these stages in his life the implicit choice between science and romance confronts the narrator with a dichotomy in which the competing strands in his make-up are torn. Marion, with her physical beauty and elusiveness, embodies all that yearning for passion and loveliness which haunts him. His uncle with his impetuousness, his enthusiasm and constant talk of 'the Romance of Commerce' embodies the quest for adventure and excitement which has for George an irresistible appeal. Beatrice, with her mystery, her spirit and aura of romance, symbolises for him the search for an enigma which exercises such a powerful emotional attraction. The conflict within himself between duty and romance, between the dispassionate quest for truth and the yearning for beauty, corresponds to a fundamental ambivalence in Wells's personality which underlies many of the crucial episodes in the novel.

An interesting illustration of this tension is the extensive use of imagery associated with water and the sea. When George as a boy is fleeing from Chatham on his journey to Bladesover House he looks back and sees the estuary of the Thames, 'that river that has since played so large a part in my life'. He is struck by a romantic vision of the sea:

> And out upon it stood ships, sailing ships and a steamer or so, going up to London or down out into the great seas of the world. I stood for a long time watching these and thinking whether after all I should not have done better to have run away to sea. (I, 2, 3)

Water as the source of life can be seen as a metaphor for George's ceaseless quest for life and purpose. His quest is frustrated by Marion, with her indifference to her own beauty (her surname Ramboat suggests a literal torpedoing of his journey), then by his uncle. It is significant that his agonising over whether or not to accept his uncle's offer to join the Tono-Bungay empire takes place along the Thames embankment: the river of life is an apt symbol for the choice George is compelled to make. The symbol stays with him to the closing chapter when, on his final voyage, it returns with overwhelming force:

> It is curious how at times one's impressions will all fuse and run together into a sort of unity and become continuous with things that have hitherto been utterly alien and remote. That rush down the river became mysteriously connected with this book.
>
> (IV, 3, 2)

Cleaving through the water in his fast-moving destroyer he hastens on to the sea, closing the book with an ambiguous and haunting sentence: 'We are all things that make and pass, striving upon a hidden mission, out to the open sea.' If life has a purpose, George suggests, then that purpose is concealed from us, but it is our duty to live our lives to the utmost, disentangling the reality which he sees 'always as austerity, as beauty'. The destroyer, 'stark and swift, irrelevant to most human interests', symbolises science with its immense potentiality for creation or destruction. The river and the sea symbolise the ceaseless flow of life, the unending quest for creativity. The ambivalence remains to the end.

David Lodge has called attention to the fact that 'We find in *Tono-Bungay* in fact, that submission of Wells's professed radical optimism to the more pessimistic intuitions of his imagination, which Bernard Bergonzi has located as a prime source of the enduring interest of Wells's science fiction'.[30] Pessimistic, sceptical, far-seeing, it is a novel dominated by the idea of civilisation in decline, of the loss of confidence engendered by society in a state of flux. In writing his personal vision of life, his 'bird's-eye view of the modern world',[31] he gave expression to his deepest convictions regarding man and society and in the process created one of his most revealing and prescient works.

7

The History of Mr Polly: Paradise Regained

Indeed, you may almost be content to read Candide, *as children read* Gulliver, *simply for the story. Almost – for no intelligent reader of* Candide *could stop there. He could not get through a page of these adventures and marvels and catastrophes without discovering what underlies them all: a suggested argument, an intellectual appeal, a tissue of ideas.*

(A. B. Walkley, preface to *The History of Candide*)

As a rule, an allegory is a story in verse or prose with a double meaning: a primary or surface meaning; and a secondary or under the surface meaning. It is a story, therefore, that can be read, understood and interpreted at two levels (and in some cases at three or four levels).

(J. A. Cuddon, *A Dictionary of Literary Terms*)

The History of Mr Polly, one of Wells's finest novels, was written in 1909 and begun in a mood in which 'he felt he could go on writing for ever'.[32] Despite the mood of golden happiness which pervades the novel it was written at a time when he was prey to phases of extreme despair due to his enforced separation from Amber Reeves, with whom he had enjoyed a passionate love-affair and who was now the mother of his daughter. The story has always been regarded as one of his happiest creations and, familiarly known as *Mr Polly*, has taken its place alongside *Three Men in a Boat* and *The Diary of a Nobody* as one of the quintessential expressions of English humour. The novel is generally seen as a straightforward realist text, a throwback to *Pickwick Papers*, and a case study in the story of a 'little man' who triumphs over his limiting environment and finds happiness in the life of a tramp. That there is much more to the novel than this is evident from an examination of its language and imagery.

The title itself surely offers a pointer to the fact that Wells intended rather more than a simple description of Mr Polly's adventures. The title is not *Mr Polly*, but *The History of Mr Polly*. This suggests two things: first, that he intends a dispassionate analysis of 'the history of Mr Polly from the cradle to these present difficulties', a detailed account of the life, thoughts and motivations of his hero, omitting nothing. Wells's stance throughout is that of the impartial historian, recording all the material facts concerning Mr Polly's life, both favourable and otherwise, for example 'I am puzzled by his insensibility to Dickens, and I record it, as a good historian should, with an admission of my perplexity.'[33] Second, and more important, the title suggests that he has in mind a literary model for his story. One could be excused for thinking that the model he has in mind is a picaresque novel on the lines of *The History of Tom Jones*. I believe, however, that he received his inspiration from a novel written in an age when it was fashionable to dress up philosophical speculations as allegorical romances professing to be 'the history of' such and such a hero.

Among the books which Wells certainly read as a young man was an allegorical story by Samuel Johnson first published in 1759, *The History of Rasselas, Prince of Abyssinia*. The story describes how Rasselas, accompanied by his sister and a poet, Imlac, succeed in escaping from 'the happy valley', a paradise, and embark on a series of travels in search of enlightenment. Rasselas is warned by one example after another that reverie, imagination, romantic love and scientific speculation are harmful influences because they raise false hopes and expectations. Disillusioned in his quest for happiness Rasselas and his companions ultimately return to the happy valley, there to pursue their various occupations in peace. It is this story, an attack on the superficial optimism of the eighteenth century, which I believe Wells took as his model. In writing *The History of Mr Polly* he was consciously seeking to present a parable on the nature of happiness which would embody simultaneously a powerful allegory on the theme of paradise regained.

This is not to suggest that Wells modelled his novel in detail on the plot of *Rasselas*, although there are a number of interesting parallels between them. In particular there are similarities between the life of Imlac and that of Mr Polly. Thus, when Imlac relates how 'At length my father resolved to initiate me in commerce' one is forcibly reminded of Mr Polly's father proclaiming 'It's time that dratted boy did something for a living.' (ch. I). The debate on marriage (*Rasselas*, chs XXVI–XXIX) which forms such an important element in Johnson's novel is paralleled by the 'Miriam' chapter of *The History of Mr Polly* and most strikingly by Uncle Pentstemon's homily (ch. VI, 7) rehearsing the arguments for and against marriage. Mr Polly's concluding reflection that 'I've never really planned my life, or set out to live. I happened; things happened to me' is strongly reminiscent of the closing paragraphs of *Rasselas*, with Imlac and his companions returning to the happy valley 'contented to be driven along the stream of life without directing their course to any particular port'.

As if to underline the parallels between the two novels Wells invents a character who is a surrogate for Samuel Johnson – wise, practical, sagacious, unimaginative – and with a pleasing sense of rightness names him Johnson: 'Johnson was the sort of man who derives great satisfaction from a funeral; a melancholy, serious, practical-minded man of five-and-thirty, with great powers of advice.' It is he who urges Mr Polly to invest his money in a shop and to read 'a good book on book keeping' instead of wasting his time reading fiction. Johnson in fact is the antithesis of all that Mr Polly stands for: he represents prudent judgement as opposed to imagination, convention as opposed to romance.

But more significant still are the marked affinities in tone and theme. Both novels are based on the idea of a journey towards enlightenment: *Rasselas* describing a journey to Cairo and other cities in which the travellers experience a series of encounters contributing to their education; *Polly* describing one man's journey through life, from happiness to disillusionment and ultimately to happiness again. Both are concerned with the theme of escape: *Rasselas* with escape from the happy valley; *Polly* with escape from a limiting environment. And both are allegories designed to illustrate a moral: as D. J. Enright has expressed it, 'the discrepancy between what is wished for and what is obtained'.[34] In his study *Novel and Reader* John Fletcher has drawn attention to 'the technique of ironic contrast – set up between an imaginary or ideal world and our own – which is the staple of Swiftean or Voltairean satire'.[35] It is this contrast between ideal and reality, between the world of romance and imagination on the one hand and that of practical realisation on the other, which provides both novels with their central theme.

Wells makes extensive use of irony in contrasting the world of Mr Polly's dreams and hopes with the world of actuality. In describing his schooling, his marriage and his years as a shopkeeper the contrast between his anticipations and reality is drawn in unmistakeably ironic terms. The contrasts extend to the use of surnames. The similarity between the name A. Polly (Alfred Polly) and Apollo can only be a deliberate irony on Wells's part. The contrast between Apollo, the god of light and youth, and Mr Polly's dyspeptic existence could not be more marked.

The History of Mr Polly, in common with Joyce's *Ulysses*, is rich in literary and mythological allusions. In the first chapter alone there are references to Shakespeare, Milton, Boccaccio and Rabelais, and in the succeeding chapters there are allusions to Sterne, Belloc, Dickens, Conrad, Stevenson and many others. Its 'literary' flavour is established, then, from the outset. Moreover the theme of life as a journey, as a quest, is underlined at numerous points in the narrative. Mr Polly's voracious reading includes Chaucer's *The Canterbury Tales*, *Purchas his Pilgrimes*, the voyages of La Perouse, and the travels of the Abbés Huc and Gabet. His wandering life in search of romantic adventure recalls the travels of Rasselas in his quest for happiness:

> He had dreamt of casual encounters with delightfully interesting people by the wayside – even romantic encounters. . . . Sunshine and a stirring wind were poured out over the land, fleets of towering clouds sailed upon urgent tremendous missions across the blue sea of heaven, and presently Mr Polly was riding a little unstably along unfamiliar Surrey roads, wondering always what was round the next corner, and marking the blackthorn and looking out for the first white flowerbuds of the may.   (V, 2)

The entire novel, with its emphasis on the imagination as 'an insatiable hunger for bright and delightful experiences, for the gracious aspects of things, for beauty', is a wish-fulfilment, a romantic quest for all those aspects of life that are conducive to happiness. In the process Mr Polly is chastened by many unpleasant experiences, and emerges from his travels a sadder, wiser and more contented individual.

Mr Polly, in common with Rasselas, yearns for happiness and is tormented by the realisation that contentment continually eludes him:

> Deep in the being of Mr Polly, deep in that darkness, like a creature which has been beaten about the head and left for dead

but still lives, crawled a persuasion that over and above the things that are jolly and 'bits of all right', there was beauty, there was delight; that somewhere – magically inaccessible perhaps, but still somewhere – were pure and easy and joyous states of body and mind. (I, 2)

In common with Rasselas, whose 'chief amusement was to picture to himself that world which he had never seen', he is haunted by a vision of another world, a world of happiness, beauty, romance and delight.

The History of Mr Polly embodies a striking amount of paradisial imagery to reinforce its underlying theme of the Fall of Man and the return to Paradise. In the opening chapter there is an idyllic description of the countryside surrounding Port Burdock (Portsmouth) in which Wells is at pains to stress the virginal, unspoilt quality of the landscape. Reference is made to its 'old-fashioned, scarcely disturbed' quality, to its 'unknown winding lanes' and 'primrose-studded undergrowths'. The account of the pastoral beauty of the scene is followed by a haunting echo of the parable of the Garden of Eden:

Once a simple-mannered girl in a pink print dress stayed and talked with them as they ate; led by the gallant Parsons they professed to be all desperately in love with her, and courted her to say which she preferred of them, it was so manifest she did prefer one and so impossible to say which it was held her there, until a distant maternal voice called her away. Afterwards, as they left the inn, she waylaid them at the orchard corner and gave them, a little shyly, three yellow-green apples – and wished them to come again some day, and vanished, and reappeared looking after them as they turned the corner, waving a white handkerchief. All the rest of that day they disputed over the signs of her favour, and the next Sunday they went there again.

But she had vanished, and a mother of forbidding aspect afforded no explanations.

If Platt and Parsons and Mr Polly live to be a hundred, they will none of them forget that girl as she stood with a pink flush upon her, faintly smiling and yet earnest, parting the branches of the hedgerows and reaching down, apple in hand. (I, 4)

The image of the Fall is reinforced by the memory of the girl 'reaching down, apple in hand', by Mr Polly falling from the wall

after his romantic encounter with Christabel, and by his sense of
'falling, falling through the aching silence' during his proposal to
Miriam. When Christabel talks to him 'her smiling face *looked down
upon him* out of the sky'. His fall reaches its nadir during his 15 years
as a shopkeeper at Fishbourne, an experience which corresponds to
the human vision of hell:

> Suddenly, one day it came to him . . . that he had been in his shop
> for exactly fifteen years, that he would soon be forty, and that his
> life during that time had not been worth living, that it had been in
> apathetic and feebly hostile and critical company, ugly in detail
> and mean in scope, and that it had brought him at last to an
> outlook utterly hopeless and grey.   (VII, 2)

The theme of emergence from a valley of happiness, and
subsequent attempts to return to the valley – a theme which
dominates *Rasselas* – is continually present in *The History of Mr
Polly*. When he first falls in love with Christabel it is as if 'the world
had given way beneath him and he had dropped through into
another, into a world of luminous clouds and of a desolate hopeless
wilderness of desiring and of wild valleys of unreasonable ecstasy'.
Throughout his adventures he is haunted by memories of beauty,
by dreams 'of delightful impossibilities' which fill him with longing.
At the end of the novel, secure in his ultimate haven at the Potwell
Inn, there is a powerful sense of having returned to the safe, friendly
paradise which has eluded him all his life:

> It was as if everything lay securely within a great, warm, friendly
> globe of crystal sky. It was as safe and enclosed and fearless as a
> child that has still to be born.   (X, 3)

Secure in this enclosed womb of happiness and peace he lives out
his life, protected against intrusions from the world outside. He has
found his happy valley.

The Potwell Inn is explicitly referred to as a paradise at several
points in the narrative. When he is debating whether to leave the
Inn or remain to do battle with Uncle Jim he is unsure 'whether he
was taking a walk to clear his mind, or leaving that threat – marred
Paradise for good and all'. And the poplar trees which provide the
Inn with its setting seemed to Mr Polly 'to touch a pleasant scene
with a distinction *almost divine*' (my italics). The use of the word

divine strengthens the analogy between the Inn and paradise. Wells derived some of his inspiration for the Inn from his childhood memories of Surly Hall, a riverside inn near Windsor, which clearly impressed him as a paradise:

> Often when I was going for walks along the rather trite and very pebbly footpaths about Bromley, thirty miles away, I would let my imagination play with the idea that round the next corner and a little further on and then a bit more, I should find myself with a cry of delighted recognition on the road that led immediately to Surly Hall in summer and all its pleasantness. . . . But this is a mere glimpse of summer paradise on the way to my first start in life.[36]

There is extensive use of mythological symbolism and imagery throughout the novel. There is, first, a frequent recurrence of symbolism based on the motif of a trinity. There are the 'three P's' – Polly, Platt and Parsons. Mr Polly has three sisters who vie for his affections – Miriam, Annie and Minnie. His war with Uncle Jim for the possession of the Potwell Inn 'fell naturally into three campaigns'. The Inn has as a backcloth three poplar trees, 'three exceptionally tall, graceful and harmonious poplars'. This repetition of motifs based on a threefold pattern reinforces some of the novel's underlying themes. The figure three traditionally represents birth, life and death (or creation, preservation and destruction). In one sense the novel can be read as an allegory on the idea of happiness: its birth in Mr Polly's transitory vision of paradise, its destruction by evil (in the person of Uncle Jim), and its preservation through his defeat of evil and ultimate possession of the Inn. This threefold pattern provides the novel with a symmetrical unity which underpins the significance of the parable.

The image of a wall is another powerful motif. Immediately before his encounter with Christabel he 'wheeled his machine along a faintly marked attractive trail through bracken until he came to a heap of logs against a high old stone wall with a damaged coping and wallflower plants already gone to seed'. Later in the novel he returns to the same scene, 'an old lichenous stone wall'. In interpreting dreams psychologists classify a wall as a mother-symbol, or as a symbol representing the feminine element of mankind. At first Mr Polly is enraptured by Christabel but the encounter soon ends in disillusionment, as he remembers when he proposes to Miriam: 'Folly not to banish dreams that made one ache of townless woods and bracken tangles and red-haired linen-clad figures sitting in dappled sunshine upon grey and crumbling walls and looking queenly down on one with clear blue eyes.' But the significance of the wall is that it is in ruins. The adjectives Wells uses are *old, damaged, crumbling, lichenous*. All Mr Polly's experiences of womankind – with the notable exceptions of the 'simple-mannered girl in a pink print dress' and the plump lady at the Potwell Inn – are tarnished by disillusionment: Christabel because of her insincerity, Miriam because of her total lack of imagination, Annie and Minnie because of their shallowness and inability to enter his mental world.

The trees which dominate the landscape surrounding the Potwell Inn have special symbolic importance:

It was about two o'clock in the afternoon, one hot day in May, when Mr Polly, unhurrying and serene, came upon that broad bend of the river to which the little lawn and garden of the Potwell Inn run down. He stopped at the sight of the place and surveyed its deep tiled roof, nestling under big trees – you never get a decently big, decently shaped tree by the seaside – its sign towards the roadway, its sun-blistered green bench and tables, its shapely white windows and its row of upshooting hollyhock plants in the garden. A hedge separated the premises from a buttercup-yellow meadow, and beyond stood three poplars in a group against the sky, three exceptionally tall, graceful, and harmonious poplars. It is hard to say what there was about them that made them so beautiful to Mr Polly, but they seemed to him to touch a pleasant scene with a distinction almost divine. He stood admiring them quietly for a long time.   (IX, 3)

As if to draw attention to their significance Wells refers to them again in the closing scene of the novel: 'the three poplars rose clear and harmonious against the sky of green and yellow'. Traditionally the poplar tree is known as the tree of life and has a special allegorical significance since the two sides of its leaf are different shades of green. J. E. Cirlot, in *A Dictionary of Symbols*, observes that the poplar is 'bright green on the side of water (moon) and a darker green on the side of fire (sun). The poplar also has a place within the general range of bipolar symbols (positive–negative).' It will be seen, then, that the poplar at this stage in the narrative – Mr Polly's first discovery of the haven which he immediately recognises as the object of his quest – is a peculiarly apposite symbol. It is the poplar trees with their positive–negative imagery which separate him both literally and metaphorically from his riverside haven. Behind him lies Fishbourne and the fire and the old life from which he has fled (dark green). Before him lies the inn and happiness and the romantic paradise of his dreams (bright green). He recognises at once that he has come to a watershed in his life and that there can be no turning back.

> He knew – he knew now as much as a man can know of life. He knew he had to fight or perish. . . . He had been muddled and wrapped about and entangled, like a creature born in the jungle who has never seen sea or sky. Now he had come out of it suddenly into a great exposed place. (IX, 7)

Other prominent images in the novel are fire and water. When Mr Polly sets fire to the shop he is not simply destroying an environment he has hated (the inferno destroys the hell in which he has been imprisoned for 15 years) but entering a new lease of life. M. Eliade in *Myths, Dreams and Mysteries* (London, 1960) observes that 'to pass through fire is symbolic of transcending the human condition'. Having triumphantly emerged from the travail of the fire he is a changed man, perceiving for the first time in his life that the solution to his unhappiness lies in his own hands:

> But when a man has once broken through the paper walls of everyday circumstance, those insubstantial walls that hold so many of us securely prisoned from the cradle to the grave, he has made a discovery. If the world does not please you, *you can change it*. Determine to alter it at any price, and you can change it altogether. (IX, 1)

After the fire he is transformed. Instead of a self-pitying weakling he assumes control of his destiny, in the process becoming aware of a world of beauty and interest which has surrounded him all the time:

> After a lapse of fifteen years he rediscovered this interesting world, about which so many people go incredibly blind and bored. . . . He felt as the etiolated grass and daisies must do when you move the garden roller away to a new place. (IX, 2)

The fire is in fact a catalyst, the agent which transforms him from a dyspeptic bankrupt intent on suicide to a heroic individual, determined to do battle with the forces of evil for the possession of his earthly paradise. In the process he has symbolically 'transcended the human condition', for he has destroyed his hell and embarked on a journey which will change the tenor of his life. As if to underline the metamorphosis the narrative states: 'He seemed transported to some strange country'. Fire clearly held for Wells a deep symbolic importance. Not only does fire play an important role in *The History of Mr Polly* but also in *The Wonderful Visit*, in which an angel visiting the earth is destroyed in a fire, and in *In the Days of the Comet*, in which a series of conflagrations (likened to the Beltane fires in Frazer's *Golden Bough*) usher in a new age of enlightenment and beauty. Fire as an image of destruction and regeneration is central to the plot of the novel and Wells makes skilful use of language and atmosphere to heighten its effect.

The river is a seminal image in the concluding chapters. The Potwell Inn stands on the banks of a river and Mr Polly's first task at the Inn is to cross the river in a ferry, the same river in which his antagonist Uncle Jim is drowned. In the symbolism of dreams a river represents the irreversible passage of time, an awareness of a sense of loss. It is while fishing in the river that he experiences his first regrets on having left Miriam and decides to revisit her. It is also the river which provides the backcloth for his concluding reflections – 'It was one of those evenings serenely luminous, amply and atmospherically still, when the river bend was at its best' – and which represents for him the paradisal setting of his longings. (It is interesting in this connection to recall the description in ch. III of Mr Polly rowing vainly against the tide on the River Stour – a prefigurement of his disposition to struggle against destiny.) For Mr Polly the river is a Rubicon which he has to cross on his journey to paradise: having crossed it, there can be no looking back. It is the dividing line between the old life of discontent and the new life of happiness.

Robert M. Polhemus, in his *Comic Faith: The Great Tradition from Austen to Joyce*, observes that 'Much of the essential quality of British fiction . . . grows out of the novelist's wishes and efforts to augment, modify, or replace the Christian "divine comedy", the scheme of redemption and resurrection to which Dante gave the name of *commedia*. . . . The basic plot of comic form, I have surmised, grew out of the process and hope of regeneration.'[37]

That this is one of the central underlying themes of *The History of Mr Polly* is clear from the extensive use of imagery suggesting a fall from a former state of grace culminating in its eventual reattainment. The point is made explicit when Mr Polly is wrestling with his conscience over whether to abandon the plump woman to her fate or return to the Inn to confront Uncle Jim:

> And while Mr Polly sat thinking these things as well as he could, he knew that if only he dared to look up, the heavens had opened, and the clear judgment on his case was written across the sky
> (IX, 7)

The deliberate use of biblical language – 'the heavens', 'judgment', 'written across the sky' – underlines the theme of redemption and resurrection which is reinforced when Wells adds at the conclusion of the same passage: 'It was as if God and Heaven waited over him, and all the earth was expectation.'

The History of Mr Polly, then, can be regarded in one sense as a Utopian romance in the vein of William Morris's *News from Nowhere* or *The Life and Death of Jason*, contrasting the world of the present with life as it might be. A more apposite analogy is with the didactic allegorical romances of the past – *Rasselas*, *Candide*, *Pilgrim's Progress*. For in this apparently simple story of a draper who abandons his wife and his shop to find contentment at a country inn lies an allegory of profound relevance to the twentieth century.

'It seems to me, said Imlac, that while you are making the choice of life, you neglect to live.' In common with Rasselas, Polly spends much of his existence drifting through life, responding to events rather than controlling them, failing to see the beauty which lies all around him. It is not until the confrontation with evil in the person of Uncle Jim that he recognises that the quest for happiness has been the essential theme of his journey:

> The reality of the case arched over him like the vault of the sky, as plain as the sweet blue heaven above *and the wide spread of hill and valley about him*. Man comes into life to seek and find his sufficient beauty, to serve it, to win and increase it, to fight for it, to face anything and dare anything for it, counting death as nothing so long as the dying eyes still turn to it.   (IX, 7, my italics)

The novel ends as it begins (as does *Rasselas*) with the image of the valley to which the hero returns. In one of the many reflective passages with which *Rasselas* abounds, Rasselas's sister, the princess Nekayah, observes:

> All that virtue can afford is quietness of conscience, a steady prospect of a happier state; this may enable us to endure calamity with patience; but remember that patience must suppose pain. . . . Long customs are not easily broken, he that attempts to change the course of his own life, very often labours in vain; and how shall we do that for others which we are seldom able to do for ourselves?

In the serene closing sequence of *The History of Mr Polly* when Wells's hero speculates on the meaning of his life he too recognises that patience must suppose pain. In acknowledging his own good fortune he accepts that he has treated Miriam badly but is realist enough to see that he had no alternative but to act as he did. He accepts that happiness cannot always be attained without sacrifice:

> Like children playing about in a nursery. Hurt themselves at times. . . . There's a sort of character people like, and stand up for, and a sort they won't. You got to work it out, and take the consequences.   (X, 3)

The novel, then, may be regarded as a secular reworking of *Pilgrim's Progress*, as an allegorical fable recounting one man's journey through life. In its insistence that man is responsible for his own destiny, that happiness has to be consciously sought for and defended, the narrative is entirely characteristic of Wells and consistent with all that we know of his life and beliefs. A novel which has until recently received surprisingly little critical attention can now be seen to be an ironic myth in the same tradition as the philosophical tales of Swift and Voltaire. For Mr Polly is not simply representative of his own age; he is an archetypal figure whose actions and aspirations bear a profound relevance to modern man. In relating the story of a sample human being who struggles valiantly against dispiriting circumstances and ultimately finds his 'sufficient beauty', Wells embodies a most potent myth of personal renewal and rebirth.

8

Boon: the Novelist Dissected

I once told H. G. Wells and, after reflection, he agreed with my analysis, that at least two people struggled inside him, Herbert and George. Bert reacted; George dreamed.

(Kingsley Martin, *Editor: A Volume of Autobiography*)

With the breakdown of specific boundaries the validity of the logical process beyond finite ends breaks down. We make our truth for our visible purposes as we go along, and if it does not work we make it afresh. We see life once more as gallant experiment.

(H. G. Wells, *Boon*)

Boon – or to give it its full title *Boon, The Mind of the Race, The Wild Asses of the Devil, and The Last Trump* – occupies a somewhat ambiguous place in Wells studies. Neither a conventional novel on the one hand nor a volume of essays on the other, it sits uncomfortably in that vague no man's land occupied by such works as *Tristram Shandy* and *Finnegan's Wake*, a literary oddity. Critics have never known quite what to make of it, and the book has been described variously as 'a rag-bag', 'a farrago' and 'a compost heap'.[38] Critical discussion of *Boon* has concentrated almost entirely on one chapter – 'Of Art, of Literature, of Mr Henry James' – in which there is a biting parody of James's style and an illuminating debate between the Jamesian and Wellsian attitudes to the novel. The chapter is certainly of fundamental importance to an understanding of Wells's approach to literature, but the bypassing of the remainder (and the substantial part) of the book has meant that *Boon* has been consistently underrated as a work of fiction.

In form it belongs to a genre made famous by William H.

Mallock's *The New Republic* (1876), a conversational novel in which the principal literary personalities of the day appear behind a series of transparent masks. The chapters in Mallock's satire are made up of conversations between the guests who discuss a range of topics suggested by the host, in the manner of the characters in Peacock's discussion novels. The genre clearly held a strong attraction for Wells and there is evidence that he experimented with the format of *Boon* for some years. 'I found myself', he wrote, 'and I got to the dialogue novel, through a process of trial and error.'[39] The book seems to have been conceived in 1901 and Wells then laid it aside, returning to it sporadically during the ensuing decade. He took it up again in earnest in 1912 and continued to make additions and refinements until after the outbreak of war two years later. He added years afterwards that he considered *Boon* to be the most 'frank and intimate' of his works.[40]

Writing to his friend Arnold Bennett on 17 October 1901 Wells confided:

> Mainly just now I'm meditating on a something which is really this time to get me all together and reconcile all my aspects – something in the form of a lax extravaganza of the Rabelais type . . . superposed on interlocutors such as one gets in *Tristram Shandy* – discourses and Peacockian dialogue – an effect of looking into a room in which a number of human beings behave and talk, with someone like Father Shandy giving a lantern entertainment with comments.

This is the earliest intimation in his correspondence that he was toying with the machinery of the work we now know as *Boon*, a book which grew slowly by a process of accretion and reveals the fluctuations in his state of mind as his moods alternated between hope and despair. The book purports to be 'a first selection from the literary remains of George Boon, appropriate to the times', prepared for publication by Reginald Bliss. In the opening chapters Bliss introduces himself as a friend of Boon, a successful novelist who had for years cherished an ambition to publish a *magnum opus*. In this work Boon had planned to develop his *idée fixe* of 'the Mind of the Race', the notion that all literature, all writing, all creative expression, is part of a living process, a continuing body of thought to which all contributed. Boon had been obsessed by the idea that the bonds which had held Victorian society and culture together were break-

ing up and that nothing had arisen to replace them. The dominating
idea of his life had been that 'a great effort of intellectual self-control
must come if the race is to be saved from utter confusion and
dementia',[41] that the function of literature in the modern world must
be to contribute to this continuing process of discussion and
clarification rather than the effort to produce perfect and symmetrical works of art. Following Boon's death, Bliss attempts to piece
together – from fragments of manuscript and recollections of
conversations – the substance of his unpublished work and to cast
this into a literary form. He presents this material in a series of
conversations or dialogues, beginning with an engaging pastiche of
the house party in *The New Republic* ('The Great Slump, the Revival
of Letters, and The Garden by the Sea') proceeding through
encounters with Henry James and George Moore to a world
conference on the Mind of the Race attended by Shaw, Hardy, Hugh
Walpole and other literary personalities of the time.

Throughout the book one is aware of a curious relationship
between the reader and the text, an effect which is achieved through
a series of framing devices. There is the convention of the 'literary
remains' prepared for publication by an ostensible editor, Reginald
Bliss, whom the reader is led to believe is someone other than Wells
himself. There are the conversations between Boon and his associ-
ates which are commented upon by the editor. There is the sense
that one is reading a satire made up of a series of satires. Above all
there is an awareness that the apparent shapelessness of the book
has itself a satirical intention and that the device of eavesdropping
on a series of imaginary conversations has been deliberately
adopted to give the appearance of fluidity. It is as if one is looking
inwards at a novel containing a novel which in turn contains a novel;
one is reminded of such metafictions as Calvino's *If on a Winters
Night a Traveller* or Gide's *The Counterfeitors*.

The book is in fact a conversational novel, a point which is made
clear at an early stage in the narrative:

> He [Boon] went on almost at once to suggest a more congenial
> form, a conversational novel. I followed reluctantly. I share the
> general distrust of fiction as a vehicle of discussion. We would, he
> insisted, invent a personality who would embody our Idea, who
> should be fanatically obsessed by this idea of the Mind of the
> Race, who should preach it on all occasions and be brought into
> illuminating contact with all the existing mental apparatus and

organisation of the world. . . . So we settled on our method and principal character right away.   (ch. 2, 3)

The 'I' here is Reginald Bliss, the literary aesthete and dilettante. The device of a narrator who disapproves of fiction as a vehicle of discussion and intersperses critical comments on the other interlocutors gives a distancing effect to the narrative, as if the reflections of Boon, Wilkins and Hallery are being sifted by an unsympathetic observer. Bliss – the editor of Boon's papers and author of *The Cousins of Charlotte Brontë*, *A Child's History of the Crystal Palace*, *Firelight Rambles*, *Edible Fungi*, *Whales in Captivity* and other works – is a caricature of the literary dilettante but is by no means a minor figure in Wells's design. Each of the scenes in the novel is presented by Bliss; the conversations between Boon, Wilkins and Hallery are in turn commented on by Bliss; it is Bliss who adds a commentary to the short stories 'The Wild Asses of the Devil' and 'The Last Trump'; and after Boon's death the reader is left with Bliss's reflections on life and literature. It is Bliss's perspective, then, which determines the 'point of view' from which the reader approaches the work as a whole and whilst there are a number of points in the narrative when Boon (an inveterate joker) makes fun of him, so that Bliss's rather pompous manner is gently deflated, it is his imaginary personality which shapes and controls the narrative.

It is with something of a shock that one realises that the book is made up of a series of parodies. The book as a whole is a parody of Mallock's *The New Republic*, but within this overall frame Wells inserts a series of interlocking parodies satirising literary devices and styles, leading writers of the day and aspects of his own personality. The result is a fantasia comparable with Fielding's *Shamela*. It is essential to grasp at the outset that Boon, Wilkins and Hallery – the leading protagonists in the novel – are all reflections of Wells's own self: facets of his temperament which are sometimes uppermost and sometimes in abeyance. Boon represents Wells the successful novelist, the buoyant public figure possessing a 'half mystical confidence in the inevitableness of human wisdom'.[42] Boon, at least initially, takes a hopeful view of human progress in contrast to the pessimism of Wilkins. Wilkins represents the sceptical, pragmatic, realist Wells – the Wells of *The Time Machine* and *The Island of Doctor Moreau*. He appears as a character in a number of novels and embodies that side of his personality which regarded life without illusions. He insists on precise statement and is impatient of rhetoric. Hallery, with his nervous intensity, his earnestness and obsession with the idea of the Mind of the Race, is a reflection of the serious, didactic Wells – the Wells of *Anticipations* and *Mankind in the Making*. He is an 'intensely serious exponent of moral values'[43] who introduces a note of obsessiveness into the novel and acts as a touchstone against which the arguments of Boon and Wilkins can be measured. The relationship between the three forms a backcloth of discussion and commentary continuing through most of *Boon*'s 10 chapters and permits Wells to dissect his own personality in a manner unique in his fiction. Boon defines the relationship between himself and Hallery in a revealing aside:

> I invented Hallery to get rid of myself, but, after all, Hallery is really no more than the shadow of myself, and if I were impersonal and well bred, and if I spoke behind a black screen, it would still be as much my voice as ever. (ch. 6, 2)

This recognition that the obsessive, moralising aspect of his make-up 'is really no more than the shadow' of himself and an integral part of his temperament is an interesting example of Wells's candour in acknowledging his limitations. Throughout *Boon* one has the sense that he is exploring his own ambivalence, debating with himself on the meaning of life and art, and that behind the conversations of which the book is composed lies a deeply divided personality. The contrasting personalities of Boon and Wilkins are expressed in these terms:

> Wilkins is a man of a peculiar mental constitution; he alternates between a brooding sentimental egotism and a brutal realism, and he is as weak and false in the former mood as he is uncompromising in the latter. I think the attraction that certainly existed between him and Boon must have been the attraction of opposites, for Boon is as emotional and sentimental in relation to the impersonal aspects of life as he is pitiless in relation to himself. (ch. 7, 1)

In this 'attraction of opposites' Wells lays bare the dichotomy in his make-up between the man of confidence and the man of doubt, between the hopeful author of *A Modern Utopia* and other speculations and the profound pessimism of the scientific romances. The gist of the book is a debate between Boon and Wilkins in which

Wilkins questions whether there is any secular intellectual growth and Boon clings passionately to his belief in human progress. Wilkins raises objections at various stages of the discussion and thus obliges Boon to continually restate and clarify his propositions. The result is a work of unusual intimacy, as if the author is thinking aloud: the reader has a sense of participating in his innermost reflections on the fundamentals of life and literature. As the debate proceeds – and with the mounting carnage of the First World War – there is a gradual shift of mood. Boon becomes slowly more pessimistic, Wilkins more optimistic, corresponding to the fluctuating phases in Wells's outlook. At last it is the war which destroys Boon's spirit and brings about his premature death. He becomes convinced that there is no hope for mankind, that evil is irrevocably unleashed over the world.

In view of the pessimism which overshadowed Wells's final illness and is reflected in *Mind at the End of its Tether* (1945), one of the most revealing passages in the book is that in which the narrator broods on Boon's sense of hopelessness:

> Boon's pessimistic outlook on the war had a profoundly depressing effect upon me. I do all in my power to believe that Wilkins is right, and that the hopelessness that darkened Boon's last days was due to the overshadowing of his mind by his illness.   (ch. 9, 7)

In this and other passages can be traced the fluctuations in Wells's attitude of mind, the shift from the intense patriotism of the first days of the war to the mounting disillusionment of 1915. He clearly sensed that the war marked a turning point in human affairs and that as a writer he had to come to grips with what it meant for his life and art. The substance of *Boon* is a debate between the optimistic and pessimistic aspects of his temperament on the nature and purpose of literature, on the function of the writer in an age when the old order was visibly crumbling away.

Within the interlocking satirical frame Wells inserts three short stories – 'The Spoils of Mr Blandish', 'The Wild Asses of the Devil' and 'The Story of the Last Trump' – each of which is a parody, either of himself or of an attitude of mind. Each story is self-contained yet each contributes to the overall theme: the continuing debate on the nature and purpose of literature.

'The Spoils of Mr Blandish' is a parody of Henry James's *The Spoils of Poynton* and is also self-parody since it is a reworking of Wells's short story 'The Rajah's Treasure'. It relates the story of a Mr Blandish, 'a man with an exquisite apprehension of particulars' who is a transparent caricature of James. He purchases the house of his dreams, Samphire House (samphire is a plant whose fleshy leaves are used in making pickles: there is clearly a satirical intention here) and fills it with antiques and treasures. Imperceptibly it dawns upon him that the house is pervaded by a presence, 'a something extra, of something not quite bargained for' which disturbs him. He senses that his butler Mutimer is party to the secret but for a long time Mr Blandish is unable to discover the source of his uncomfortable awareness of a presence. There are intimations that its source may lie in buried treasure but at last it is revealed that the presence is a hoard of vintage brandy hidden in a disused cellar of Samphire House, a hoard which Mutimer has been surreptitiously sampling for years. Mr Blandish tries to dispose of the remaining brandy but before he can do so is compelled to the realisation that Mutimer has consumed the last drop. In writing this amusing parody Wells seems to have had both a literal and an allegorical intention. The lampooning of James's ponderous style – which is likened to 'a magnificent but painful hippopotamus resolved at any cost, even at the cost of its dignity, upon picking up a pea which has got into a corner of its den' – is brilliantly done and conveys as nothing else could his exasperation with the convolutions of James's later fiction. Behind the satire one can detect the accumulated frustrations of an uneasy friendship in which James, whilst appearing to admire the work of the younger novelist, had in reality disparaged him.

Beneath the surface the story is also capable of a symbolic interpretation. The fact that the cellars of Samphire House are filled with the wine of life, that Mr Blandish is the last person to realise this and that, having discovered it, he is determined to exorcise it, can be read as an allegory for Wells's conviction that the creation of perfect works of art in the Jamesian sense forms only a small part of life and that by excluding 'those deeply passionate needs and distresses from which half the storms of human life are brewed'[44] James was turning his back on aspects of living of fundamental importance. As an antagonist to the view that literature should be 'alive with passion and will' Wells posits an artist:

> this man who seems to regard the whole seething brew of life as a vat from which you skim, with slow, dignified gestures, works of art. Works of art whose only claim is their art.   (ch. 4, 3)

'The Spoils of Mr Blandish' is not simply a good-humoured satire on Henry James. It is a critique of the view that life can be excluded from art, that prodigality and emotion can have no place in the novel. Mr Blandish, who 'went about elaborately, avoiding ugliness, death, suffering, industrialism, politics, sport, the thought of war, the red blaze of passion', symbolises for Wells the notion that life can be kept at arm's length, that all that does not fit neatly into the novelist's scheme can be excised from his picture. The story is a plea for the rich discursiveness of Sterne and Dickens as against the tidy symmetry of James or Austen.

'The Wild Asses of the Devil' marks a return to the pessimism of *The Island of Doctor Moreau*. It tells the story of a successful author who encounters a devil disguised as a stoker. The devil confesses that he has inadvertently permitted a herd of wild asses – 'unruly, dangerous and enterprising beasts' which have the ability to assume human form – to escape from hell and that these are now at large and intent on unleashing evil into the world. The story is self-parody in the sense that the author 'who pursued fame and prosperity in a pleasant villa on the south coast of England' is recognisably Wells himself and the setting is Sandgate, near Folkestone, his home from 1899 to 1909. What is so revealing about 'The Wild Asses of the Devil' is its insight into his frame of mind following the outbreak of war and the evidence it affords of his growing awareness of evil. The devil fails to recapture the wild asses, violence and destruction are rampant in Europe until Boon is compelled to accept that 'continually it is clearer that there *were* diabolical Wild Asses loose and active in the affairs of the world'. The story culminates in a nightmare in which Bliss has a terrible vision of himself surrounded by the wild asses:

And then suddenly there I was amidst all those very asses of which I have told you. There they were all about me, and they were more wild and horrible than I can describe to you. It was not that they were horrible in any particular way, they were just horrible, and they kicked up far over head, and leapt and did not even seem to trouble to elude my poor ineffectual efforts to get within salting distance of them. I toiled and I pursued amidst mad mountains that were suddenly marble flights of stairs that sloped and slid me down to precipices over which I floated; and then we were in soft places knee-deep in blood-red mud; and then they were close to my face, eye to eye, enormous revolving eyes, like the lanterns of lighthouses; and then they swept away, and always I grew smaller and feebler and more breathless, and always they grew larger, until only their vast legs danced about me on the sward, and all the rest was hidden. . . .

I saw the sward they trampled, and it was not sward, it was living beings, men hurt by dreadful wounds, and poor people who ran in streaming multitudes under the beating hoofs, and a lichenous growth of tender things and beautiful and sweet and right things on which they beat, splashing it all to blood and dirt. (ch. 9, 7)

This nightmare, which links so clearly to themes he was later to develop in *Mr Blettsworthy on Rampole Island* and *The Croquet Player*, is an unforgettable picture of twentieth-century warfare and its indiscriminate slaughter. The Houyhnhnms of *Gulliver's Travels*, the noble and rational horses, have become the wild asses of the devil – reason has given way to madness – and horror on an unprecedented scale is at large. What begins as a genial tale in the manner of his early short stories becomes a Kafkaesque vision of evil, a haunting representation of human bestiality. One of the many ironies of the book is that this unforgettable vision comes not to Boon but to Bliss, a man whose sensitive nature is 'oppressed with peculiar and melancholy dreams' and who cannot rid his mind of the spectre of a world laid waste.

'The Story of the Last Trump', which is described significantly as Boon's 'epitaph upon his dream of the Mind of the Race', is a caricature of his short story 'A Vision of Judgment'. A child, playing in an attic in heaven, finds the trumpet of Judgement Day and drops it over the battlements to the earth. Centuries later it is found and sounded by two men who discover it in a junk shop, and for an instant there is a vision in the sky of God surrounded by angels. The story relates the impact of this startling vision on a representative sample of human beings: a little old lady, a rector, a bishop and a wealthy parishioner. Each has a momentary sensation of the presence of God but each subsides into the normal routines of life, apparently unwilling or unable to grasp the meaning of the experience. Of those who have seen the fleeting glimpse of the divinity it is the rector, Mr Parchester, who is most disturbed but he is persuaded by the bishop to take a sedative and read a calming and purifying book. The story concludes with the reflection that as it was with Mr Parchester so it was with all the rest of the world: 'If a thing is sufficiently strange and great no one will perceive it.' The story reflects Wells's sense of the immense importance of the war and his conviction that its significance had dawned only on a minority. Bliss's comment that in the story Boon had 'mocked at the idea that under any sort of threat or warning whatever men's minds can move out of the grooves in which they run' is a reminder of this conviction and of his fear that after the war men would slip back into the outmoded routines of the Edwardian era. For Wells the war was a dividing line, a crucial turning point demanding a sea-change in approaches to life and art.

Boon occupies a central place in Wells's intellectual pilgrimage and in his approach to the novel, since both thematically and artistically it marks a watershed in his work. Thematically it can be seen as the attempt of a sensitive, troubled, divided mind to come to terms with the reality of war: a reluctant acceptance that the old order has passed away.

> The struggle began to assume in our minds its true proportions, its true extent, in time, in space, in historical consequence. We had thought of a dramatic three months' conflict and a redrawn map of Europe; we perceived we were in the beginnings of a far vaster conflict; the end of an age; the slow, murderous testing and condemnation of whole systems of ideas that had bound men uneasily in communities for all our lives.   (ch. 9, 4)

There is an obituary quality about the work, as if Wells consciously intended something in the nature of a memorial volume. In the closing pages Bliss sadly reminds the reader that 'Boon is dead and our little circle is scattered.' For Wells the coming of the war meant a realisation that literature must be relevant to the needs of his own age and that he must sever himself irrevocably from the notion – cultivated by James and his circle – that the role of the novelist was to produce aesthetically pleasing, enduring works of art. Boon's death is symbolic of a final parting of the ways. Wells had always held the view that the novel must be by its very nature anarchic, that it could not be circumscribed by rules and conventions; the war strengthened this conviction with overwhelming force. From now onwards, he realised, his role must be to write for his time, to discuss through the medium of fiction the social, personal and moral issues of world in a state of flux: 'We see life once more as gallant experiment.'[45]

Artistically it represents a brave attempt, through the medium of a dialogue novel, to expose the ambivalence in his mind concerning the human condition and to think aloud on the issues he and James had been debating for more than a decade. There are few more revealing passages than the debate between Boon and Wilkins, between Wells the optimist and Wells the pessimist, on the reality of progress:

> 'The Mind of the Race,' said Wilkins, 'seems at times to me much more like a scared child cowering in the corner of a cage full of apes.'
> Boon was extraordinarily disconcerted by these contradictions.
> 'It will grow up,' he snatched.
> 'If the apes let it,' said Wilkins.   (ch. 7, 2)

Again we are reminded of *The Croquet Player* and *Mr Blettsworthy* and the stark Swiftian realism of so many of his parables. That he chose to discuss some of the fundamental problems of life and literature in the form of a conversational novel, a dialogue between conflicting aspects of his own temperament, is an indication of his debt to Sterne. He could so easily have framed his riposte to James in the form of a volume of essays, an extended version of 'The Contemporary Novel'. Instead he conceived the idea of a dialogue, a work which by its experimental nature, by its apparent shapelessness, would embody a denial of all that James stood for and at the same time demonstrate the continuing versatility of the novel as a form of expression.

Viewing *Boon* as a novel in its own right it can be seen that, far from signalling Wells's departure from literature, it demonstrates his continuing commitment to artistic concerns.

9

Men Like Gods: End of Innocence

He had a vague feeling that a very delightful and wonderful dream was slipping from him. He tried to keep on with the dream and not to open his eyes. It was about a great world of beautiful people who had freed themselves from a thousand earthly troubles. But it dissolved and faded from his mind.

(H. G. Wells, *Men Like Gods*)

At best it is a cry of distress, a plea for things to be other than they are. Men Like Gods *is in reality an altogether pessimistic book.*

(Anthony West, *Principles and Persuasions*)

Men Like Gods, written in 1921–2 after Wells had completed his monumental *Outline of History*, has been largely bypassed by modern academic criticism. Because its apparent tone is one of facile idealism – the novel describes a visit by a group of representative Englishmen and women to a Utopian paradise – it has been bracketed with his other Utopian speculations and dismissed as Wells at his most fanciful. Read as a straightforward text it is difficult to quarrel with this judgement. What has escaped the attention of most critics is that this 'somewhat dull and undistinguished romance'[46] is very far from straightforward. In common with *The Time Machine* and many of his stories it is rich in mythopoeic imagery of direct relevance to the twentieth century and to Wells himself as man and writer.

On first examination there is little to alert the reader that the story is anything other than a conventional piece of story-telling. The novel describes an overworked journalist, Alfred Barnstaple, 'sub-editor and general factotum of the *Liberal*, that well-known organ of the more depressing aspects of advanced thought', who embarks on a motoring holiday for the sake of his health. While travelling between Slough and Maidenhead his car seems to hit something and skids. From this point onwards he finds himself in a strange, Utopian world in which war has been eradicated and many of the problems which beset mankind in 1921 have been solved. As he learns more of the history and organisation of the idyllic world he becomes increasingly attracted to it and is content to remain there. Some other contemporaries who are with him, however, regard the planet as decadent and attempt to mount an armed revolt against their hosts. The Utopians imprison the Earthlings in a castle on a high crag and, learning of the abortive coup, destroy the castle and its occupants. Mr Barnstaple succeeds in making his escape from the crag and is ultimately returned to his own time. He returns to his wife and home feeling thoroughly refreshed though filled with nostalgia for the world he has left behind him.

On closer perusal the reader is aware of a note of irony in many of the descriptive passages – this is increasingly evident in the lyrical eulogies of Utopian laws and institutions – and a careful use of names for characters and places reminiscent of those in allegorical works such as *Pilgrim's Progress* and *Candide*. The tiresome editor of the *Liberal* is called Mr Peeve, a mercenary doctor is named Pagan, the valley where Mr Barnstaple convalesces after his illness is called the Valley of Rest, and so on. One is increasingly aware of a transparent quality in the text, as if one is being invited to look at both the surface narrative and a metaphor – or rather a series of metaphors – lying behind it. Gradually it dawns on the reader that the story seems vaguely familiar and that the reason for this apparent familiarity is that *Men Like Gods* is an elaborate parody in which the author caricatures both his own Utopian speculations and the mythical quest for an earthly paradise. Wells seems to have intended the novel to be both a parody and an allegory – and when viewed in either of these aspects it can be seen to be a rewarding and stimulating work of considerable thematic importance.

In his autobiography Wells tells us that *Men Like Gods* 'frankly caricatures some prominent contemporaries'[47] and that he laughed aloud when writing it. The party of Englishmen includes Cecil Burleigh [Arthur Balfour], Rupert Catskill [Winston Churchill] and Freddy Mush [Edward Marsh]. The book is a parody not simply in the sense that it caricatures a number of contemporary figures but in that it parodies some of Wells's own writings, including most notably *A Modern Utopia* and 'The Door in the Wall'. In doing so it forms a revealing contrast between the Wells who was writing before 1914 and the Wells who had lived through the holocaust of the First World War.

The title of the novel is clearly ironic and should be compared with an observation in his philosophical work *First and Last Things* (1908). After reminding the reader of the beauty of the earth Wells remarks: 'I do not know why he [man] should not in response fling his shabby gear aside and behave like a god; I only know that he does not do so' (Book IV, 6). The holocaust of 1914–18 and its aftermath – the formation of the League of Nations (which he regarded as the flimsiest of barriers against war) and the subsequent outbreaks of violence in Ireland, Italy and elsewhere had convinced him that the idealism of the Edwardian years was now outmoded. Man, he sensed, was very far removed from God-like behaviour. Angry and disillusioned he set to work to write an ironic fable which would express his profound misgivings concerning the human condition.

One's first impression of the narrative is of a loss of direction, of a journey being thrown off course. At the beginning of the novel the car 'skidded round so violently that for a moment or so Mr Barnstaple lost his head'. When he regains consciousness after the episode of Quarantine Crag he has a momentary loss of memory, for 'he had been knocked over and stunned in some manner too big and violent for his mind to hold as yet'. This sense of a physical jar, of being concussed, symbolises Wells's uncertainty in the years following 1914. For it is difficult to exaggerate the impact of the war on his outlook and imagination, the sense of being thrown out of gear by immense forces beyond his control. In the concluding essay of *An Englishman Looks at the World*, written before the outbreak of war, he had written: 'Never, it would seem, has man been so various and busy and persistent, and there is no intimation of any check to the expansion of his energies.' With the coming of war, confidence of this kind became immediately obsolete, as if written in a different age. For Wells the war meant an immense dislocation, the crumbling of a world that had seemed familiar and secure. His hero's confusion and debility in the opening chapter is symptomatic of this malaise.

The landscape described in the story is strongly reminiscent of that depicted in *A Modern Utopia*:

There were few houses and no towns or villages at all. The houses varied very greatly in size, from little isolated buildings which Mr

Barnstaple thought might be elegant summer-houses or little temples, to clusters of roofs and turrets which reminded him of country chateaux or suggested extensive farming or dairying establishments. Here and there people were working in the fields or going to and fro on foot or on machines, but the effect of the whole was of an extremely under-populated land.   (I, 3, 4)

What is being parodied here is not only the landscape of *A Modern Utopia* and *The Time Machine* – there is a terrace adorned 'with squat stone figures of seated vigilant animals and men' which recalls the memorable image of the sphinx – but that of William Morris's *News from Nowhere* and a number of other Utopian romances including Bulwer Lytton's *The Coming Race* and Bellamy's *Looking Backward*. In the description of the idyllic, garden-like scenery of Utopia, Wells is both caricaturing himself and the paradisal accounts of Eden in the Bible and mythology.

There are echoes of his allegorical short story 'The Door in the Wall' in Mr Barnstaple's nostalgic longing to return and in his haunted sense of belonging in the world of the enchanted garden. When he returns to his own time he reflects sadly that 'the door that had opened so marvellously between that strange and beautiful world and our own had closed again'. This explicit reference to a door – a well-known symbol for the threshold between conscious and unconscious, outer and inner – is a further reminder of his short story and of the dividing line between the world of actuality and the imagination.

What is so noticeable about *Men Like Gods* is that it is in itself a parody and has in turn been frequently parodied. George Orwell's *Coming Up For Air*, James Hilton's *Lost Horizon* and Aldous Huxley's *Brave New World* each caricature aspects of Wells's novel. It has also spawned a whole genre of Utopian and dystopian novels including B. F. Skinner's *Walden Two* (1948), and David Karp's *One* (1953). The fact that it has proved to be such a fertile source of inspiration strongly suggests that, in common with other novels which are much imitated, it makes use of imagery and metaphor to convey a series of truths concerning the human condition. *Men Like Gods* is in fact a myth – a parable which invites comparison with other twentieth-century myths including Kafka's *The Castle* and John Fowles's *The Magus*. It is at once a metaphor and an ironic fable.

Throughout the novel there is extended play on the themes of duality and mirror imagery. The road on which Mr Barnstaple is travelling is transformed into one 'apparently made of glass, clear in places as still water and in places milky or opalescent'. The glass road is followed by a series of encounters in which duality is a key element: there are *two* apple trees, the bodies of *two* dead experimenters, the visitors are greeted by *two* Utopians, the roses Mr Barnstaple admires so much are *double* roses. In a speech Mr Burleigh announces that 'we conceive ourselves to be living in a parallel universe to yours, on a planet the very brother of your own'. It is apparent that not only is Utopia a twin planet to earth but *Men Like Gods* is a mirror image of *The Dream* (in the former a man from the twentieth century finds himself in the world of 3000 years hence; in the latter a citizen of the future dreams through a lifetime covering the late nineteenth and early twentieth centuries). The theme of duality is reiterated by a series of linguistic puns emphasising the idea of a mirror reflection: Mr Barnstaple's home is in Sydenham, the location of the Crystal Palace; his close companions in Utopia are Lychnis (likeness) and Crystal; the Utopians' pronunciation of Barralonga is Long Barrow, a mirror image of the name. There are no displayed mirrors in Utopia but when Mr Barnstaple opens a cupboard door on the morning after his arrival 'he found himself opening a triple full-length mirror'. The book itself is a mirror in the sense that its two halves exactly complement one another. The novel consists of 16 chapters divided into three Books; Book One comprising eight chapters and Books Two and Three four chapters each. The crisis on which the story hinges – the evacuation of the 'Earthlings' to Quarantine Crag – occurs at the exact midway point, the point of fulcrum. The story is one of the most neatly balanced and symmetrical of all his novels, Mr Barnstaple's journey to Utopia occurring in the first chapter and his return to earth in the last. His journey is also an exact mirror: at the moment of entry into the dream he sees a little country inn on his *right*; on his return the inn is on his *left*. His acclimatisation to the familiar routines of his life in chapter 16 is the reverse of his departure from these routines in chapter 1.

The continual interplay of the idea of dualism reinforces the notion that a dominant theme of the novel's symbolism is the idea of the divided self. Interwoven through the novel is a continual contrasting of opposites:

conscious	unconscious
masculine	feminine
thinking	feeling

pessimism	optimism
ego	shadow
outer	inner

Through the allegory of Mr Barnstaple's journey to the enchanted garden Wells is exploring the cluster of divisions within his own mental and emotional self.

There are a number of indications to suggest that Mr Barnstaple's sojourn in another world is a vivid dream rather than a reflection of an actual experience. At the moment when his sojourn commences he is aware of a familiar sound:

> Afterwards he remembered that at this point he heard a sound. It was exactly the same sound, coming as the climax of an accumulating pressure, sharp like the snapping of a lute string, which one hears at the end – or beginning – of insensibility under anaesthetics. (I, 1, 3)

The sound is repeated at the instant he returns to earth in the final chapter: 'came that sense again of unendurable tension and that sound like the snapping of a bow-string'. This sound is heard by Job Huss in *The Undying Fire* at the beginning and end of his dream and strongly suggests that the chapters describing Mr Barnstaple's journey to a perfect world are impressions of an *imaginary* experience.[48] We are repeatedly told in the opening chapters that he is suffering from overwork and neurasthenia, and that he is overwhelmed by a desire to escape from the world of his daily routines. Once he leaves the familiar world behind him there are frequent allusions to dreams and dream-like states of mind: 'He was extraordinarily happy with the bright unclouded happiness of a perfect dream' (I, 1, 4), 'He had a vague feeling that a very delightful and wonderful dream was slipping from him' (I, 8, 1), 'Mr Barnstaple awoke slowly and reluctantly from a dream'. (II, 4, 1). The only tangible reminder of his journey, a flower, crumbles into nothingness when he takes it from his pocket. Though he has been away for more than a month there is no mention in the newspapers of his missing companions, even though these include a number of prominent public figures. When he returns to his wife and she asks him where he has spent his holiday he replies: 'Oh! just drifting about and dreaming. I've had a wonderful time . . . I just wandered and dreamt. Lost in a day-dream' (III, 4, 7).

At times when reading *Men Like Gods* one is aware of a feeling of unease, as if something about the narrative is askew. This disorientation has its origin, I suggest, in this dream-like quality, the sense of a lack of solidity in the events being described: 'Mr Barnstaple had a sense of floating from star to star and from plane to plane, through an incessant variety and wonder of existences' (III, 1, 1). Despite the hero's apparent conviction that he has been miraculously transported to another world one senses that the narrator is much less sure: that whilst Mr Barnstaple imagines himself to be in Utopia in reality he remains throughout in the Thames valley. On awakening after the destruction of the castle he looks around him and sees that 'all the land fell at last towards a very broad valley down which a shining river wound leisurely in great semi-circular bends until it became invisible in the evening haze'. This is so unmistakeably a description of the Thames – it bears a close resemblance to the scenery in the neighbourhood of Surly Hall, a much-loved haunt of Wells's boyhood – as to confirm the impression that Mr Barnstaple's journey is mental rather than actual.

There are frequent reminders of Wells's awareness that in describing Utopia he is depicting a dream world, a society that is unattainable. The sketches of Utopian scenery – 'the landscape . . . was garden pasture with grazing creamy cattle and patches of brilliantly coloured vegetation' suggest the dream-like landscapes of childhood reading, of an impossible wonderland. Morris's *News from Nowhere*, with its pastoral vision of an ideal society, is described as 'a graceful impossible book'. On his first arrival in Utopia Mr Barnstaple reflects that at half past ten that morning he had been travelling along the main road through Slough 'and now at half past one he was soaring through wonderland with his own world half forgotten'. The phrase 'soaring through wonderland' strongly suggests that what is being described is an *imaginary* landscape: the fanciful, haunting scenery of reverie and dreams.

This is, of course, no ordinary dream but an extremely vivid mental journey, a trauma, which affects Mr Barnstaple emotionally and intellectually. It is in a sense a symbolic death. When he is trapped while attempting to descend Quarantine Crag he spends a considerable time contemplating his own death and thinking back on his past life. During this interval time seems to pass more and more slowly: 'Presently he caught himself looking at his wrist watch. It was twenty minutes past twelve. He was looking at his watch more and more frequently – or time was going more slowly . . . Should he wind his watch or let it run down?' This sense of arrested time, of a turning point midway between life and death, is mirrored in his realisation that he is trapped and can neither climb nor descend:

> He fingered the smooth rocks about him. 'But this is absurd', he said breaking out into a cold perspiration. There was no way out of this corner into which he had so painfully and laboriously got himself. He could neither go on nor go back. He was caught.
>
> (II, 3, 6)

This sense of being caught in a dilemma, 'with unclimbable heights and depths above him and below', can be seen as a reflection of the sense of ambivalence which troubled Wells increasingly during the years following the First World War. The novels of this period – *The Undying Fire*, *The Secret Places of the Heart*, *Men Like Gods* and *The Dream* – veer uneasily between optimism and pessimism as his moods fluctuated. Emotionally he yearned for the ideal world of Plato's *Republic* and his own *A Modern Utopia*; intellectually he knew that this was a dream. He expressed this ambivalence in a revealing aside written at about this time: 'Temperamentally he is egotistic and romantic, intellectually he is clearly aware that the egotistic and romantic must go.'[49]

Mr Barnstaple's eventual escape from the crag and descent down a rope ladder is an apt symbol of Wells's descent from impractical dreams to a realistic awareness of the human condition. 'Romance is not reality', confesses Mr Barnstaple at one point, reluctantly acknowledging the transitoriness of Platonic speculations.

The whole of Book Two, 'Quarantine Crag', can be read as a metaphor for Wells's journey from illusion to enlightenment. At its centre is the description of the castle on the crag:

> The high crag which was their destination stood out, an almost completely isolated headland, in the fork between two convergent canyons. It towered up to a height of perhaps two thousand feet above the foaming clash of the torrents below, a great mass of pale greenish and purple rocks, jagged and buttressed and cleft deeply by joint planes and white crystalline veins. The gorge on one side of it was much steeper than that on the other, it was so overhung indeed as to be darkened like a tunnel, and here within a hundred feet or so of the brow a slender metallic bridge had been flung across the gulf. . . . The crag was surmounted by the tall ruins of an ancient castle. (II, 2, 1)

The description is so strongly reminiscent of the castles of fairyland as to suggest a deliberate allusion to the romantic castles of childhood reading. This is reinforced by the account of the journey to the crag – 'The flying ship passed down the valley and over the great plain and across a narrow sea and another land with a rocky coast and dense forests, and across a great space of empty sea' – a description which seems to echo the magical journeys of *The Arabian Nights* and *Vathek*. It is as if the reader is floating through space across a dream-like landscape culled from romance and mythology. What is even more striking about the description of the crag is Wells's careful use of language charged with imagery: the crag stood out 'in the fork between two convergent canyons' (in a later passage we are reminded that 'Sheer and high the great headland rose like the prow of some gigantic ship between the two deep blue canyons'); the rock is cleft with 'white crystalline veins'; the gorge on one side 'was so overhung as to be darkened like a tunnel'; below the summit of the gorge 'a slender metallic bridge had been flung across the gulf'. Throughout the passage a dual process is in evidence: the physical description of the castle and the crag is echoed by a series of metaphors for the conscious and unconscious mind. The impregnable castle on its high fortress is a fitting image for the inner self, for the irrational, romantic elements within Wells's makeup. The situation of the castle in a fork between two convergent ravines symbolises its importance as a point of fulcrum, as a watershed in Mr Barnstaple's journey towards enlightenment. It stands at the dividing line between romanticism and reality; between naïve optimism on the one hand and stoical endurance on the other. When the 'slender metallic bridge' linking the two is destroyed Wells is reluctantly acknowledging the impossibility of co-existence – the fragile harmony between the two states of mind could no longer be sustained. The white veins which cleft the rock symbolise the sensitive, feminine aspects of his nature: those elements in his make-up which produced the delicate fantasies of 'The Beautiful Suit' and 'Mr Skelmersdale in Fairyland'. There was much in his temperament which responded to beauty; Wells was fully aware that his outward self of the man of science was deeply cleft with sensitivity.

It is interesting to contrast Mr Barnstaple's *descent* down the mountain with the *ascent* of Nunez in 'The Country of the Blind' (1904). Nunez escapes from his uncomprehending pursuers by ascending; Barnstaple by descending. The comparison neatly encapsulates Wells's symbolic journey from the unconscious to the conscious mind; in descending from the inaccessible crag to earth he is abandoning facile romanticism and returning to a pragmatic recognition of man's animality. (Mr Barnstaple enters his dream at Slough: the casting off of his depression not only parallels Bunyan's account of Christian crossing the Slough of Despond, but echoes Wells casting off – sloughing – his outmoded Utopianism. The play on words here, as elsewhere in the novel, is interesting and suggestive.) Mr Barnstaple's return to earth at the conclusion of the novel is also accompanied by a physical descent – 'the car seemed to fall a foot or so' – an echo of his descent from flights of the imagination to the uncomfortable world of reality.

It is not only *Pilgrim's Progress* that is being parodied here but the conventional vision of heaven and hell exemplified in such works as Dante's *The Divine Comedy*. Instead of climbing the mountain of purgatory in order to enter paradise the process is inverted: he *descends* the mountain and, having reached the base of the crag, enters an Eden-like garden where he is tended by angelic figures: 'Two gentle goddesses had given him some restorative in a gorge at the foot of high cliffs. He had been carried in a woman's arms as a child is carried.' The language and imagery are strongly reminiscent of *Mr Blettsworthy on Rampole Island* and suggest that the novel is an allegory of a journey – the journey of a mind from innocence to disillusionment. As the poet in *The Divine Comedy* encounters those doing penance for envy, lust, sloth and so on, so the characters encountered by Mr Barnstaple represent the forces which had contributed to the First World War: intolerance (Father Amerton), prejudice (Barralonga), xenophobia (Burleigh), pride (Greeta Grey). The revelatory language at the moment of his awakening from unconciousness – 'Then they had turned him over, and the light of the rising sun had been blinding in his eyes' – reinforces the notion of enlightenment, of a progression from darkness to perception. His awakening marks the beginning of the end of his symbolic death.

The destruction of the castle and its fairyland setting can be read as a symbolic ending of Mr Barnstaple's (and Wells's) innocence. With the destruction of the castle comes the ending of romance, the abandonment of illusion. Though he still longs to return to Utopia, his acceptance of its inaccessibility – 'That dear world of honesty and health was beyond the utmost boundaries of our space, utterly inaccessible to him now for evermore' – suggests that Wells has come to terms with reality and acknowledged the impracticality of his Edwardian dreams.

It should be noted in passing that the novel contains not one castle, but two. Almost the last sight he sees before he enters his dream is 'a distant view of Windsor Castle'. When he returns to earth at the end of his strange experiences he sees the same view:

> On the far side of the road were level fields against a background of low wooded hills. Away to the left was a little inn. He turned his head and saw Windsor Castle in the remote distance rising above poplar-studded meadows. (III, 4, 6)

The romantic castle of his Utopian dreams is no more, but Windsor Castle remains, as real and tangible as ever. Mr Barnstaple has quite literally come down to earth. (The reference to poplar trees, a well-known bipolar symbol, recurs in *The History of Mr Polly* and again in *The Brothers*. The reference is a further reminder of the bifurcation which confronts his hero: a symbolic parting of the ways between dream and reality.)

It is significant that the final chapters describing Mr Barnstaple's experiences after the destruction of the castle are entitled 'A Neophyte in Utopia'. In the context of Wells's apparent intentions the title is suggestive. A neophyte (from the Greek *neophytos*, newly planted) is a tiro, novice or beginner. The term suggests an acknowledgement of his innocence in imagining that man could ever attain to a Utopian society. The innocence which produced *The Discovery of the Future* and *A Modern Utopia* was swept away in the battlefields of Europe – in *Joan and Peter*, written in the last year of the war, he wrote: 'In August, 1914, that detachment of human lives from history, that pretty picaresque disorder of experiences . . . which had gone on for thousands of years, came to an end.' Without exception those who accompany Mr Barnstaple into Utopia are consumed by malice, stupidity or dreams of imperial grandeur. He is compelled to recognise the emptiness of his vision until at last, before returning to the world of everyday, he says aloud: 'Dear Dream of Hope and Loveliness, Farewell!' The destruction of his innocence is complete.

The epidemic which breaks out in Utopia as a result of the arrival of the 'earthlings' is an apt symbol for Wells's sense of contagion overrunning the planet. Mr Barnstaple's conviction that 'seven-eighths of the world seemed to be sinking down towards disorder and social dissolution' is paralleled by the outbreak of 'physical depression and misery' consequent on his arrival in Utopia. His awareness that Europe was capsizing into conflict and unreason brought to the forefront of his mind the nightmare of the Wild Asses which had haunted him while writing *Boon*. Violence and cruelty were increasingly endemic and, Wells remarks, for Mr Barnstaple and men of his temperament 'hope is the essential solvent without which there is no digesting life'. Clearly the novel was begun in a mood of pessimism and disillusionment: for both Wells and his *alter ego* the book was an act of exorcism.

The metaphorical discarding of Utopian dreams is accompanied by a symbolic process of growth. On his return to the world of everyday, Mr Barnstaple's wife remarks that he has grown: 'It's not simply that your stoop has gone. You have grown oh! – two or three inches.' Yet simultaneously Utopia has shrunk. Before returning to his wife he gazes longingly at the flower he has brought back with him: 'The lovely world from which he had been driven had shrunken now to a spot of shining scarlet.' The dream world has diminished while he himself has grown. This contrasting image can be seen as a reflection of the process of change within Wells's consciousness. With the ending of the dream Mr Barnstaple becomes a different person: he has increased in stature. Wells was deeply aware that for him the First World War and its aftermath meant that Utopian speculations were henceforth of diminishing importance. From now onwards his energies must be channelled in other directions.

In *Men Like Gods* there is extensive use of symbolism associated with colour. When Mr Barnstaple first crosses the threshold between the world of actuality and that of his dreams he finds himself on a road bordered by 'a mass of some unfamiliar blossom of forget-me-not blue'. Later, when he is being cared for by Lychnis after his illness, he is struck again by the vividness of the colours:

> He was too feeble and incurious to raise his head and look to see where she had gone. But he saw that she had been sitting at a white table on which was a silver bowl full of intensely blue flowers, and the colour of the flowers held him and diverted his first faint impulse of curiosity. . . . Beyond the table were the white pillars of the loggia. A branch of one of these eucalyptus-like trees, with leaves bronze black, came very close outside.
>
> (III, 1, 1)

Blue, in the language of symbolism the colour of innocence, represents his naïvety and romantic longing for the world of his imagination. Almost his first impression of Utopia is of the mass of blue flowers and at the end, as he takes his last look at his surroundings, 'the blue blossoms that had charmed him on arrival still prevailed'. The contrast of the white pillars with the black leaves is a reiteration of the conscious–unconscious imagery which is a powerful motif in the 'Quarantine Crag' chapters. This imagery is further reinforced by the friendship between Mr Barnstaple and Lychnis. Lychnis, a tender, loving woman who tends him during his convalescence, symbolises the feminine, sensitive elements in his make-up:

> Since she was always close at hand, she filled for him perhaps more than her legitimate space in the Utopian spectacle. She lay across it like a shadow.   (III, 2, 7)

The repeated references to the 'shadow' (in the same paragraph Wells regrets that she possessed 'the dark sacrificial disposition that bows and responds to the shadow') leave no doubt that for him Lychnis is an Anima figure, the embodiment of the female, emotional aspects of his temperament. Weena in *The Time Machine* and Rowena in *Mr Blettsworthy on Rampole Island* are similar figures: each complements the masculine, conscious ego by ministering to the protagonist and reminding him of the duality in his temperament. Before he returns to earth Mr Barnstaple climbs to a viewpoint Lychnis has directed him to and surveys the prospect for the last time:

> For a time he noted little of the things immediately about him. Then the scent of roses invaded his attention, and he found himself walking down a slanting pergola covered with great white roses and very active little green birds. He stopped short and stood looking up at the leaves, light-saturated, against the sky. He put up his hands and drew down one of the great blossoms until it touched his cheek. (III, 4, 4)

His reluctance in leaving the world of his dreams, in admitting to himself the imaginary nature of his sojourn, is aptly reinforced here: 'He put up his hands and drew down one of the great blossoms.' His powerful emotional attraction for the white roses is mirrored by his passionate response to Utopia, his longing to delay his sojourn there. But the whiteness of the roses is contrasted with the green birds and the green leaves. Birds are a familiar psychological symbol for the imagination, for man's ability to engage in flights of fantasy. Green represents the cycle of birth and death: in this context a fitting reminder of the symbolic death of the imagination (the Utopian experimenter who is killed at the moment of Mr Barnstaple's entry is named Greenlake) and of the intimate association between imagination and the feminine, unconscious aspects of his make-up. On returning to his own time he finds himself in a field separated from the road by an open black gate. Driving his car on to the road 'he left the black gate open behind him'. The gate, a repetition of the idea of a threshold, represents the unconscious. In passing through it Mr Barnstaple leaves behind him an essential part of his make-up; his failure to shut it suggests a recognition of his ambivalence – and a reluctance to sever the links with his innermost imagination.

Considerable use is made of feminine–masculine imagery, most strikingly in the numerous references to roses. Mr Barnstaple encounters two Utopian gardeners armed with hooks and knives engaged in pruning a thicket of roses.

> Their wood was in long, thorny, snaky-red streaked stems that writhed wide and climbed to the rocky lumps over which they grew. Their great petals fell like red snow and like drifting moths and like blood upon the soft soil that sheltered amidst the brown rocks. (I, 8, 4)

Here Wells reinforces the obvious bipolar symbolism of the roses (the hard, penetrating quality of the thorns contrasted with the softness and beauty of the petals) by juxtaposing a series of contrasting images: thorny, snaky-red, rocks; snow, drifting moths, soft soil. The dualism of the roses is an apt metaphor for the thesis–antithesis contrast that underlies so much of the novel's imagery and contributes to its symmetrical structure.

Reinforcing the repeated allusions to roses there is considerable play on the image of the circle. The Utopians follow the teachings of a great prophet who had been tortured on a wheel. Literal followers of his teachings 'turned his wheel into a miraculous symbol, and they confused it with the equator and the sun and the ecliptic and indeed with anything else that was round'. The castle on the crag stands within a *circular* wall. Immediately before its destruction it rotates upon its axis, 'exactly as though some invisible giant had siezed the upper tenth of the headland and was twisting it round'.

The rose, the wheel and the circle are all figures patterned after the mandala (a circle enclosed within a square), a symbol for the inner and outer aspects of life. The repeated use of mandala imagery in the novel can only be deliberate – Wells had made a careful study of religious and psychological imagery in the writing of *The Outline of History* and strengthens the impression that in *Men Like Gods* he is seeking to unfold a series of metaphors to suggest the fracturing of man's psyche. The immense disillusionment of 1914–18 had caused a great divide in his response to reality.

The parallels between *The Time Machine* and *Men Like Gods* are numerous. In both novels the vehicle in which the traveller has journeyed is retained by the captors:

> I stepped through the bronze frame and up to the Time Machine. I was surprised to find that it had been carefully oiled and cleaned.
> *(The Time Machine*, XIII)

> His old car, the Yellow Peril, looking now the clumsiest piece of ironmongery conceivable, stood in the road. He went and examined it. It seemed to be in perfect order; it had been carefully oiled and the petrol tank was full. *(Men Like Gods*, III, 4, 5)

In both there is a discussion on the idea of time as the fourth dimension. In both the traveller has a female companion (Weena and Lychnis, respectively). In both the traveller is given a flower as a reminder of his sojourn. In both the traveller is smitten with regrets on returning to his own time and wishes to return. But the differences between the two novels are equally striking. Whereas the Time Traveller wishes to bring Weena back to his own time, Mr Barnstaple makes no plans to persuade Lychnis to accompany him. Whereas the flowers which Weena thrusts into the Time Traveller's pockets survive his journey back to 1895, those Mr Barnstaple attempts to keep wither into dust. And, most suggestive of all, these flowers in *The Time Machine* are white; those in *Men Like Gods* are red. White symbolises the feminine realm; it is the colour of the moon and for this reason is associated with symbols of the anima. The white petals are a reminder of Weena's sensitivity and receptiveness. Red, the colour of blood, symbolises passion and romance. When it disintegrates in Mr Barnstaple's hand – 'It had lost its glowing red, and as he held it out . . . it seemed to writhe as it shrivelled and blackened' – there is a moment of both actual and metaphorical destruction. Romance has given way to a sombre awareness of reality.

A comparison of *Men Like Gods* and 'The Door in the Wall' is equally revealing, particularly in the close analogy between the two stories at the moment of crossing the threshold:

> Wallace mused before he went on telling me. 'You see', he said, with the doubtful inflection of a man who pauses at incredible things, 'there were two great panthers there. . . . And I was not afraid. There was a long wide path with marble-edged flower borders on either side, and these two huge velvety beasts were playing there with a ball. . . . It was, I tell you, an enchanted garden.'   ('The Door in the Wall')

> On either side was a band of greensward, of a finer grass than Mr Barnstaple had ever seen before . . . and beyond this a wide border of flowers . . . a big and beautifully marked leopard had come very softly out of the flowers and sat down like a great cat in the middle of the glass road at the side of the big car.
>
> (*Men Like Gods*, I, 2, 3)

The feline imagery here is particularly interesting. Throughout his 10-year love-affair with Rebecca West (1913–23) he referred to himself as 'Jaguar' and Rebecca as 'Panther'.[50] For him a panther represented all that is embodied in the feminine side of life, all that is soft, emotional and receptive. The presence of the panther at the commencement of both stories and its direct association with the image of the garden suggests an acknowledgement on Wells's part of the central importance in his life of such feminine qualities as sensitivity and imagination. When, later in *Men Like Gods*, the animal dies – 'it was found unaccountably dead on the second morning' after Mr Barnstaple's arrival – its death represents an admission that a vital element in his personality has been lost. His innocence has been destroyed by the trauma of 1914–18. (Note that this theme is strongly reinforced by his name: Barn, staple = literally, the burning of the pillar. The name suggests the destruction of a central element of belief and also prefigures the violent end of the castle on its rock.)

The entire novel can be read as an extended allegory on the theme of loss of innocence. On entering the dream Mr Barnstaple is impressed with the whiteness of his surroundings:

Beyond this gloriously coloured foam of flowers spread flat meadows on which creamy cattle were grazing. . . . From these benign creatures Mr Barnstaple's eyes went to a long line of flame-shaped trees, to a colonnade of white and gold, and to a background of snow-clad mountains. A few tall, white clouds were sailing across a sky of dazzling blue. (I, 2, 1)

The repetition of whiteness – the creamy cattle, the white colonna-de, the snow-clad mountains, the white clouds – is clearly deliberate. In psychological terms white is a familiar symbol of innocence and loss; it also symbolises the feminine realm. Its reiteration underlines the association of innocence with imagination and sensitivity. His entry into the dream is accompanied by an explosion in which a stone house is demolished. Beside the ruins of the house (it may be noted in passing that ruins are themselves a symbol of the destruction of ideas or sentiments) were 'two large apple trees freshly twisted and riven, as if by some explosion'. Wells's extensive use of religious imagery in the scientific romances and short stories leaves little doubt that the reference here is to the apple of the Tree of Knowledge. The destruction of the apple trees at the moment the dream commences is a fitting metaphor for the corrosive power of knowledge (see in this connection his suggestive short story 'The Apple') and the loss of innocence consequent on its unleashment.[51] Note also that the destruction of Quarantine Crag is accompanied by an outburst of apocalyptic imagery:

And then it vanished. As it did so, a great column of dust poured up into its place; the waters in the gorge sprung into the air in tall fountains and were splashed to spray, and a deafening thud smote Mr Barnstaple's ears . . . he fell amidst a rain of dust and stones and water. (II, 4, 4)

The destruction of the castle is accompanied by a violent explo-sion of dust and stones in which 'the waters in the gorge sprung into the air in tall fountains'. The dissipation of the waters (a symbol of life and of the feminine unconscious) represents the death of innocence and of that romantic longing that had sustained Wells so powerfully since he had read Plato's *Republic* as a boy at Up Park. It represents his reluctant admission that a phase in his life has come to an end and that henceforth he must abandon the faith in progress implicit in such works as *The World Set Free* and *An Englishman Looks at the World*.

On examination it is apparent that *Men Like Gods* is a highly complex piece of writing in which Wells draws freely on the symbolism of dreams, mythology and psychology to create a myth of enduring relevance to our times. Implicit within it is a note of profound disillusionment. At the commencement of the novel Mr Barnstaple reflects that 1921 was an even sillier year than 1913, which he had 'hitherto regarded as the silliest year in the world's history'. At both the opening and closing of the story he is saddened and distressed by newspaper reports of war and violence. When Crystal, one of the Utopians, remarks that politicians 'produced the most preposterous and unworkable arrangements in the gravest fashion' he immediately responds 'Like Tristram Shandy's parish bull – which set about begetting the peace of the world at Versailles.' For Wells the Treaty of Versailles and its aftermath marked the collapse of his hopes for world reconstruction. The trauma of the war followed by the vindictive peace and the rise of Nazism and Fascism confirmed his worst fears for the future of mankind; the Wild Asses of the Devil were now irreparably at large.[52] After *Men Like Gods* his Utopian writings become increasingly rare. Instead he returned more and more to the pessimism of his early work, to the Swiftian polemic of *Mr Blettsworthy on Rampole Island*, *The Croquet Player* and *The Camford Visitation*. The carnage of 1914–18 had swept away the optimism of his middle years.

10

The World of William Clissold: a Writer Surveys his World

For in this long digression which I was accidentally led into, as in all my digressions . . . there is a master-stroke of digressive skill, the merit of which has all along, I fear, been overlooked by my reader . . . it is this: That tho' my digressions are all fair, as you observe, – and that I fly off from what I am about, as far, and as often too, as any writer in Great Britain; yet I constantly take care to order affairs so that my main business does not stand still in my absence.

(Laurence Sterne, *Tristram Shandy*)

This book, which contains religious, historical, economic and sociological discussions, which expresses fits of temper and moods of doubt, is at any rate submitted as a novel, as a whole novel, and nothing but a novel, as the story of one man's adventure, body, soul, and intelligence, in life. If you are the sort of person who will not accept it as a novel, then please leave it alone.

(H. G. Wells, *The World of William Clissold*,
'A Note Before the Title Page')

The 1920s was a period of experimentation in the European novel. James Joyce's *Ulysses* was published in 1922, Franz Kafka's *The Trial* and Virginia Woolf's *Mrs Dalloway* in 1925, Hermann Hesse's *Steppenwolf* in 1927 and D. H. Lawrence's *Lady Chatterley's Lover* in 1928. T. S. Eliot's *The Waste Land* (1922) reflected the disillusionment of the post-war generation and paved the way for a new mood in literature. Whilst many novelists were content to produce material in the conventional pattern (J. B. Priestley's *The Good Companions* appeared in 1929) there was clearly a spirit of innovation abroad. Writers were seeking for new departures, for a fresh sense of direction in a world in which the old order was visibly passing away. Wells was by no means immune to this spirit of experiment. He had read and admired much of Joyce's work and liked to keep abreast of contemporary developments in the novel.[53] His friendship with Rebecca West had made him more aware of a new generation of younger writers and brought him within the ambit of influential critical journals such as *Adelphi* and *The English Review*. Following the immense popular success of his novel *Mr Britling Sees It Through* (1916) and the comparative failure of *Joan and Peter* (1918), a novel on the grand scale, he seems to have felt the need for a mental stocktaking. 'The huge issues of the War and the Peace held my mind steady and kept it busy for some years', he wrote in his autobiography, but 'a phase of great restlessness and discontent came upon me in 1923–24'.[54] He solved the problem of his discontent in characteristic fashion by purchasing a house near Grasse in the south of France and settling down to write a long, discursive novel in which he could review his world and attempt to get his ideas in perspective. The result was *The World of William Clissold*, a book which he described at the end of his life as 'a vast three decker, issued in three successive volumes of rigmarole, which broke down the endurance of readers and booksellers alike'.[55] This extraordinarily neglected novel (it has received almost no critical attention since its publication in 1926), the longest Wells wrote, bears all the hallmarks of a modernist text: density of symbolism, shifts in time sequence and acute psychological insight. Moreover in presenting the inner life of his divided narrator, his *alter ego*, and in looking at him *from the outside*, he succeeded in breaking new ground in the English novel by portraying a rounded picture of a mental world.

The book is presented in the form of a first person narrative by William Clissold, a successful businessman of Wells's generation who sets out at the age of 60 to write an account of his life and ideas. Clissold confesses at the outset, in a manner reminiscent of George Ponderevo in *Tono-Bungay*, that he has written a number of technical reports but has not attempted to write an autobiographical manuscript before. He explains that he intends to begin with his metaphysics and, after a sketch of his beliefs, 'so to the immediate affairs of everyday life, to moods, passions, experiences' . . .

It is not exactly an autobiography I want to write, and not exactly a
book of confessions. . . . I should say that a description of my
world best expresses what I have in view; my world and my will. I
want it to be a picture of everything as it is reflected in my
brain.   (I, 2)

In entering any novel there are two processes simultaneously at
work in the mind of the reader: first, the unfolding of the novel as a
story and, second, the point of view from which the story is
presented. The reader is usually more aware of the first process than
the second, since the narrative impinges much more immediately
on the reader's consciousness than the individuality behind it. In
The World of William Clissold the two processes are inseparably
fused. The device employed is of an autobiographical manuscript
written by an invented personality, William Clissold, who sets out
to review his world. This approach permits a degree of introspection
and discursiveness unusual in Wells's fiction. On entering the novel
the reader embarks on a journey into a mind, a mind which ranges
over beliefs, passions, attitudes and experiences in an effort to
explain itself.
   Wells deliberately opts for a discursive style which reveals once
again his indebtedness to Sterne. Indeed at first glance the book
seems to consist of a series of digressions. Many of the devices
employed in *Tristram Shandy* are evident again here. There is, for
example, the device of the novel apparently in the process of being
written, as in Book One, 6:

I wish I knew more of the practical side of literature. . . . I have
been beating about the bush for five sections and making notes for
various matters that must come in later, and still I doubt if I have
told anything at all about my world. Instead I have written about
my childhood and made a sketch of my host at lunch.

There are the interruptions which prevent the narrator from
getting on with the story: 'For a time I must discontinue making
these notes altogether, for old Sir Rupert York has rung me up' (I, 4).
'This morning my work has been interrupted. I have been raided
and assaulted by Clementina' (II, 10). There are the continual
digressions on all manner of subjects ranging from religious belief to
Marxism and from advertising to universities. There is the same
sense of peering into the author's mind, of being a participant in the

writer's mental world. In fact Clissold is careful to stress his view that the digressions are important, that far from being asides they have an important place in the scheme of things: 'It is true that the last three or four sections have been mainly devoted to Marx and Socialism, but that is no more a digression from the account of my world than the theology of the First Book. Why should one entertain the idea that a man is no more than his face, his mannerisms, and his love affairs?' (II, 10). This insistence that in order to present a fully rounded picture of a character the portrait must include an account of his philosophy, his metaphysics, is interesting and marks a fundamental departure from the work of contemporaries such as Bennett. Clissold has both an *outer* life – the story of his friendships, love-affairs, marriage and career is described in detail – and an *inner* life in the sense that his outlook and beliefs and the drives that motivate him are set down. What appears on first reading to be a series of essays, a patchwork quilt of digressions and asides, can be seen on examination to be an integral part of the overall design. The apparent discursiveness is a deliberate device, an attempt to convey a comprehensive picture of the world as it appears to a representative Englishman of Wells's time. Seen in its totality the novel is an attempt to build up a picture of Clissold's consciousness in all its aspects and in the process to demonstrate, as Sterne seeks to do, the interconnectedness of all human experience.

The book is dominated by the idea of time. The opening paragraphs reveal Clissold obsessed by the passing of time and by his expectation of life. 'In the face of these figures I cannot hide from myself that the greater part of my life has been lived. So far I have had but few physical reminders of the ebb of the years.' Time returns to the forefront of his thoughts when looking back on his childhood. When tragedy (the suicide of Clissold's father) compels the family to leave the peace and beauty of Mowbray his mother removes him to Bruges, which he remembers as 'cobbled, with grass and moss between the cobbles, as built of very worn red brick and having a great number of courts in which big trees grew and into which one went through great archways' (II, 2). There is an echo here of the communal halls described in *The Time Machine*, a suggestion of ruin and decay. The grass and moss growing between the cobbles suggest the inevitable encroachment of time, the hand of corruption on all things. The town is dominated by a belfry containing a carillon which chimes at frequent intervals: 'It showered chimes and airs at the hours and the half-hours and quarter-hours.' His memories of the tragedy which uproots their lives are associated in his mind with the continual chiming of the bells (Wells emphasises the point by entitling the chapter 'Carillon and Tragedy') and the memory of the overgrown cobbles. Time is thus established as an important element in the novel, a motif which is never far from the surface of the narrative. At his home in Provence, Clissold surveys his world and reminds the reader of his obsession with time.

> It is only because I may sit at this window for so brief a time that I do not see this scene dissolve visibly and pass and give place to other unprecedented and equally transitory apppearances. Of one thing only can I be sure, that all this goes, peasants and pleasure cities, ships and empires, weapons, armies, races, religion, and all the present fashions of man's life. Could my moment be enlarged to the scale of a thousand years, my world would seem less lasting than a sunset and the entire tragedy of this age the unimportant incident of an afternoon. I can discover in all my world nothing enduring, neither in the hills nor in the sea, nor in laws and customs nor in the nature of man, nothing steadfast except for this – a certain growth of science, a certain increase of understanding, a certain accumulation of power.
>
> (I, 15)

Time as the inevitable concomitant of change is Clissold's theme. War, disasters, pain, the tragedy of our individual lives, all are transitory things, incidents in the measureless passage of the years. It is this perspective – that of a narrator who is both aware of time and yet outside it – which accounts for the novel's unusual detachment, the sense that Clissold is viewing his life and thought from a dimension remote in space and time. The tone of the book is of a man looking back on his past life from a vast perspective of time and presenting a distillation of his experience. In the process he reviews both his individual experience and the social history of his age. His theme throughout is the inexorable passing of time, the unseen hand of change resting on all things. His detachment is that of a man who has lived a full and active life but has now removed himself from the pressures of time and chance to think over all that life has taught him. The result is a text of unusual intimacy, as revealing about Wells as *The Private Papers of Henry Ryecroft* is about Gissing.

In considering *Clissold* in relation to the modern novel what impresses the reader most strongly is the divided nature of its central character. A common criticism of Wells's novels is that his characters have no depth, that they are uncomplicated, static – 'flat' in E. M. Forster's terminology. There is some substance in this criticism in the early work – *The Wheels of Chance* and *Kipps* for example – yet again and again in the later novels we find instances of acutely differentiated personalities. Arnold Blettsworthy in *Mr Blettsworthy on Rampole Island*, Theodore Bulpington in *The Bulpington of Blup* and Brynhild Palace in *Brynhild* each possess a divided temperament, an ambivalence which is explored in the course of the novel. William Clissold is a further example of a character who is divided against himself and much of whose life is spent in seeking to reconcile the conflicting aspects of his personality. In a revealing chapter, 'Trouble in the Night', Clissold refers to the 'sleepless nights when all our mental restraints have been put off with our daytime clothes' and describes the agonising of a soul in torment:

> I return to this inner and hidden life. This is what feels, this is what responds, this is what matters, this is what is. This is the life that in the daytime and commonly we hide even from ourselves. The night is its time for revelation. Then for all our resistances we find ourselves taken and stripped and put upon the rack of these blundering contradictions of standard and desire. Then come writhings and cries. The angel and the ape appear. The morning finds us already most sedulously forgetting that dreadful interview with our bare selves. We dress, we examine our faces in the glass to be sure that we are masked before we risk the observation of our fellow masqueraders.   (VI, 8)

It is this recurring theme of the 'inner and hidden life', of the contrast between 'the angel and the ape', which renders the novel such a seminal text in understanding Wells. He had been deeply interested in the psychological ideas of William James (the brother of Henry James and author of *The Varieties of Religious Experience* and *The Principles of Psychology*) and as early as *The New Machiavelli*, written in 1908–9, had laid great stress on the 'mental hinterland' of his characters, the deep recesses of the mind in which ancestral images recur. James was instrumental in formulating the idea of the stream of consciousness, the technique which seeks to record the random flow of impressions through the mind of an individual.

What Wells is seeking to do in *The World of William Clissold* is to present the thoughts, ideas and impressions of a sample human mind – not merely his surface mental states but the innermost drives and fears which haunt his unconscious.

Clissold insists that his own case is by no means exceptional, that he is typical in many respects of his class and generation. In asserting that 'the ordinary personal life is still a sensitised meeting place of conflicting forces that rather imagines itself to be, than is as yet, an individual'[56] he touches on an important psychological truth which links the novel to the work of Hesse, Kafka and Camus. Clissold is typical of his time in his introspection, his self-honesty, his loneliness. All his life he is seeking with varying degrees of success to explore the contradictions within himself – between male and female, passion and rationality, instinct and intelligence, doubt and belief. To some extent these contradictions mirror the ambiguities within Wells himself but their exploration and discussion in the novel is elaborated with disarming frankness. In the preface he observes: 'And it is a point worth considering in this period of successful personal memoirs that if the author had wanted to write a mental autobiography instead of a novel, there is no conceivable reason why he should not have done so. Clearly he did not want to do so.' In writing *Clissold*, then, he chose to analyse the personality and attitudes of a sample human being in the form of a novel, and in doing so to explore a cluster of traits and drives which formed a dominant part of his own makeup.

Far from being an integrated personality, Clissold's temperament is fractured by competing demands. In all his experiences – his childhood and adolescence, his relationship with his brother Dickon, his friendships with women, his marriage – can be discerned his attempts to come to terms with this dichotomy. Clissold expresses his inner conflict in these terms:

> This book, however, is not to tell of my social and economic imaginations and desires, but about the conflict of motives that has gone on in me, beneath the surface of my very considerable business activities. . . . I try to lay bare in myself the soul of a successful business man.   (IV, 11)

It is precisely this sense of a baring of a soul, of the dissection of a complex personality, which provides the novel with much of its interest. Much of the book has the air of an intimate diary, a confessional after the manner of *Amiel's Journal*. It is as if the narrator is confiding to the reader thoughts and impressions he is reluctant to admit to himself: at numerous points in the story the reader has an awareness that he is looking at Clissold from the inside and the outside simultaneously. At an early stage in the novel Clissold compares the world of reality to a crystal:

> There are times when I feel as though it was less the sphere that enclosed me and made my all, than a sort of magic crystal into which I peered and saw myself living. I have, as it were, a sense of externality. . . . It is the world in the crystal I want to write about, this crystal into which I seem to have been looking now and living for nine-and-fifty years.   (I, 2)

The analogy of life as a transparent sphere 'into which I peered and saw myself living' holds true throughout the novel. Time and again one has the sense that Clissold is describing himself from the outside, scrutinising his motives and actions as if he is observing a specimen under a microscope. This is particularly evident in parts Three and Four – 'Essence of Dickon' and 'Tangle of Desires' – where the account of his life and experiences is described with a detachment unusual in Wells's fiction. In 'Essence of Dickon' he is seen largely from Dickon's point of view (and again in the epilogue), while in 'Tangle of Desires' the description of his marriage to Clara and her infidelity is told with marked restraint, as if he is anxious that the reader should see his behaviour from her point of view as well as from his own. This objectivity is in sharp contrast to the solipsism of Richard Remington in *The New Machiavelli* and is an indication of Wells's desire to present a comprehensive picture of his hero, warts and all.

What is the relationship between Wells and Clissold? Wells states in his autobiography that 'I dramatised myself as William Clissold, an industrialist in retreat – the prophet Hosea could not have been more thorough in his dramatisation.'[57] It would be easy to assume from this that Clissold is simply a dramatised version of Wells himself rather than a fictional character. The evidence of the text suggests that Clissold is neither the one nor the other but is a second self, a shadow figure who embodies the contradictions and ambivalences in Wells's own make-up. Such a shadow personification enables the writer to see himself from outside with a degree of objectivity that first person narration does not normally permit. In discussing Clissold's relationships with women, for example, there is a revealing passage describing his search for a compensating self:

> And still there was something more. I think that I have been the victim of one of those exaggerations of promise that our restless, purblind old mother Nature never hesitates to put upon us. Always through my fuller years there was a feeling, a confidence I never had the power or will to analyse, that somewhere among womankind there was help and completion for me. How shall I express it? The other half of my androgynous self I had lost and had to find again. You remember the fable Aristophanes told in the Symposium.　(IV, 11)

'The other half of my androgynous self I had lost and had to find again' might almost be taken as the key to the understanding of the novel. In common with his creator, Clissold embodies both male and female characteristics. In his passion for political ideas, his stoicism, his flair for economic activity he displays many masculine traits. Equally in his sensitivity, his response to beauty, his love of order and yearning for feminine companionship he reveals the female aspects of his personality. The novel as a whole is an exploration of this ambivalence, using Clissold as a vicarious self whose personality can be dissected at will. A similar process is at work in the chapters describing his love-affairs. Sirrie Evans, Helen and Clementina embody characteristics recognisably belonging to actual people (Jane Wells, Rebecca West and Odette Keun, respectively) but in each case the portrait differs significantly from life. None of the portraits is a photographic likeness but is rather a fictionalisation. (In his 'Note Before the Title Page' Wells hits on the truth of the matter when he states: 'But all novelists rearrange, sublimate, intensify. One turns over the sketchbook of one's memories and uses what one needs.') In a sense, then, the novel is an exploration of an egotism, a journey into the mind. It is an attempt to view as comprehensively as possible one man's world, to see the totality of all that has made him what he is.

Clissold builds up an elaborate edifice of his political philosophy, his dream of an open conspiracy of leading men and women inspired by a vision of world order (Wells in his autobiography asserts that this is the most important part of the novel) but the abiding impression left in the mind of the reader is of Clissold's fallibility, his humanity, of a man haunted by the contradictions within himself and the central role of hazard in human affairs:

At the end, as at the beginning of every individual thing, stands careless, irresponsible Chance, smiling at our rules and foresight and previsions. The great life of the species has, it may be, some other law – I more than half believe it has some other law – but this is the quality of its atoms, our individual lives. (VI, 13)

The contrast drawn by the narrator between his rational self – the 'methodical, anxious, planning fellow' who writes didactic essays – and his impulsive, romantic self, the self who responds to beauty and companionship, echoes an ambivalence in Wells's nature which is evident in *Tono-Bungay* and many other novels. The ambivalence is present throughout *Clissold*, for the dreamer who speculates about the future of mankind is also a man who loves and desires and responds to beauty.

Loss as a motif is a frequently recurring element in the novel. Much of Clissold's life is a quest – for beauty, for order, for companionship, for faith. In describing the world of his childhood he asserts 'I am no longer the young man I was. He and I have almost lost identity. Nevertheless, I am still intensely the child I used to be' (I, 3). The child-like sense of wonder and release he has experienced at Mowbray is never recaptured, yet his attempts to bring order and stability into his life can be seen as an effort to regain the peace and security he had known at the great house. Clissold writes his manuscript in a remote house near Grasse, lovingly described in 'View from a Window in Provence', a house notable for its sunlit peace and beauty. The story of his relationships with women is a continual search for completion, for 'the mixture of sexual need and the hunger for a dear companion that has so disturbed me' (I, 5). And the quest for a personal philosophy which consumes so much of his energy is, in a sense, a search for a secular equivalent of the religious belief which has played such a disproportionate role in his youth.

In the chapters entitled 'Disintegrating Protestantism' and 'The Religious Mind' he describes his disillusionment with religious belief and his gradual loss of faith, a loss of faith he shares with many intelligent men and women of his generation. The story of his subsequent attempts to find a satisfying personal philosophy can be

seen as a series of not wholly successful attempts to fill the vacuum
left by the abandonment of belief. Despite moods of self-confidence
he is aware of phases of unhappiness when he is compelled to admit
his discontent:

> When I go back among my memories I find the partially effaced
> evidences of profound conflicts. These are largely effaced,
> because that is the self-protective habit of the mind. . . . . Much of
> my subsequent life . . . has often been far from happy. There were
> long phases of sustained strain and dissatisfaction.   (IV, 1)

Clissold, then, is aware of moods of doubt and introspection in
which he questions his outward image and is conscious of a deep
yearning for completion.

Wells stresses this sense of loss through extensive use of imagery
associated with leaves and flowers. In *Tono-Bungay* he employs an
image of fallen leaves to suggest a sense of regret, an image which
recurs in 'The Door in the Wall' and again in *Mr Blettsworthy on
Rampole Island* where the death of the narrator's mother is associated with a memory of 'a multitude of crimson petals soddened in a
gutter'.[58] In the chapter entitled 'The Treacherous Forget-Me-Nots'
Clissold plunges into reminiscences of his childhood, memories
which are prefaced with the remark that 'I suppose it is the sodden
horse chestnut leaves scattered over the wet stone pavement in the
yard behind this house that have released this group of memories'
(I, 3). There follows an account of how he was 'awakened quite
suddenly to beauty and wonder' in the park at Mowbray (Up Park).
Here he is surrounded by wild flowers and the beauty of trees and
parkland. He discovers forget-me-nots for the first time in his life
and is overwhelmed by 'the clouds of flowers of a divine, incredible
blue'. But the forget-me-nots are half hidden amongst clumps of
sedges:

> There was an afternoon at Mowbray, it must have been earlier in
> the year, in the summer, when I first discovered forget-me-nots.
> At the upper end of the pond near where the stream came in there
> were shallows and floating masses of green weed with pink
> blossoms and thick, widespread clumps of sedges, and half
> hidden amidst these sedges were clouds of flowers of a divine,
> incredible blue. Either I had never seen forget-me-nots growing
> before or I had never observed them. I went to and fro peering

from the bank, and then took off my shoes and stockings and waded into the water and mud until my knickerbockers, in spite of all the tucking up I gave them, were soaked. And I picked handfuls of these the loveliest of all English wild-flowers.

Then suddenly came horror, the unqualified horror of childhood. My legs were streaming with blood. The sharp blades of the sedge leaves had cut them in a score of places. Fresh gouts of blood gathered thickly along the cuts, and then darted a bright red ribbon down my wet and muddy skin. 'Oh! Oh!' I cried in profound dismay, struggling and splashing back to the bank and still holding my forget-me-nots with both hands.

Still do I remember most vividly my astonishment at the treachery of that golden, flushed, and sapphire-eyed day.

That it should turn on me! (I, 3)

This contrast between the beauty of the flowers and the pain of the sedges forms an apposite symbol for the duality of his life, for his continual search for beautiful responses. Clissold is a highly successful businessman, but he is also a man of sensitivity, a man who has devoted years of his life to a quest for 'something hard to name, a kind of brightness, an elation, a material entanglement with beauty' (IV, 11). Behind his commercial exploits and pursuit of social and political ideas lies a man who is constantly searching for beauty and order.

His memories of the summer loveliness of Mowbray are prefaced by the reflection that 'a hundred times, perhaps, in the course of my life and in a score of places, I have seen autumnal horse-chestnut leaves reflected in brown water and the branches of a horse-chestnut tree coming down close to that still mirror' (I, 3). The juxtaposition of the autumnal leaves (an allegory of lost happiness) and the mirror (an image of the Shadow or the unconscious) is another potent symbol, a foreshadowing of his lifelong quest for loveliness. Later in the novel (IV, 12, 'Mirage and Moonshine') he returns to the image of the mirror in a description of Helen and himself gazing into the lake at Virginia Water:

The still water reflecting the slumbering trees and a hemisphere of afterglow becomes a magic mere in a world of infinite peace. . . . I thrust an oar into the reasoning liquid and turned its argument to quivering ecstasy. The reflection danced upon her face. And I, too, was all a-quiver with love for her.

But he is dwelling on memories almost too painful to recall, for his love for Helen is doomed. Clissold senses this for he adds significantly 'How vividly I remember that quiet moment side by side . . . yet it was as unreal as a picture painted on glass.' By thrusting his oar into the still surface of the water he destroys the pattern of the reflections, erasing the moment from his sight but not from memory. It remains locked in his mind with 'the intense, irrational significance of some of my childish memories'. The transcience of love forms one of the dominant themes of the novel. The story of his love-affairs is one of a continual quest for beauty, a search for perfect happiness which eludes him. The quotation by Heraclitus which forms the book's motto – all things pass, there is no enduring thing – is symbolised by the leaves, an image which for Wells clearly held a powerful emotional appeal. (His childhood memories of the lost happiness of Surly Hall, an inn near Windsor where he had spent many happy hours, were tinged with the recollection of 'the lawn with its green tables sodden and littered with dead leaves'.[59]) For Clissold the beauty of the forget-me-nots is inseparably associated in his mind with the treachery of the sedges. Beauty must always be accompanied by sorrow; happiness must always be transitory.

A further strand of imagery is associated with water. When describing his home in Provence he dwells on the fact that 'there is always a sound of running water about this house'. The garden contains a stream and fountains; the flow of water is a constant backcloth to his writing. Water as a symbol of life is an apt metaphor for the flow of existence, the constant flux which forms the novel's leitmotif. In psychological terms water is also a feminine symbol, representing the female aspects of the unconscious. In linking the description of the water with his love for Clementina, 'protecting me against a score of imaginary onslaughts upon my peace and comfort'[60] and his love for the ordered tranquillity of his home, he is responding to the softer, feminine aspects of his personality and his need for beauty and reassurance. Clissold is a man in search of completion. His attempts to find himself through a 'tangle of desires' form the substance of the novel.

Roland Barthes draws a useful distinction between two basic types of literary text: the readerly (*lisible*) and the writerly (*scriptible*). The readerly work is one which seems to offer a realistic picture of characters and scenes, a picture which does not require interpretation or analysis since the meaning is conveyed in the text itself. The text is consumed passively by the reader who is apparently looking at a description of the real world. In this sense the novels of Trollope and the earlier novels of Dickens may be regarded as readerly texts. The writerly text, in contrast, is one in which the meaning is less clear, which draws attention to its own fictionality and relies both on a surface narrative and a secondary narrative of imagery and metaphor. My thesis is that *The World of William Clissold* is an interesting example of a writerly text, a text which will repay careful study because of its extensive use of symbolism, its continual experimentation in narrative method and the oblique relationship between author and narrator. Its apparent lack of organisation conceals a comprehensive design: an attempt to present the whole range of experience – psychological, social and emotional – as it confronts an intelligent human being and to place this before the reader in the form of an intimate journal.

The World of William Clissold is innovative in that it consists of a series of experiments in methods of narration, ranging from reverie to reminiscence, from homily to historical essay to excursus. There is no straightforward structure, no logical progression in the framework of narrative. Moreover the expectations raised in the mind of the reader are not fulfilled. The expectation implicit in the opening pages – that the reader has before him a completed work – proves to be unfounded; the book ends abruptly before Clissold has completed his design. Instead of ending with the mature vision of his life and work it concludes with his death, with an epilogue written by his brother. There is also far more emphasis on the mind of the narrator than students of Wells's work had come to expect, far more dwelling on the inner life of the central character. The substance of the book is an exploration of Clissold's persona – his feelings, thoughts, attitudes, desires, doubts. The abiding impression left in the mind is of a disappearance of confidence, a doubting of ultimate reality:

I find most of the world that other people describe or take for granted much more hard and clear and definite than mine is. I am at once vaguer and more acutely critical. I don't believe so fully and unquestioningly in this 'common-sense' world in which we meet and exchange ideas, this world of fact, as most people seem to do. I have a feeling that this common-sense world is not *final*. (I, 2)

Clissold's lack of certainty is evident in his agnosticism, in the provisional nature of many of his statements, in the very shapelessness of his narrative. A comparison with the confident opening of a realist novel such as *Middlemarch* with the markedly diffident opening paragraphs of *Clissold* reveals at once the immense differences between the Victorian novel and that of the twentieth century. Between the two lies the great divide of the First World War, of the work of Jung and Freud, of man's realisation of his terrifying loneliness. This is aptly symbolised in the quotation which Wells inserts on the title-page: 'flux eternal, all things pass'. In a lengthy chapter, 'View from a Window in Provence', Clissold includes a description of his home in the south of France and of the serene beauty of the surrounding landscape. After remarking that 'one could think that here if anywhere in the world was peace and permanent adaptation' he adds significantly:

> But, indeed, this fair and spacious scene is a mere mask of calm beauty upon the face of change. As I sit writing I hear the sounds of chopping and sawing and ever and again a shout and a crash. (I, 15)

The apparently unchanging scene is deceptive: because of changing fashions in perfume the farmers of Provence are uprooting their olive trees and planting jasmine. There is no enduring thing. Wells leaves the reader to draw the inference that change applies not only to landscapes, to fashions, to social and political ideas but to the novel itself. What he is saying in *Clissold* is that the novel as a literary genre is as subject to flux as any other aspect of life and art. The book's subtitle, 'A Novel at a New Angle', expresses his conviction that in writing it he was feeling his way towards a new and fruitful approach to the art of fiction.

11

Mr Blettsworthy on Rampole Island: the Novel as Fable

> I would like to suggest, then, that a literary game may be seen as any playful, self-conscious and extended means by which an author stimulates his reader to deduce or to speculate, by which he encourages him to see a relationship between different parts of the text, or between the text and something extraneous to it.
>
> (Peter Hutchinson, *Games Authors Play*)

> *The gist of Rampole Island is a caricature-portrait of the whole human world.*
>
> (H. G. Wells, *Experiment in Autobiography*)

From the beginning to the end of his literary career Wells was an experimental novelist, continually seeking fresh forms for the expression of his ideas. Throughout the decade following the immense upheaval of the First World War he continued to experiment with fiction, producing a number of promising novels and fantasias and testing out a variety of approaches in fictional form. *The Undying Fire: A Contemporary Novel* (1919) is a flawed but brave attempt to recast the Book of Job in a form appropriate to the needs and problems of the twentieth century. In *The Dream* (1924), a fine and much neglected work, the narrator looks back on a typical Victorian lifetime from the perspective of twenty centuries hence. *Christina Alberta's Father* (1925) explores in the form of a comic novel the theme of self-delusion, whilst *Meanwhile: The Picture of a Lady* (1927) is a dialogue novel in which the guests at a house party discuss a range of contemporary issues against the background of the General Strike.

Mr Blettsworthy on Rampole Island (1928) marks a return to a genre made famous by Swift in *Gulliver's Travels* and *The Tale of a Tub*: the satire written in the form of an allegory. It tells the story of Arnold Blettsworthy, an effeminate, rather precious young man who is brought up in the sheltered home of his Pangloss-like uncle, a rector who professes a genial, kindly version of Christianity in which 'evil was very far away and hell forgotten'.[61] Following an unhappy love-affair and after he has been deceived by his close friend, Lyulph Graves, Blettsworthy has a breakdown and embarks on a sea voyage for the sake of his health. The voyage ends in disaster when the engine of the *Golden Lion* fails during a violent storm and Blettsworthy finds himself taken prisoner by savages on Rampole Island. The island and its people and topography are described in detail, including a vivid account of the giant sloths which still survive and whose flesh is held to be taboo. Blettsworthy rescues one of the native girls from drowning and falls in love with her but is pursued by the islanders for his failure to support the war against a neighbouring tribe. The pursuit rises to a frenzied climax during which he is shot by an arrow, but awakens from delirium to find himself in New York. He learns that he has been in New York for the past five years, living bodily in the real world but mentally in an imaginative reverie of his own making. He returns to civilisation to fight as a soldier in France (it is now 1916) but is wounded and returns stoically to England, where he befriends Graves once again. The book concludes with a discussion between the two men in which they debate the prospects for the future of mankind.

The book is dedicated 'to the Immortal Memory of Candide' which surely offers a hint that Wells intended the book to be rather more than a straightforward piece of story-telling. The whole of the third chapter (the account of Blettsworthy's sojourn on Rampole Island) is allegorical, and the entire novel is written with an irony and detachment he rarely excelled. The literary progenitors of *Mr Blettsworthy* are Poe and Swift. As if to emphasise his indebtedness to the author of *The Narrative of Arthur Gordon Pym* there is a veiled reference to Poe at the end of his life in the description of Blettsworthy in a state of delirium:

My movements for three weeks are untraceable. At the end of that time I was found wandering along a back street in the outskirts of Norwich. I was found at three o'clock in the morning by a policeman. I was mud-stained, hatless and penniless and in a high fever. I gather I had been drinking hard and taking drugs and I had evidently been in low company. I smelt strongly of ether. (I, 7)

Some of the details of the sea voyage derive from incidents in *Pym* and from 'MS. Found in a Bottle'. Poe in turn had been influenced by Defoe and there are echoes of *Robinson Crusoe* in the detailed summary of contents on the title page, in the matter-of-fact opening with its autobiographical particulars and in the verisimilitude of the account of the sea journey (there is a particularly Defoe-like passage in Chapter II, 12, in which Blettsworthy describes with pleasing exactitude the contents of the ship's pantry). In both *Pym* and *Blettsworthy* the narrator is placed in a heuristic mill through which he gradually sheds his illusions. In both there is an exciting account of mutiny and murder at sea. In both there is a circumstantial description of an island inhabited by savages and a detailed account of their customs and way of life: an account which in each case is capable of an allegorical interpretation. And in both there is a recurring pattern of confinement and release. Throughout the narrative Pym seeks to escape from one restricting situation after another – from the coffin-like box in which he is confined as a stowaway, from the hold of the ship, from starvation and death aboard the *Grampus*, from the avalanche of rocks precipitated by the islanders, from the island itself and lastly from the vortex of the pole. Similarly Blettsworthy seeks release from his aimless life, from the cabin in which he has been imprisoned by the captain, from the *Golden Lion*, from the gorge of the island. 'In this gorge we must live hatefully', he writes, 'driven by ignoble stresses, and in this gorge we shall presently die' (IV, 6). But Wells's debt to *Pym* is more than a matter of surface similarities; it is in the emotional affinity between the two novels. Wells shared with Poe a wish to describe both a literal and a metaphorical journey, a journey which would symbolise his hero's quest for fulfilment. Each succeeded in his own way in creating a myth appropriate to his time: Poe in writing a profoundly serious allegory on the release of the imagination from oblivion; Wells in rendering in allegorical form his deep unease concerning the malaise of civilisation.

Swift exercised a seminal influence on Wells's writings and his shadow looms large over *Mr Blettsworthy*. Writing to Julian Huxley during its composition Wells described it as 'my fantastic pseudo boys' adventure story which will be my *Candide*, my *Peer Gynt*, my

Gulliver'.[62] Swift's influence is evident in the biting satire and invective with which Wells lampoons the politicians and rulers of the day, in the richness of his allegory and the skill with which the satirical and allegorical chapters are placed within a narrative frame. One of Mr Blettsworthy's first observations on landing on Rampole Island is to remark that

> Moreover in common with unenlightened people the whole world over, they have an awe of the mad. Insanity they think is a peculiar distinction conferred by their Great Goddess. (III, 1)

The reader is reminded irresistibly of Gulliver's adventures among the Lilliputians and the Yahoos. Wells confided in his autobiography that he laughed when writing *Mr Blettsworthy on Rampole Island*. At times his humour takes the form of Swiftian condemnations of his fellow men – 'These people I had fallen among seemed just dirty, greedy, lazy, furtively lascivious, morally timid, dishonest, stupid, very yellow, tough and irritable, and very hard, obdurate and cruel' (III, 3) – at other times he adopts a pose of barbed irony: 'I contrasted our kindly constitutional monarchy with the superstitious cultivation of a breed of inferior animals, and our popular church, comprehensive enough to embrace almost every type of belief, with the bloodstained ritualism of the goddess' (III, 4). Whether he is describing the Great Goddess welcoming her slaves (the Statue of Liberty), the dreary Megatheria (the state, the church, institutions), the discourse with the five sages or love on Rampole Island, the irony is deliciously effective. In a characteristic passage the narrator describes the campaign of vilification against the alleged enemies of the tribe:

> In the tirades of our speakers three main accusations constantly recurred, our grievances against our foes, their master crimes. The first of these was that they were cannibals. This charge never failed to evoke the most impassioned indignation. The speaker would lean over and ask impressively: '*Do you* want to go into these up-river cooking pots?'
>
> Their second offence was that they were uncleanly in their persons and habits. The third was that they kept a family of loud-croaking bull-frogs as their mystic rulers, a thing all our people found incredibly disgusting and degrading. The offensive noises made by the parental bull-frog and his loud-splashing leaps hither

and thither were contrasted with the louse-like movements and inoffensive gentleness of our own dear tribal totem. (III, 8)

Not until the publication of *Animal Farm* in 1945 has irony been employed with such artistry. Wells had clearly been deeply depressed by the carnage and futility of the First World War, by the mounting evidence of intolerance towards freedom of thought, by the apparent aimlessness of civilisation in the aftermath of the war. Brooding on these things he produced one of the richest and most memorable of his satires. In a preface to a collected edition of his romances he remarked 'Now and then, though I rarely admit it, the universe projects itself towards me in a hideous grimace.'[63] The mood which had come upon him with overwhelming force in the writing of *The Time Machine* and *The Island of Doctor Moreau* returned powerfully in 1927–8 and, though he was working simultaneously on the monumental *Science of Life* (a summary of modern biological knowledge), he worked with feverish energy on this tale of a modern Gulliver in quest of enlightenment. The result is a remarkably sustained satire which embodies a mythopoeic vision of modern civilisation in Swiftian terms: it is Dr Moreau's island writ large. Disillusioned by the war, repelled by the cruelty and horror all around him, Blettsworthy is compelled to admit 'I realised more than ever I had done, that Rampole Island had indeed now spread out and swallowed all the world.'[64] (The very name 'Rampole' suggests *rampant*, the spreading of unrestrained forces and influences.) Most striking of all is the manner in which the novel anticipates the regimentation and organised hatred of Orwell's *Nineteen Eighty-Four*:

Every few days there would be orgiastic War Dances, in which slaughter and victory were rendered with great animation, or there would be Howling Meetings against the enemy. These gatherings were supposed to keep up the spirit of our people. In them the sages and leaders of our tribe denounced the vices and crimes of our antagonists amidst the applause and indignation of the tribe. The sentences of the speakers were punctuated by violent howling, and it was extremely unwise to betray any slackness in these responses. (III, 8)

Seen in these terms the novel can be seen to be a dystopia, a worthy descendant of *The Time Machine* and the early romances, an allegory in which Wells sought to repay his debt to Swift in a contemporary fable.

Whilst Swift and Poe can be traced as direct influences on the tale – and also Coleridge, whose *Rime of the Ancient Mariner* (1798) seems to brood enigmatically in the background – in a deeper sense its origins lie buried in the human psyche, in the dark wells of the unconscious from which such tales as Conrad's *Heart of Darkness* derive. At one point the narrator refers to 'the dark streaks of fear and baseness that have been revealed in my composition'.[65] These streaks of terror and evil lie like a shadow across the narrative, as if this story of a lonely outcast marooned on an island of savages strikes a responsive chord in the ancestral memory. Never far beneath the surface of the novel is a translucent quality, a mental unease which makes the reading of it a disturbing – almost an extraliterary – experience. There is something dream-like about the narrative, as if Wells is trying to render a mental state, a nightmare which is painful to recall. 'It was as if the whole universe, and I with it, had become something different, as if the self I had known hitherto had been a dream in a dream world, and this now was reality' (I, 5). In the chapter entitled 'Old Horror Recalled' Blettsworthy vividly relates his efforts to prevent his mind from returning to the island and conveys the mixture of fascination and terror with which he recalls his experiences: 'I have never to forget Rampole Island, I feel, I have to settle my account with it . . . The island lies in wait for me.' To glimpse the human condition in its stark reality, without illusions – to return metaphorically to the island – was to be haunted by an awareness of man's animality, by a bitter sense of the madness which lay like a shadow across human affairs. At times Blettsworthy's nightmare becomes an obsession which torments his life:

Gradually as I brooded over the intricate developments of this case the sense of Rampole Island resumed its sway in my brain. The world's transparency increased. The tall cliffs and the ribbon of sky above, appeared more and more distinctly through the dissolving outlines of surrounding things. I would sit behind my morning newspaper in the London train and hear the comments of my fellow business men, and it would seem to me that the rattling of the train was the noise of the torrent in the gorge and that I sat once more at the round table in the upper eating-house while the ancients delivered judgment on the safety of the state. (IV, 13)

A number of Wells's later novels – *The Bulpington of Blup*, *Brynhild*, *Apropos of Dolores* – are explorations of egotisms. *Mr Blettsworthy on Rampole Island* shares with these its preoccupation with mental states. At an early stage in the story the narrator confides to the reader his awareness that his is a deeply divided personality.

I am divided against myself – to what extent this book must tell. I am not harmonious within; not at peace with myself as the true Blettsworthys are. I am at issue with my own Blettsworthyness. I add to my father's tendency to a practical complexity, a liability to introspective enquiry. . . . I have great disconnected portions of myself. (I, 1)

Blettsworthy is one of the more complex of Wells's characters in his sense of internal moral conflict, in his continual attempt to reconcile his feeling of isolation with his 'perpetual search for a logical and consoling presentation of life'.[66] Longing for friendship and yet unable to establish lasting relationships he drifts through life, an outcast from his fellow men. As a child he is rejected by one relative after another. During the sea voyage he is shunned and ridiculed by the crew, whilst his periods ashore are lamentable failures in communication. The dominant impression is of a man isolated from his kind, a man adrift, a misfit in a world of misfits.

Mr Blettsworthy is characteristic of modernist writing in its stress on alienation and discord, on the distress and dislocation which lie at the heart of much twentieth-century fiction and imbue the work of Kafka and Conrad. The narrator describes his sense of alienation in a memorable passage during his sea voyage aboard the *Golden Lion*:

The broadest fact, the foundation fact so to speak, of the situation, was this, that I had started out in life with the completest confidence in myself, mankind and nature, and all that confidence was gone. I had lost all assurance in my personal character; I had become alien to and afraid of my fellow creatures and now my body was in hideous discord with the entirely inhospitable world into which it had come. (II, 5)

All his experiences serve to destroy his simple, naïve faith in the innate goodness of his fellow creatures. The shallowness of his friend, Graves, the deceit of the girl he loves, the treachery of the captain, the horror of his sojourn on Rampole Island, all undermine the confidence in humanity instilled into him by his uncle. At last he is obliged to confess that he is living in a universe which 'had neither benevolence nor purpose with regard to me. . . . There is no kindly Human God, no immanent humanity in this windy waste of space and time.'[67] It is not simply that he loses his religious beliefs. In common with Edward Prendick in *The Island of Doctor Moreau* he is permanently scarred by his experiences, an outcast, a man at odds with the world. His personal disaster mirrors the distress and confusion of Europe on the brink of war in 1914. Continually while reading *Mr Blettsworthy* one has the sense of a world out of gear, an overcrowded, disjointed civilisation hurrying onwards to disaster. The sea voyage culminating in the storm and engine failure symbolises this angst, this nightmarish awareness of impending catastrophe. At the height of the storm Mr Blettsworthy remarks that each member of the crew 'was more or less starved, drenched, eviscerated, bruised and tormented during that clinging life while the waves hunted for us and the very ship seemed trying to fling us out'.[68] The leading impression which remains in the mind is one of humanity adrift, a civilisation dislocated by war and blundering from crisis to crisis.

The novel is a mirror not only in the sense that it is transparently allegorical but also in that it reflects themes and insights peculiar to Wells as man and writer. It is significant that it was written in the immediate aftermath of the death of his wife Jane in 1927, his loyal companion and helpmate over a period of 34 years. To Wells, Jane had always been a mother-figure, a source of solace and reassurance he could not do without. Interwoven with the political and social satire of *Mr Blettsworthy* is a secondary layer of imagery related to themes of motherhood, the womb and rebirth.

In the course of his explorations the narrator discovers a huge cave or fissure which impresses him as an ideal refuge if he should ever be pursued by the savages. The fissure is described as

> a cave of very considerable size. I advanced discreetly and was very soon in what I could feel was a large airy darkness. . . .
> Everything about me was pallid, with a sort of phantom clearness, even in the brightest places, and water dripped from untraceable

origins upon the face of the rock. The rock shone in that twilight an alabaster white.   (III, 9)

This womb-like cavern, with its suggestions of concealment and security, does indeed prove to be an effective hiding place for he flees to it when he is pursued by warriors: 'the great cave is cool and safe and dark'. The cave is, moreover, the means of his release for it is while resting within it, tended by Wena, that he awakens from his reverie and finds himself in the real world. He emerges from the womb a man reborn. Linked to the imagery of the womb (which is echoed in the safe, enclosed, benevolent world of his Wiltshire childhood) is a complex web of symbolism associated with water. In psychological terms water is a symbol of the female side of the personality, the feminine unconscious. When Blettsworthy has an adolescent disagreement with Graves (he surprises Graves embracing the girl he, Blettsworthy, has loved) he hurls at him a vase filled with water. The broken vase, which 'burst with a gulp and fell about him in water and fragments',[69] symbolises the dissipation of his dreams of female companionship, dreams which are not realised until years later. On Rampole Island there is a vivid account of his rescuing a native girl from drowning – a deliberate echo of the recovery of Weena from drowning in *The Time Machine* – in which Blettsworthy and the girl are totally immersed in water. The account of their immersion is strongly suggestive of baptism, with its associations of rebirth and regeneration. On reaching the bank and safety Blettsworthy 'spouted water like a Roman fountain'; the fountain has long been recognised in Jungian psychology as a symbol of life and energy. From this point onwards he is indeed a man reborn. 'So the tenor of my life was changed', he adds, '. . . suddenly my destinies turned about. It was as if I was baptised to a new life when I plunged into the water' (III, 10). The girl he has rescued (who appears significantly in the guise of a water maiden, a well-known symbol of the anima, the female shadow figure in a man's psyche) is a familiar figure in Wells's novels, the consoling, reassuring presence who comforts and sublimates:

It was a friendless failure and a hunted thing I pulled out of the water. And also it had in it, locked away and untouched, that treasure of gratitude, possessive love, loyalty and tenderness I have found inexhaustible. . . . She gave herself to me in a passion of gratitude and took me into her life so soon as she realised the isolation of reverie in which I was living. For it is the supreme function of the lover to come between the beloved and the harsh face of reality.　(IV, 3)

All Wells's life was a search for a mother-figure, the woman who is at once passionate and gentle, loving and protective. At the moment when Blettsworthy first sees the girl he sits brooding 'above one of the largest and deepest of the lonely tarns' and becomes aware of her at first from her reflection. She is wandering 'knee-deep in deep green weeds'. The imagery here is richly suggestive and reinforces the theme of rebirth. Lewis Carroll in *Alice Through the Looking Glass* explores the idea of a mirror as a door through which one may pass to a different world. When Blettsworthy contemplates the mirror-like surface of the pool he sees not only himself, Narcissus-like, but the reflection of a girl. Her reflected image, upside down in the water, is an apt symbol for the opposing forces within the psyche; he is seeing his female shadow, the soulmate who will complement his needs and satisfy his desires. In the symbolism of dreams the mirror is interpreted as an image of consciousness and revelation. The duality of its image symbolises perfectly Blettsworthy's (and, by implication, Wells's) divided personality and his lifelong search for a shadow-figure who would reconcile his competing impulses. The deep green vegetation surrounding the girl complements the suggestion of a sympathetic and responsive companion. Green not only suggests fertility and life but also, in psychological terms, sympathy and adaptability. Wena becomes the girl of his desires, the loving partner who has eluded him hitherto.

Mr Blettsworthy on Rampole Island is one of the most powerful of Wells's novels in the sense that it marks a fusion of themes and approaches which appear and reappear in his work. The biting satire which he imbibed from Swift and Voltaire, and which had lain dormant for many years, now rose to the surface in a fable which merits much wider critical attention than it has yet received. The chapters describing Blettsworthy's sojourn on the island are written with an incisive fluency he had not attained since the romances of the 1890s, unforgettable in their power. This deep strand of irony is wedded to the themes of alienation and distress which are so characteristic of twentieth-century fiction. *Blettsworthy* is in one sense a novel about loss of confidence, about the end of faith in an age of doubt and confusion. It has a sombre, dark quality, redeemed by flashes of puckish humour when Wells cannot resist mocking his hero's plight or pouring scorn on the human condition. The exploration of Blettsworthy's divided character and its reflection of the author's own temperament is deeply interesting and anticipates the fuller treatment the theme receives in such works as *The Bulpington of Blup* (1932). These strands are woven together in a narrative which is rich in psychological insights and which will well repay further study by readers interested in the language of symbolism. *Mr Blettsworthy on Rampole Island* is a dystopia which anticipates the work of Orwell and Koestler and is also a novel which forms a landmark in Wells's development as an artist. It marks a return to some of his earliest concerns as an imaginative writer and offers significant evidence of his willingness to experiment with literary forms in an effort to widen the scope of the novel.

12

The Croquet Player: the Heart of Darkness

> *I tried to break the spell – the heavy, mute spell of the wilderness –
> that seemed to draw him to its pitiless breast by the awakening of
> forgotten and brutal instincts, by the memory of gratified and
> monstrous passions.*
>
> (Joseph Conrad, *Heart of Darkness*)

> *Everything he told you was true and everything he told you was a
> lie. He is troubled beyond reason by certain things and the only
> way in which he can express them even to himself is by a fable.*
>
> (H. G. Wells, *The Croquet Player*)

'I may write a story or so more – a dialogue, an adventure or an
anecdote. But I shall never come as near to a deliberate attempt upon
The Novel again as I did in *Tono-Bungay*.' Thus wrote Wells in his
autobiography.[70] Following its completion in 1934 he embarked on a
series of promising experiments in the novella form: *The Croquet
Player* (1936), *Star Begotten* (1937), *The Camford Visitation* (1937) and
The Brothers (1938). The novella as a literary genre was one he had
hitherto left virtually untouched, apparently preferring the ampler
scope of the novel. But he cannot have been unaware that during the
years when he was working on long, discursive novels such as *The
Research Magnificent* and *Joan and Peter* a new generation of writers
was producing memorable fiction on a much tauter canvas.
Lawrence in such works as *The Fox* (1920) and *The Woman Who Rode
Away* (1925) had demonstrated the possibilities of the genre as a
means of artistic expression, whilst Conrad in *The Secret Agent* and
other works had been experimenting with shorter fictions over a
period of many years.

When *Heart of Darkness* was written in 1899 Conrad may well have been influenced by Wells's *The Island of Doctor Moreau*, a Swiftian fable on the beast in man, which had appeared three years earlier. Wells and Conrad enjoyed a close friendship which commenced in 1896 (a year earlier Wells had enthusiastically reviewed *Almayer's Folly*, Conrad's first novel), a friendship which continued for many years. For some time the two novelists met frequently and held earnest discussions on each other's work and on the craft of fiction. Wells had certainly read *Heart of Darkness* which, coming so soon after his own allegorical works, must have struck a responsive chord. Conrad's novella, an intensely felt account of a journey into the Congo jungle which is also a metaphorical description of a journey into the mind, is a deeply pessimistic work which is said to have influenced T. S. Eliot in the writing of *The Waste Land*.[71] Remarkably Wellsian in the density of its symbolism and imaginative power, *Heart of Darkness* embodies a terrifying vision of man's bestiality, a moment of ultimate horror when the depths of human degradation are revealed. *Moreau* was written in much the same mood, a mood which returned in 'The Wild Asses of the Devil' and again in *Mr Blettsworthy on Rampole Island*. Now in 1936, against a background of torture, concentration camps and the emergence of total warfare, the mood returned powerfully in a short allegory of impressive force.

The novella form was comparatively new to Wells. He had of course been an accomplished writer of short stories, and earlier in his literary career had produced some of the finest short stories in the language including 'The Door in the Wall' and 'The Country of the Blind'. But the novella of 18,000 words or so is a very different medium from both the short story and the full-length novel and imposes quite different restraints on the author. Whereas the novel permits a generous degree of discursiveness in the development of character and incident, the novella imposes the discipline of economy. The author is compelled to work within a much more restricted canvas and to achieve his effects with the minimum of elaboration. It is a medium in which each word and sentence has to contribute to the overall design and which demands the utmost clarity of expression. At the same time it is a genre which, by its very nature, demands lucid, descriptive prose:

There can be no disputing the stillness of that district. Sometimes I would stop my car on one of the winding dyke roads and stand listening before I went on again. One would hear the sheep upon the lavender-coloured hills, four or five miles away, or the scream of some distant water-fowl, like a long, harsh scratch of neon light across the silent blue, or the sound of the wind and the sea, a dozen miles away at Beacon Ness, like the world breathing in its sleep. At night of course there were more noises: dogs howled and barked in the distance, corncrakes called and things rustled in the reeds.   (1)

Again and again in *The Croquet Player* one is struck by the astringent quality of the writing. The language has a cutting edge which permits its use as a vehicle for conveying irony, suspense or foreboding; it is difficult to believe that it stems from the same pen as *The Research Magnificent* or *The Passionate Friends*. It is written in a spare, tense prose of impressive energy and power: 'A long, harsh scratch of neon light across the silent blue', 'the sound of the wind and the sea . . . like the world breathing in its sleep'. One is reminded irresistibly of Conrad in *Heart of Darkness*:

The water shone pacifically; the sky, without a speck, was a benign immensity of unstained light; the very mist on the Essex marshes was like a gauzy and radiant fabric, hung from the wooded rises inland, and draping the low shores in diaphanous folds.

Or of Stevenson in *Weir of Hermiston*:

All beyond and about is the great field of the hills; the plover, the curlew, and the lark cry there; the wind blows as it blows in a ship's rigging, hard and cold and pure; and the hill-tops huddle one behind another like a herd of cattle into the sunset.

There is the same quality of limpid precision, the same ability to convey a vivid word picture with the utmost economy of expression, the same gift for achieving an effect beyond the literary. In *The Croquet Player* Wells recaptured the extraordinary vividness of his early romances – the terse, documentary style of *The Time Machine* and *The War of the Worlds*. The adoption of this clear, controlled, economical style results in one of the most memorable of his shorter fictions, a tale which is remarkable for the fact that so much of its weight is carried by symbol and metaphor and yet remains a fine example of the art of the story-teller.

In this short tale of haunting power, Wells returns to the device of the story within a story he had used so effectively in *The Time Machine*. The story is narrated by George Frobisher, an ineffectual young man who leads a life of cultured idleness in the shadow of his paternal aunt. He tells the reader that 'I am probably one of the best croquet players alive . . . my life has always been an extremely sheltered and comfortable one.' He is 33 in 1936 and therefore belongs to the same generation as Orwell and Waugh, the generation which was too young to serve in the holocaust of 1914–18, and for whom the Spanish Civil War came as a terrifying revelation of modern warfare. A skilful word picture is built up of Frobisher's personality and attitudes so that the reader quickly comes to feel secure in a familiar, recognisable world. It is a world of croquet and archery, of pottering from his home in London to his 'modest little place in Hampshire', of travelling round the world with his aunt attending conferences (his aunt is an obsessive supporter of the Women's World Humanity Movement though Frobisher has 'never clearly understood what it is all about'), of playing tennis, dining, and recuperating on the French Riviera. 'I have soft hands and an ineffective will', he adds. 'Like most well-born, well-off people, we have taken inferiors for granted, servants for granted, and the general good behaviour of the world towards us.' Frobisher clearly represents an outlook on life that Wells found uncongenial (the choice of surname is surely ironic, for there could hardly be a sharper contrast than that between the intrepid explorer and the effeminate croquet player),[72] yet as the narrator he plays a crucial role in the story. His personality remains consistent throughout and it is from his point of view that the events are depicted.

He is sipping a pre-lunch vermouth in a cafe at Les Noupets when he is accosted by a talkative stranger who engages him in conversation. The stranger introduces himself as Dr Finchatton, a doctor who has abandoned his practice in the Fens to receive treatment at the hands of a nerve specialist. He proceeds to relate to Frobisher the disturbing story of 'the brooding strangeness that hangs over Cainsmarsh', a miasma of fear and tension which has wrecked his health. The doctor had bought a practice in a country district near Ely but had soon become aware of a contagion of terror infecting the local people:

Beneath the superficial stolidity a number of these people were profoundly uneasy. There was fear in the Marsh for them as for me. It was an established habitual fear. But it was not a definite fear. They feared something unknown. It was a sort of fear that might concentrate at any time upon anything whatever and transform it into a thing of terror. (1)

With mounting earnestness the doctor describes how he in his turn became infected with the atmosphere of miasmatic horror, how he began to suffer from terrifying dreams and to share the universal horror of darkness. He relates how, unable to stand any longer the unbearable, pervading tension, he confides in the vicar, an elderly recluse obsessed by the notion that Cain ended his days in the marsh and that it is his evil spirit that haunts the district, 'something remote, archaic, bestial'. Dismissing this idea as the ravings of a madman, the doctor visits a natural history museum where he examines the bones and implements of prehistoric men who had roamed the marshes. The curator discusses with him the atmosphere of evil which pervades the district and reminds him that 'Millions of these brutish lives had come and passed. . . . Do you think it had anything you could call a spirit? Something that might still be urgent to hurt and torment and frighten?' Greatly disturbed by this conversation and by nightmares in which the palaeolithic skull assumes gigantic proportions, the doctor resolves to consult a London nerve specialist, Dr Norbert, who has a clinic at Les Noupets.

It is at this point in the narrative that the conversation between Frobisher and the talkative stranger is interrupted. Dr Norbert appears on the scene, anxious to learn the croquet player's impressions of Finchatton's strange story. Frobisher arranges to return at the same time the following day, when Norbert explains to him that the story he has heard is a fable, a myth designed to convey the idea that mankind is plagued by 'a sickness in the very grounds of our lives, breaking out here and there and filling men's minds with a paralysing, irrational fear'. Norbert's thesis is that civilisation is a delusion, that progress is a mere façade that is breaking down everywhere and the spirit of man's animal past is rampant. The croquet player, instinctively disliking Norbert and his aggressive manner, succeeds in escaping from the conversation on the plea that he has arranged to meet his aunt, who has a horror of being kept waiting. But he confides to the reader that he has been deeply unsettled by the encounter:

I have been talking to two very queer individuals and they have produced a peculiar disturbance of my mind. It is hardly an exaggeration to say that they have infected me and distressed me with some very strange and unpleasant ideas.   (1)

The indelible impression left by the story on the reader's mind (in common with James Hilton's *Lost Horizon* or Poe's 'The Fall of the House of Usher' it is one of those tales that is never forgotten) owes much to Wells's indirect method of narration. The haunting story related by Finchatton is retold to the reader by Frobisher, so that throughout the narrative the strange events described are filtered through Frobisher's consciousness. The device recalls the distancing effect achieved by the employment of Reginald Bliss as the narrator in *Boon*. The effect is to distil the doctor's terrifying story through the croquet player's scepticism, to subject his nightmare experiences to the critical acids of a man who has never known tension, worry or fear. Wells might have chosen to have the story narrated by Dr Finchatton or by Norbert but wisely opted to present his narrative through the eyes of a disinterested and sceptical observer.

Though this work is so compact it is unusually rich in imagery, particularly in that associated with time, paradise and darkness. The obsession with time which had haunted Wells since *The Time Machine* and his student writings on the fourth dimension is continually present in *The Croquet Player*. He was 70 in 1936 and with the attainment of this landmark in his life must have been more than usually aware of the passing of time. The discovery of man's evolutionary origins had opened up an immense vista of the past, and this had been accompanied by an awareness of man's animal ancestry. This is expressed in a vivid metaphor of a magic sphere that is now broken:

We lived in a magical sphere and we felt taken care of and safe. And now in the last century or so, we have broken that. We have poked into the past, unearthing age after age and we peer more and more forward into the future. . . . We have broken the frame of the present, and the past, the long black past of fear and hate that our grandfathers never knew of, never suspected, is pouring back upon us.   (3)

The concept of the present as a broken frame is reinforced by a series of metaphors associated with time. An old lady terrified of the darkness hurls a clock at the shadows and the narrator stands 'rigid and expectant staring at the broken clock in the corner'. A skull, a powerful symbol of man's mortality, looms larger and larger in the story until at last 'it became as vast as a cliff, a mountainous skull in which the orbits and hollows of the jaw were huge caves'. The croquet player escapes his conversation with the intolerable psychiatrist Norbert when he is reminded of the passing of time by the sudden striking of a clock. He escapes again at the end of the story by announcing that 'I have to play croquet with my aunt at half-past twelve.' Time, mortality, punctuality – Wells, no less than his characters, was deeply conscious of the inexorable passing of the years and that for man, no less than for himself as an individual, the sands of time were running out.

As in *The Time Machine* Wells makes extensive use of paradisal imagery. Finchatton's first sight of Cainsmarsh in the height of summer recalls the enchanted garden of 'The Door in the Wall' and is an echo of the romantic idea of the Garden of Eden:

> It looked as good as any possible world for me, and going there in summer-time with the wild flowers out and a hundred sorts of butterfly about, dragon flies and an abundance of summer birds . . .I would have laughed if you had told me that I had come into a haunted land.   (1)

The image is reinforced by Frobisher's description of Cainsmarsh as 'a magic marshland into which a man might go sane and confident, admiring the butterflies and the flowers', a description which immediately becomes a longing for a lost paradise, for he adds: 'and out of which presently he would come running again frantic with fear and rage'. The theme of an Eden overcome with evil recurs in the notion of earth poisoned by Cain and the worst of his sons.

Interwoven with the biblical imagery is a secondary layer of symbolism drawn from mythology and literature. When Norbert tries to restrain Frobisher from eluding him Frobisher remarks: 'I had an absurd feeling that I was like that wedding guest who was gripped by the Ancient Mariner.' The reference is a reminder that the croquet player – like the wedding guest in the poem – is a reluctant listener, that he is cornered by Norbert against his will. The allusion also provides a link with the poem's themes of loneliness and loss, with the mariner's strange account of lost grace and the revelation that he is 'alone on a wide wide sea'. As Europe slid ominously towards war, Wells became increasingly alarmed at the prospects for mankind, and may well have seen an echo of man's predicament in Coleridge's enigmatic poem. The mariner, with his hypnotic eye and compulsive manner, is a fitting surrogate for Norbert, a man obsessed with a single idea.

The description of the museum, with its locked glass cupboard containing the skull, recalls the derelict science museum in *The Time Machine* and its abandoned collection of artefacts. The inference is that it is not simply man's inventions which are a thing of the past but man himself: *Homo sapiens* has become an exhibit in a museum. In the back garden of his home at 13 Hanover Terrace, Regent's Park, Wells had drawn a frieze depicting various stages of evolution culminating in man. Beneath man he had posed the question: 'Time to Depart?' His sense of *Homo sapiens*'s precarious foothold at the apex of the evolutionary process is strikingly evident in the metaphor of the skull, an image which is described in unforgettably Poesque terms:

More and more did the threat of that primordial Adamite dominate me. I could not banish that eyeless stare and the triumphant grin from my mind, sleeping or waking. Waking I saw it as it was in the museum, as if it was a living presence that had set us a riddle and was amused to hear our inadequate attempts at a solution. Sleeping I saw it released from all rational proportions. It became gigantic. It became as vast as a cliff, a mountainous skull in which the orbits and hollows of the jaw were huge caves. He had an effect – it is hard to convey these dream effects – as if he was continually rising and yet he was always towering there. In the foreground I saw his innumerable descendants, swarming like ants, swarms of human beings hurrying to and fro, making helpless gestures of submission or deference, resisting an over-powering impulse to throw themselves under his all-devouring shadow. Presently these swarms began to fall into lines and columns, were clad in uniforms, formed up and began marching and trotting towards the black shadows under those worn and rust-stained teeth. From which darkness there presently oozed something – something winding and trickling, and something that manifestly tasted very agreeable to him. Blood.   (3)

This passage is remarkable both for its nightmarish quality and the intensity of its imagery. The comparison of the skull 'to a living presence that had set us a riddle and was amused to hear our inadequate attempts at a solution' recalls the motif of the sphinx in *The Time Machine*. (Later in the story Frobisher refers to the skull as 'an explanation that was itself an enigma'.) The skull is a tantalising riddle, at once a reminder of man's mortality and a potent symbol of his atavistic past. The narrator likens the orbits and hollows of the jaw to 'huge caves', in Jungian psychology an image of the shadow or unconscious. The skull with its 'all-devouring shadow' and blood-stained teeth represents man's animal ancestry, the compound of hatred, fear and cruelty which was now welling up in Spain, Germany and elsewhere.

The frequent references to dreams and nightmares (Finchatton confesses that he is a prey to 'quite peculiar dreams, like none I had ever dreamt before'), the dream-like landscape of Cainsmarsh and the continual allusions to the unconscious create an atmosphere of subliminal unease in which images from Victorian literature rise and pass. Frobisher, sceptical though he is, has to admit that 'ever since I discovered Edgar Allan Poe in my early boyhood I have had a taste for the weird and the eerie', and there are powerful reminders of Poe in the atmosphere of menace and suspense, the emphasis on shadows and darkness, and the haunting quality of the skull in the museum. Something of the cruelty of *The Island of Doctor Moreau* recurs in the image of the mutilated dog and the attempted murder of the vicar's wife, whilst the transparency of the narrative (for example 'I read evil things between the lines in the newspapers, and usually very faintly but sometimes quite plainly I see, behind the transparent front of things, that cave-man face') vividly recalls the allegorical texture of *Moreau*.[73] There are faint reminders of *Alice in Wonderland* in the references to croquet (the Queen of Hearts), the fact that twice Frobisher hears a clock striking and says he must leave (the White Rabbit) and the description of Rawdon with his 'bleary old eyes' (Father William). Dominating these images is the landscape and atmosphere of Conrad's *Heart of Darkness*, a brooding sense of 'the deep fountains of cruelty in the human make-up':

> After all. – It is in just such a flat, still atmosphere perhaps – translucent, gentle coloured, that things lying below the surface, things altogether hidden in more eventful and colourful surroundings, creep on our perceptions. (1)

As in *Heart of Darkness* there is a continual interplay of imagery contrasting darkness and light. Frobisher remarks that 'I felt such a dread of unfamiliar shadows as I had not known even in childhood.' He relates that 'one evening I found an old lady stiff with dread at a shadow in a corner' and that throughout his sojourn in Cainsmarsh 'there was an unusual terror of the dark'. He first becomes aware of Dr Norbert when his shadow darkens the terrace and he confesses to the reader that 'I disliked the shadow of Dr Norbert even before I looked up and saw him.' The frequent references to darkness serve both as a reminder of Conrad's novella and a potent symbol of the relentless march of evil.

Scattered through the narrative are hints of the tropical landscape of *Heart of Darkness*. The vicarage is situated in a remote spot on a sort of 'crocodile back of land'. One of Frobisher's nightmares is of 'a black snake wriggling out from under the valance of an armchair'. And when he sees an old man bending down in a ditch he imagines 'a hunched, bent and heavy-jawed savage'. But the affinity between *The Croquet Player* and *Heart of Darkness* is emotional rather than textual. It lies in their shared atmosphere of brooding suspense, in their sense of an imminent revelation of unspeakable horror.

One may speculate why *The Croquet Player* was chosen as the title, when a more descriptive title such as *The Haunting* might be thought more appropriate. The explanation lies, I believe, in a series of critical articles written by Wells's former mistress Odette Keun shortly before the novella was written.[74] In 1934 *Time and Tide* published a number of articles accusing Wells of shallowness and inconsistency, of shifting 'almost from one moon to another, his ground, his angle, and his solutions'. The articles appeared under the title 'H. G. Wells – The Player'. Odette Keun's thesis was that Wells had never been in earnest, that in all his novels and dreams he had simply been toying with his readers, idling with them with the inconsistency of a chameleon. Wells took his revenge in *Apropos of Dolores* (1938), a savagely funny novel in which he portrayed Odette as a shrewish virago, but it is not difficult to see in his choice of title for *The Croquet Player* an oblique reference to their quarrel. The real players, he asserts, are those who persist in playing futile games while the bombs are dropping, those who ignored the increasingly ominous signs of a return to barbarism. Moreover, by returning to the themes and preoccupations of his earliest romances, he demonstrated his own consistency, his unswerving adherence to the evolutionary pessimism he had imbibed as a student. The pessimism which haunts *The Croquet Player* is the same which permeates *The Time Machine* and his early student writings: a corrosive sense of man's unchanging nature.

One of Wells's most profound convictions was his sense of man's animality, his conception that *Homo sapiens* was a transitory phase in the evolutionary process. He had studied biology under T. H. Huxley and had emerged with 'man definitely placed in the great scheme of space and time. I knew him incurably for what he was, finite and not final, a being of compromises and adaptations.'[75] His conviction that man was essentially unchanged since the age of unpolished stone, that civilisation was a veneer which could be rolled back at any time to reveal the animal beneath, found expression in *The Island of Doctor Moreau*, *Mr Blettsworthy* and many other writings. It is evident in a number of his early scientific essays – for example 'Human Evolution, an Artificial Process' and 'Morals and Civilisation' – and in the short stories 'The Reconciliation' and 'The Cone'. This deep awareness of the evil in humanity, of 'the aimless torture in creation',[76] returned powerfully in 1936 with the writing of *The Croquet Player*. It was written against the background of the Spanish Civil War and the ominous rise of Nazism and Fascism. Beneath its terse, troubled prose there is a haunting consciousness of torture and violence, of the recrudescence of organised cruelty. When Finchatton remarks in a horrified aside 'Little children killed by air-raids in the street' one senses Wells's foreboding at the collapse of civilised values and the rapid slide of Europe into barbarism. When the croquet player is shown the Neanderthal skull the curator reminds him that

> His sort had slouched and snarled over the marshes for a hundred times the length of all recorded history. In comparison with *his* overlordship our later human rule was a thing of yesterday. (3)

It is this sense of man's inherent animality, a realisation that 'the cave-man was becoming more and more plainly a living presence', which haunts one of the finest and most carefully written of his stories.

13

The Brothers: the Shattered Mirror

We are just prisms who sort out the rays of life in our way, bent mirrors that reflect them into relevant forms. Our minds are distorting mirrors. . . . Prisms and mirrors. That is all we are. Shatter the mirror and the story ends.

(H. G. Wells, *The Brothers*)

With many novels, our proper work as readers cannot begin until we have begun to discover the 'figure in the carpet', that is, the form and pattern that give meaning to the whole.

(John Colmer, *Approaches to the Novel*)

The Brothers, a short novel of about the same length as *The Time Machine*, was written in 1937 and published early in 1938. The Spanish Civil War was raging throughout its composition and is reflected in the conflict which forms its backcloth. That Wells had an allegorical intention is clear from the note he inserted on the title page: 'If you like this story you will probably also like *The Croquet Player, Star Begotten, Mr Blettsworthy on Rampole Island, The Time Machine, Men Like Gods* and such short stories as "The Pearl of Love", "The Country of the Blind", "The Beautiful Suit" by the same author.' This selection of novels and short stories is suggestive. The common denominator is that each is an allegory, a fable which seeks to explore the relation between fiction and reality through a series of metaphors. The genre had interested Wells since his boyhood at Up Park when he had read *Gulliver's Travels*, *Rasselas* and Voltaire's *Candide*. *The Brothers* is a significant addition to the genre, for within a narrative which ostensibly describes an ideological conflict between two warring factions he interweaves a rich tapestry of symbolism in which the duality of his own temperament is explored.

The story describes a civil war in an unnamed European country, a conflict which has reached a decisive stage. The two sides in the war are not directly named, though it is clear that one side, led by Ratzel, is broadly 'left' and the other, led by Bolaris, is broadly 'right'. The faction led by Bolaris is supported by the monarchy, the aristocracy and the church; Ratzel and his followers represent the dispossessed and disadvantaged, the party of protest. At a crucial stage in the conflict when an important battle is imminent Ratzel is taken prisoner by Bolaris's forces. The two men meet and are astonished to find there is a strong physical resemblance between them. They have a long private conversation during which it becomes evident that, behind the rhetoric of their political attitudes, the two leaders have much in common. Despite the differences in their experience of life they share the same basic attitudes and the same aspirations. Eventually they realise that they are in reality twin brothers who have been separated since infancy. Bolaris, grasping that it would be unthinkable to have his brother executed, conceives a bold plan to permit his prisoner to escape. The plan is opposed by Bolaris's advisers and, in a moment of confusion when his head-quarters is under attack, Ratzel is shot dead by Handon, one of Bolaris's most loyal supporters. In a rage Bolaris turns on Handon and in the ensuing struggle is himself shot dead. The story ends with Catherine, Bolaris's lover, clasping his lifeless body and murmuring 'It cannot end like this. We were just the first. We were just the beginning.'

Ostensibly *The Brothers* is a novella concerned with the futility of ideological conflict. A recurring theme in Wells's writings was the danger of misunderstandings and confusion caused by the careless use of language. In a number of his essays – 'Scepticism of the Instrument', *First and Last Things* and 'Psychoanalysis of Karl Marx' – he had drawn attention to the inadequacies of language as a means of communication and definition, and elaborated his assertion that a number of historical schisms had their origins in clumsy definitions or misstatements. In his essay 'The Future of Labour' he had stated categorically:

I believe this conflict between Capital and Labour is like that great struggle between Arianism and Trinitarianism, which tore the Roman world to pieces thirteen or fourteen centuries ago; that is to say, I regard it as a struggle about theoretical definitions having only the remotest relationship to any fundamental realities in life.[77]

In the story of the two brothers who find themselves with far more in common than they thought and who realise that much of their disagreement is based on arguments over words it seems, then, that Wells is writing a simple fable about the illusory nature of political conflict. Such a reading is entirely permissible. Yet there are good grounds for believing that more than one interpretation is intended and that beneath the façade of the outward narrative is an allegory concerned with the means and ends of literature.

When reading any novel one has to be aware of the relationship between author and reader. Unlike some of his earlier allegorical novels, *The Brothers* is told in the third person and for the most part Wells is content to let the story tell itself. Direct authorial intervention occurs only twice, each time to draw the reader's attention to the fact that lengthy conversations have not been reproduced verbatim and that 'the storyteller has stripped and simplified what they had to say'. These interventions apart, Wells follows the convention of the omniscient narrator. Yet although the story is in the third person, it is Bolaris who dominates the narrative and from his perspective that much of the action of the story is seen. In his conversations with his brother and with his lover, Catherine Farness, he is continually obliged to soften and explain his somewhat dogmatic views (in a manner reminiscent of the dialogues between Boon and Wilkins) so that the effect is of a dialogue novel after the fashion of Plato's *Republic* or the parodies of W. H. Mallock.[78] But whilst much of the story consists of conversation the dialogue is enclosed within a narrative framework of considerable complexity. Throughout the text one is aware of a continual interplay between the symbolic and the real.

The 'real' consists of a story of adventure and intrigue in the midst of a civil war. The reader is constantly aware of a background of war and strife, reflected in the immediacy with which the story is written. The opening paragraph, set in a crisp, economical style, sets the tone of the novel:

The immense beauty of the starry night seemed lost upon the man at the window. His attention was concentrated on the gap in the black hills far below him and far away, where a quivering blood-red glow marked the burning suburbs and gardens of the beleaguered city. The smoke flickered still with gun-flashes and the crepitation of the rifle-fire rose and fell and never ceased altogether. Every now and then a momentary incandescence intimated a fresh extension of the conflagration. But the big guns had desisted. Gammet's attack had been held. Gammet was done for. (I, 1)

One is reminded of the Hemingway of *A Farewell to Arms* or the Orwell of *Homage to Catalonia*. The reference to 'the man at the window' immediately draws attention to one of the central protagonists of the story, Richard Bolaris, yet the manner of his introduction is sufficiently enigmatic to arouse curiosity (the word 'seemed' in the first sentence sets a tone of ambiguity characteristic in Wells's fiction). This introductory scene, in which Bolaris is seated in a darkened room gazing through an open window, links the narrative with the glass/reflection motif which forms one of its dominant themes. As with *The Time Machine* one has an unusual sense that the text is transparent, that one is looking through it to a different reality.

At times when reading *The Brothers* the reader has the strange sensation of observing a dream landscape, a scene from a half-forgotten film:

The three cars using no lights travelled slowly down through the dark woods below the chateau, and more swiftly over the flank of the mountain, above the darkened encampments of the Black Legion and the old ninth regiment. In the open the road became more plainly visible as a faint streak on the grey starlit ground. Ever and again there was a challenge, a halt and the scrutiny of an electric torch. They passed through a silent and deserted village and between a mile-long row of still, dark poplars, until the white walls of the old convent turned hospital were reached. There was no pretence of calling there. Bolaris, with his cars and escort, passed straight on through the gates of the little villa beyond and descended at the entrance. Two sentinels appeared from the shadow of the portico and saluted. A tall dark woman in a white dress appeared in the doorway. (I, 3)

The 'row of still, dark poplars' is a powerful image presaging the theme of duality which forms the novel's leitmotif. In the language of dreams the poplar is a bipolar symbol, suggesting positive/ negative imagery or the contrast of opposites. The passage also contains a remarkable number of contrasting references to darkness and light: the cars are using no lights and travelling through dark woods; the encampments of the Black Legion are darkened; torchlight flashes across the starlit ground; the walls of the convent are painted white; a dark woman in a white dress appears. The repetition of dark/light imagery is interwoven throughout the text. In Bolaris's chateau, 'gigantic ebony negresses sustained clusters of electric lights'. Whilst he watches the battle through the window 'the glare of the distant conflagration' is contrasted with 'the black silhouette of the motionless agaves'. This repetition reinforces the dualism of the narrative by continually juxtaposing a pattern of opposites.

The dream-like texture of the narrative, reminiscent of the tales of Kafka and Poe, is occasionally pierced by moments of structural dislocation. At one point Bolaris complains to his brother: 'My head's spinning faster and faster. And yet not fast enough for me. I want to talk this out with you and nothing will wait for us to talk. Have you ever thought, Ratzel, how the poor human mind is being left behind nowadays by the rush of events?' (III, 2). This Sterne-like plea to arrest the relentless march of time, to halt the scenario to enable a dialogue to take place, is a reminder of the reality which lies behind the text, the world of the 'real' and actual. Towards the end of the story comes a moment of transition, an abrupt change in the flow of events:

Abruptly everything stood still. It was as if a motion picture suddenly ceased to turn over.
'What's that?'
Before Bolaris could give any directions a swift run of shots, crack, crack, crack, had come from the direction of the ravine. This whiff of firing brought everybody to rigid attention, and then as they stood and stared, silence closed upon them. . . .
The picture began to move and talk again. Bolaris was the first to speak. 'Could that have been Handon?' he said. (V, 5)

The transition from dialogue to gunfire occurs so suddenly that the reader is caught unawares. It is as if the text has come to an end and one has veered away from it into a different dimension. The moment recalls the experience of reading a metafiction by Calvino, a curious sensation that the text is not solid, that it is capable of metamorphosis into a different level of perception. The analogy of a motion picture underlines this sense of otherness, an awareness that one is both the reader of a story and an audience at a fabulation. The reader is a participant in an extraliterary experience.[79]

In this short tale Wells is expressing, in the form of a metaphor, the divisions within his own personality. The moment when Bolaris grasps the truth that 'we two people, who may be almost identically alike inside, find ourselves here in the most direct antagonism' (III, 2) is a pivotal point in the narrative, one of those moments of self-revelation which recur at intervals throughout his fiction. The brothers encapsulate the competing elements within his personality – on the one hand, the romantic, the dissenting, the anarchic; on the other, the sceptical, the scientific, the realist. Behind their discussions lies a continual contrast between these two attitudes.

When Ratzel tries to explain the reason for his attitude of discontent he makes use of romantic imagery:

> I began with tremendous expectations – as all young creatures do. And I discovered I belonged to a frustrated class before I was fourteen. I had been given life and I had been cheated of life. My promised world, the beautiful toy ball they taught me about, had been stolen from me almost as soon as it had been put into my hands. I was, I realized, condemned to live in need and humiliation, toiling, wanting, caught in that vile township with not one chance in a hundred thousand of escape. Everyone about me, everyone of my sort, seemed to be in much the same plight. So I looked round to see who had stolen my world.   (III, 2)

Behind the ideological patina with which Ratzel surrounds this statement can be discerned the romantic yearning of Lionel Wallace in 'The Door in the Wall' – 'my promised world, the beautiful toy ball they taught me about, had been stolen from me. . . . I looked round to see who had stolen my world.' Ratzel is a critic and a dreamer; Bolaris is a realist and a pragmatist.

The 'figure in the carpet' which illuminates the story and provides its frame of reference is the mirror. A mirror is a potent psychological symbol since it creates an illusion of a second self, a self which in reality has no separate existence. The mirror acts as a dividing line between opposites: between the ego and its shadow, thesis and antithesis, conscious and unconscious. In Jungian terms the ego confronts its own shadow as a figure reflected in the glass. For all these reasons the mirror is a frequently recurring image in literature, symbolising the opposing forces within the human psyche. Poe in 'William Wilson', Stevenson in 'Markheim' and Conrad in *The Secret Sharer* had written powerful stories exploring the notion of a second self, and Wells in his turn came to be obsessed with the idea. A number of his short stories describe the agony of a figure tormented by a *doppelgänger* – 'The Stolen Body' and 'The Story of the Late Mr Elvesham' are extremely suggestive in this connection – while *Christina Alberta's Father* is the story of a man obsessed by the idea of a second self.

When Bolaris looks at his prisoner, his twin brother, he realises he is seeing a mirror image of himself. Ratzel is in fact a projection, a double who embodies qualities his captor has always publicly condemned but with whom, he comes to realise, he has much in common. A projection has been defined as those 'qualities, feelings, wishes, objects, which the subject refuses to recognise or rejects in himself [and which] are expelled from the self and located in another person or thing'.[80] When this is applied to Wells it can be seen that *The Brothers* embodies an extremely apt metaphor for his own dualism. In a sense there were always two Wellses. The public figure presented an image of a critic, a dissident, an iconoclast who was indifferent to art and consistently adopted a radical posture to the social and political issues of his time. Ratzel embodies in his attitudes this dissenting, critical stance: the continual questioning of the thing that is. The private Wells was a very different figure, a man who loved the music of Mozart and the English countryside, who lived in a succession of gracious houses and appreciated wealth and all that wealth could buy. Bolaris, who enjoys the support of the aristocracy and the establishment, represents the conservative tradition in human affairs: the view of those who do not accept the need for fundamental change. In artistic terms the duality in Wells's temperament found its expression in his ambivalent attitudes to literature. The public figure consistently protested that he was a journalist rather than an artist, that he did not care whether his work endured or not, that he had to admit that most of his fiction 'was written lightly and with a certain haste'.[81] Behind the outward protestations the reality was that over a period of many years his work was most carefully written and revised and that despite his claim that he was 'outside the hierarchy of conscious and deliberate writers altogether'[82] he continued to produce memorable and coherent works of art. Wells's son, Anthony West, a perceptive critic of his father's work, has observed that his public stance 'reflected a troubled inner sense that there was something profoundly wrong about his own course of development' and adds:

> He knew in his bones that the aesthetes were right, and that the writer's sole duty is to state the truth which he knows. At the close of his life, from *The Croquet Player* onwards, he was trying to recapture the spirit in which he had written *The Island of Doctor Moreau*, and what haunted him, and made him exceedingly unhappy, was a tragic sense that he had returned to the real source of what could have been his strength too late.[83]

In *The Brothers* these two aspects of his temperament, the journalist and the artist, confront one another for the first time and come to terms with their existence. Bolaris's recognition of the reality of his second self, that the two attitudes are not mutually exclusive, forms a turning point in the novel (his very name suggests Polaris: the Pole Star, a point of fulcrum). His recognition that little differentiates their points of view, that 'the left and right in any age are just the two faces of the Common Fool, and nothing more, and you have been on one face and I the other' leads to a daring plan for him to impersonate his prisoner. The identification between the two is now complete: physically and mentally it is as if they have become one. Catherine, Bolaris's lover, pleads with him to escape from his past. In response he asserts his belief that henceforth he and his brother will be linked, that human beings are 'just prisms who sort out the rays of life in our way, bent mirrors that reflect them into relevant forms. . . . Shatter the mirror and the story ends.' Moments later, when Bolaris and Ratzel are both dead, comes a climacteric scene when the mirror is destroyed by a bullet:

> With a sound like tearing cloth a bullet came flying into the room and a mirror with a frame of cut-glass flew into a cloud of sparkling dust.
> Her eyes went to the broken fragments of glass that rolled and slid and spread and scattered on the floor. It was as if they were explaining something. Until they ceased to move.
> 'Prisms and mirrors,' she whispered. 'Our picture vanishes as the mirror breaks! You were saying that, darling. Five minutes ago you were saying that.'　(VI, 4)

The shattering of the mirror symbolically destroys the illusion of the second self. The pretence that the two are separate and distinct can no longer be sustained.

The chateau which Bolaris makes his headquarters, formerly owned by a wine merchant, is a baroque affair surrounded by a disused moat 'choked with agaves and litter'. A rococo palace linked to the outside world by underground tunnels, it is an apt metaphor for the other self, the shadow self which can only be reached with difficulty. As Bolaris descends the 'florid and redundant staircase' of the chateau he passes symbolically from one level of his mind to the other:

> He had a queer feeling that he was not altogether there, as though something had been left behind with Ratzel, and exchanged for something else. Or as if long-neglected parts of his brain had been awakened to an unaccustomed activity. Or as if he had a new sort of stereoscopic vision, seeing round things a little because now he had two heads to see with.   (IV, 2)

The phrase 'something had been left behind with Ratzel, and exchanged for something else' is revealing in this connection. Wells was intensely aware of the dichotomy within his make-up and, despite his protestations to the contrary, recognised that in his public sparring with the aesthetes he had done less than justice to himself. In one sense the chateau represents this awareness of a divided self (similarly in *The Castle* Kafka employs an inaccessible castle as a metaphor for the self which cannot be reached).

On a different level of interpretation the chateau, with its ornate decoration and needlessly elaborate architecture, becomes a fitting symbol for the intensely wrought novel which James had impressed many times on Wells as the artistic ideal. Earlier in the story the two brothers hold a discussion on literature and on the nature and quality of 'the great European literatures'. Ratzel asserts that in the past literature has been an essentially aristocratic activity:

> It has been written mainly for people who wanted to feel secure, to please and reassure them. It has been leisure reading. Bric a brac. Tapestry. Stylistic or gentlemanly sham-careless. The English Jane Austen is quite typical. Quintessential I should call her. A certain ineluctable faded charm.   (II, 1)

When Bolaris descends the chateau's fantastically ornate staircase he meditates on the architecture and traditions of the wine merchant's palace:

> For an instant in the doorway, the staircase idea made a phantasmal reappearance. What a jumble of weak appeals to ancient prestige, unintelligent acquiescence, grandiose traditions and large unsubstantial claims to present importance, this room presented! The chateau of a wine-peddling, market-rigging merchant pretending to be a kingly palace! If any palace had ever been kingly! Could one ever hope to turn this sort of thing into a rational home for human beings? Maybe after all there was something to be said for revolutionary destructiveness, and beginning from the ground upward. While the upstairs room was silver this was all gilt. Over the fireplace was a vast pseudo-Correggio, very appetising for the diners, representing Elijah fed by the Ravens. The ceiling and walls were fussy with gilt pilasters, cornices, massive mouldings, suggesting imaginary thrusts against quite impossible strains. There was a number of big shining jars of porcelain, on brackets and pedestals. 'The world has always been making big empty jars since Cnossos,' he thought. 'And sweating and enslaving and murdering to get them. . . . A civilisation of empty pots. . . . The world made safe for crockery.' These were preposterous ideas to have streaming across a mind that ought to have been clenched like a fist ready to deliver a blow. Criticising furniture!   (IV, 2)

The passage and its context make it extremely probable that in describing the chateau – an empty palace from which the wine of life has departed – Wells intended the reader to infer a comparison with the Jamesian novel (cf. the description of the memorial building in the short story 'The Pearl of Love'). The chateau is quite literally a castle in Spain. In castigating the chateau as 'a jumble of weak appeals to ancient prestige' making 'large unsubstantial claims to present importance' he is renewing his critique of the intensely art-conscious novel advocated by James and his followers. The description of the ceiling and walls 'fussy with gilt pilasters . . . suggesting imaginary thrusts against quite impossible strains' recalls the discussion of James's style in *Boon* and its comparison to 'a water-boatman as big as an elephant', whilst the analogy with a room filled with large, empty jars has relevance when viewed against the context of so much of the pretentious popular fiction of the time. What Wells is criticising in this passage, and disassociating himself from, is the notion of the novel as 'tapestry', as a means of relaxation. Throughout his career as a writer and critic he had remained consistent to the view that the novel is, or could be, a powerful instrument of moral suggestion, a means of criticising and discussing aspects of contemporary life. But by insisting that the novel must be relevant to its time he saw that he had unwittingly been responsible for polarising attitudes to literature in a needlessly divisive manner. There need be no inherent conflict, he saw, between the two approaches to his art. The future lay in a fusion between them – as Ratzel expresses it, 'here and now, we are tearing up life by the roots and anything we write – when we get to writing again – will be fundamental – vital, black, red, vibrating'.

The Brothers is a deceptively compact work, concealing beneath its outward simplicity a complex interweaving of metaphor. Its disturbing effect lies in its continual attempt to transform the relationship between the symbolic and the real, to question the boundary between allegory and realistic narrative. To read it is to be aware that the text is never quite what it seems, that one is reading a work imbued with the spirit of Swift and one in which scenes, conversations and names each have symbolic relevance.

In coming to terms with his own ambivalence Wells was attempting to reconcile the apparent contradictions between his public and private attitudes to his art. At intervals throughout the 1930s Wells had been musing on his approach to the novel. His autobiography (written 1932–4) included a long section entitled 'Digression about Novels' in which he speculated on whether or not he was a novelist. Throughout his debate with Henry James, he added, 'I had a queer feeling that we were both incompatibly right.'[84] Each of the major novels he wrote during this period – *Brynhild, Apropos of Dolores, Babes in the Darkling Wood* and *You Can't Be Too Careful* – is prefaced with an introduction in which he looks again at the complex relationship between fiction and reality. His work as president of PEN, an international association of writers, had brought him into contact with many young European authors and impelled him to consider afresh his approach to literature. Now in *The Brothers* he came to grips with his ambivalent attitudes to the novel and explored his troubled sense of doubt in an allegory. Faced with gathering war clouds and ominous signs of the collapse of European civilisation, he was compelled to admit that arguments over the means and ends of literature were futile. What mattered in the final analysis was the freedom of the creative artist to express himself in whatever form he found conducive to his art. It says much for Wells that despite his increasing preoccupation with problems of world order and his uncomfortable awareness that the sands of time were running out he chose to express his growing sense of futility not in the form of a lecture or a volume of essays but in a metaphor of memorable power. In doing so he was returning to the richness and fertility of his earliest work and creating a fable of continuing relevance to our age.

14

You Can't Be Too Careful: the Novel as Parody

> This is the story of the Deeds and Sayings of Edward Albert Tewler. From his point of view. But like those amusing pictures you find in books on Optics that will turn inside out as you look at them, it is equally the story of this whole universe of Edward Albert Tewler, and he is just the empty shape of a human being at the centre of it – its resultant, its creature.
>
> (H. G. Wells, *You Can't Be Too Careful*)

> And what of this new book the whole world makes such a rout about? – Oh! 'tis out of all plumb, my lord, – quite an irregular thing! – not one of the angles at the four corners was a right angle.
>
> (Laurence Sterne, *Tristram Shandy*)

Wells's last novel *You Can't Be Too Careful*, published in 1941, is today almost completely forgotten. Appearing at a time of wartime paper shortage, it was overwhelmed by the Second World War and has been largely bypassed by modern literary criticism. By 1941 his reputation as a novelist was at its lowest ebb. A new generation of younger writers – D. H. Lawrence, J. B. Priestley, Graham Greene, Aldous Huxley, Evelyn Waugh – had ousted him from the commanding position he had once shared with Bennett and Galsworthy (the death of James Joyce and Virginia Woolf in the same year may well have led him to speculate afresh on the nature of the novel), and in a cynical moment he confessed that none of his later novels 'did more than make his decline and fall unmistakeable'.[85] But *You Can't Be Too Careful* does not merit its current critical neglect. In the postscript to his autobiography he claims that he had tried to make it 'my best and most comprehensive novel',[86] and there are many indications that he intended it to be a summation of all that he felt and believed about the novel as a didactic instrument.

It is cast in the form of a *Bildungsroman*, a genre he had employed in *Tono-Bungay* and *The New Machiavelli* and, more recently, in *The Bulpington of Blup*, and relates the life story of Edward Albert Tewler, a Cockney born in 1901. Wells insists in the Introduction that 'no dissertations, no arguments, above all no projects nor incitements nor propaganda shall break the flow of our narrative; this is to be a novel free of ideas':

> You shall have him unadorned; you shall have his plain unvarnished record. Nothing fulsome about it. This is a plain straight story of deeds and character – not character in general but the character you get in characters.

The Introduction then goes on to raise the question whether free will exists: is Edward Albert a free agent, shaping his life in accordance with his own desires or is he manipulated by pressures and forces beyond his control? 'Plain story we have to tell, but if, in spite of that resolution, plain story leads at last to an insoluble dualism, thither we must go.' To illustrate his thesis of an insoluble dualism in human affairs – the interplay between the individual and society – Wells portrays the modern novel in the form of a diagram:

Here we have a picture of the modern novel.
Look at it hard and alternately you see the
vase, the social vessel, and nothing else, and
then the social vessel vanishes and you see
individuals and nothing more.

The interplay between Edward Albert's individuality and the constraints imposed upon him by society forms one of the novel's dominant themes. His childhood, adolescence, emotional development and marriage are described in pitiless detail but always with reference to the wider social forces which impinge on him. At intervals Wells intervenes *in propria persona* to draw together a framework of descriptive and didactic commentary and to remind the reader of the duality which lies behind the narrative: that between the central character as an individual and the complex of forces – social, psychological and emotional – which have shaped his life and attitudes.

The language of the novel – simple, colloquial, direct – suggests a text devoid of literary pretensions. But such an impression would be totally misleading. As with Defoe's *A Journal of the Plague Year* and Orwell's *Down and Out in Paris and London* what appears on a casual inspection to be a rapid, loosely assembled text is in reality a most carefully wrought whole. The terse, conversational style conceals an artistry which surrounds the plain story of Tewler's life and times with a web of descriptive and literary allusion, a continual awareness of an authorial presence. The reader has the odd sensation that he is being observed in the act of reading by Wells himself, an observer who asks disturbing questions, inserts digressions and pauses to add speculations and allusions to psychology, history and science. The effect is of a continuous *conversation* between novelist and audience, a dialogue commenting on the characters and their interrelationships. The reader is not merely a passive consumer, he is an active participant sharing with the author in the total experience of the novel.

There are a number of indications which suggest that *Tristram Shandy* is the principal inspiration behind the novel. Whereas Tristram commences his narrative with the moment of his conception, *You Can't Be Too Careful* commences with the instant of Tewler's birth. Wells repeats the Shandean devices of scatological imagery, typographical oddities, censored passages and pretences that the censor has intervened. In place of the interpolated tales added by Sterne he inserts occasional passages of homily, continually attempting to place Tewler in a wider perspective of space and time. There are quirks such as a Book containing only one chapter (*Tristram Shandy* contains several chapters consisting of a single sentence), an Introduction in which the hero and his son argue on the value of ideas, a chapter on man's ancestry and an Appendix on

'The Evolution of the Placental Mammals'. There are numerous asides strongly reminiscent of Sterne:

> The preceding Book in the life of Edward Albert Tewler has been a long one. Now by way of relief the reader shall have a very short one. (IV, 1)

There is, as with Sterne, a constant awareness of the flexibility of language (for example: 'It is only in the past few years that the sciences of Significs and Semantics have opened men's eyes to the immense inaccuracies and question-begging of language', III, 13). There is a Shandean bawdiness, a propensity to discuss sexual behaviour through a series of 'circumlocutions, metaphors and gestures' (I, 2). There is a stress on Edward Albert Tewler's 'sentimental education' – Peter Quennell in *Four Portraits* argues that the word sentimental may well have been coined by Sterne[87] – and a continual awareness of the author looking over one's shoulder while reading, a sense of participation between novelist and text. As Tristram constantly addresses himself to the reader and confides to him his thoughts and emotions, so Wells addresses observations and asides to his unknown audience. The effect of these authorial interventions is to throw into relief a question which had haunted him since his earliest speculations: the relation between fiction and reality.

When reading *You Can't Be Too Careful* one continually has a sense of entering into the novelist's workshop. At a number of points Wells echoes Sterne and shares with the reader his thoughts concerning his characters and their behaviour, as in the following passage:

> I have told my tale but ill if I have failed to convey that if this most natural and excellent of mothers had any fault at all in her, it was a certain disposition to excessive solicitude, and, associated with that and integral to that, an element of fear. I will not discuss whether these qualities were innate or the infection of her generation, for that would be a breach of the undertaking given in the Preface. She was not afraid herself, but her protective motherliness extended to everyone and everything that appertained to her. And it came to a focus upon young Albert Edward, who was always central to her thoughts and dreams and plans and speeches. She was not you must understand an unhappy

woman. She lived a life of intensely concentrated anxious happiness. There was always some new menace to excite her.

(I, 2)

When reading a Wells novel one is normally aware to a greater or lesser degree of a narrative voice, a controlling presence guiding and shaping the story. But a comparison of *You Can't Be Too Careful* with *Brynhild*, for example, reveals at once the marked difference between his last novel and his earlier fictions told in the third person. For here, as with Sterne, the author is much more emotionally involved with his characters. Tewler disgusts him yet at the same time engages his sympathy. The 'I' in this paragraph, the narrative voice, takes no part in the action of the novel yet is intimately associated with it, commenting on it, introducing digressions, expressing doubts, sharing confidences. The 'I' becomes almost a character in his own right, a participant in the total experience of the novel. One would need to go back to Dickens to find a comparable instance of authorial intervention. At one point Wells comments apropos himself: 'I know of no other writer so anxious to share his troubles and limitations with his readers' (III, 8). Throughout the experience of reading the novel one is aware of this unusual sense of participation, of sharing in its making. It is as if the voice of the novelist is constantly within hearing, reminding, confiding, speculating, suggesting.

Above all he weaves around the novel a complex and Shandean frame of reference in which the relationship between author and text is constantly called into question. It is in the intricate nature of this relationship that so much of the interest of the novel lies. For we are faced here with a text in which the relationship between author and reader is decidedly unusual. What are we to make of a novel in which the author continually addresses the reader with homiletic commentary, in which the novelist discusses the actions and motivations of his characters and confides his thoughts on the technical problems of authorship? Not only is *You Can't Be Too Careful* a text rich in Shandean devices and asides but it continually seeks to widen the scope of the novel to accommodate an examination of the hero's place in space and time. It is apparent that a novel containing discussion of man as a political animal and an analysis of his origins, nature and place in the scale of evolution must be less straightforward than appears at first sight. The closer we look at it the more we perceive that we are dealing here with a novel which is at once a parody of an orthodox realist text and a metafiction which anticipates the work of Italo Calvino and John Fowles.

As in *Tristram Shandy* the novel sets in motion a series of parodies which caricature some of the conventions of realistic fiction. The device of the omniscient narrator, of the author intervening in his own person, of the author taking the reader into his confidence, of tying up the loose ends at the conclusion of the story – all these commonplaces of the realist novel are guyed in a manner which continually draws attention to the fictiveness of the text. In doing so Wells is not only parodying himself (Tewler's adolescence and emotional life recalls some of the incidents in *Kipps*) but Dickens and Thackeray and, above all, Sterne, the man he described as 'the subtlest and greatest *artist* . . . that Great Britain has ever produced in all that is essentially the novel'.[88] There are parodies of the Dickensian novel (the descriptions of Doober's boarding house and Tewler's wedding), the Orwellian novel (the account of Tewler's marriage and divorce closely parallels the style and plot of *Keep the Aspidistra Flying*), the public school novel (Mr Myame's school and the cricket match) and the novel of suburban life so fashionable in the 1930s ('Morningside Prospect'). The titles of the 'Books' – for example, 'How Edward Albert Tewler Was Overtaken By A Storm of War and Destruction and What He Saw and Did In It' – recalls the descriptive titles familiar in Victorian fiction, whilst the novel's formal organisation caricatures his own 'Prig' novels of the Edwardian years. The manner in which characters are introduced and described deliberately echoes Dickens (the description of Pip Chaser in Book III, 12, might almost be taken from *Pickwick Papers*) and it is surely no accident that discussions of Dickens and Thackeray are introduced into the text. Clearly these references are intentional. The overall impression is of a novel which looks backwards to nineteenth-century fiction and forwards to the self-conscious fiction of our own time. In achieving this effect Wells demonstrates the malleability of the novel as a literary form and its continuing relevance in an age of fundamental social and political change.

The opening paragraph describing the birth of Edward Albert Tewler is an irreverent pastiche of the first chapter of a *Bildungsroman*:

> It took Mrs Richard Tewler, his mother, three and twenty hours to bring her only son into the world. He came shyly, not head-first but toe-first like a timid bather, and that sort of presentation

always causes trouble. It is doubtful if his reluctant entry into this fierce universe could have occurred even then if it had not been for the extreme inadequacy of the knowledge of what are called preventatives that prevailed in the late Victorian period. People didn't want children then, except by heart's desire, but they got them nevertheless. One knew there was some sort of knowledge about it, but one couldn't be too careful whom one asked, and your doctor also in those days couldn't be too careful in misunderstanding your discreet hints and soundings. In those days England was far behind Polynesia in that matter. So there you were – and do what you could, you were liable to be caught.

(I, 1)

There is clearly a note of irony here, a sense that the Tewler household is being both described and satirised. One is aware of an authorial presence behind the text, a presence commenting on the story as it unfolds – 'It is doubtful', 'One knew', 'So there you were'. The opening establishes the tone which Wells maintains throughout the novel, that of a group of specimen human beings being examined under a microscope. In his early romance *The War of the Worlds* he draws an analogy between mankind and 'the infusoria under the microscope' going to and fro about their little affairs, serene in their dominance over the planet.[89] His technique in *You Can't Be Too Careful* is to focus on a representative individual and to describe with complete frankness the forces which mould him through childhood, adolescence and manhood.

At intervals Wells offers a 'summing up', a moment of reckoning in which he shares his thoughts concerning the characters he has created:

Now this was a very cardinal moment in the development of *Homo Tewler Anglicanus*. In this one specimen the type has unfolded, slowly but surely, and here we have it now with all its distinctive qualities displayed. In spite of serious initial disadvantages, Edward Albert had made good. We have traced his education in that peculiar blend of sexual modesty and enterprise that has made the Englishman the world's lover; we have watched the natural awakening of his imperialism, have seen him become a cricket fan and a broad and intermittent but sincere Churchman; we have pursued his growing craving to become clubable and to get together with fellows in the know; and now

here we have dawning that realisation of the extreme evil of
'ideers' which more than anything else has made our England
what it is today. (III, 18).

Similar passages can be found in both Dickens and Sterne,
moments of reflection when the author passes judgement on his
creations or pauses to take stock. The early Wells was particularly
prone to such passages and to the pretence that his characters are
beyond his control. At one stage in *The Wheels of Chance* (1896) the
narrative voice comments: 'There are occasions when a moralising
novelist can merely wring his hands and leave matters to take their
course.'[90] This suggestion that the novelist is simply a recorder, a
passive observer describing scenes and events beyond his jurisdic-
tion is characteristic of much twentieth-century fiction. The point is
made explicitly in John Fowles's *The French Lieutenant's Woman* (ch.
13) and is implicit in much of the work of Calvino and Nabokov.

What is interesting about *You Can't Be Too Careful* as an example
of modernist fiction is Wells's use of language and the unusual
perspective from which the story is narrated. Such phrases as 'In
this one specimen', 'We have traced his education', 'the extreme evil
of "ideers"' are reminders that Edward Albert Tewler is a case
study, a microcosm of human life. The novel's subtitle 'A Sample of
Life 1901–1951' makes clear Wells's intention to focus his scrutiny
on a small group of individuals and to do so with the dispassionate
spirit of enquiry of a scientific experiment. This intention is
sustained throughout the vicissitudes of his story yet simultaneously he adheres to the conventions of realist fiction – even to the extent
of sharing with the reader his technical problems as a novelist. A
dual process is thus set in motion. On the one hand the reader is
invited to accept that the novel is a conventional realist text and that
the Tewlers and their circle are *real* – 'I am merely recording facts';
'This is before all things a truthful novel.' On the other hand he is
continually reminded that the story is *fiction*, that the characters are
the creatures of Wells's imagination. The resulting tension is oddly
disturbing: the text becomes counterpoised between the real and the
imaginary.

Midway through the story there is an illuminating passage in
which the author confides a serious technical difficulty:

I doubt whether in an English novel I am justified in assuming
that either I or the reader knows French, as a Frenchman might

know it. But Miss Birkenhead at this phase in her career had a curious disposition to use French under the most unexpected circumstances – and I do not feel that either I or the reader has the right to set up as a judge of the sort of French she spoke or to pretend to translate what she was saying. So the proper thing to do here seems to be to report as exactly as possible what she said, to note several occasions when it seemed to produce reactions other than those she had anticipated, and to say no more about it. And if most of what she said remains incomprehensible, then the effect on the reader will be virtually the effect on Edward Albert, and he after all is our story. (III, 8)

One is reminded of the moment in *Tristram Shandy* when Tristram confesses to the reader the discrepancy between the slowness of his narrative and the pace of the events he is attempting to describe: he feels compelled to make an observation 'upon the strange state of affairs between the reader and myself, just as things stand at present' (Book IV, 13). In his critical study of *Tristram Shandy* Max Byrd has drawn attention to 'the sheer process of writing that he displays, as if the novel had a glass window into which we could peer and see its workings'.[91] A similar transparency is evident here, a sense of looking at the machinery of the novel and being a confidant in the creative process.

Though the story is related with the utmost detachment it is written in a style which accommodates contrasts of emotion. There is a crucial moment at the end of the novel (V, 5) in which Tewler's wife Mary is lying on her death-bed, having been gravely wounded in an air raid. Tewler has spent the day in London being awarded the George Cross for heroism. On his return he is summoned to the hospital to see her before she dies. This last conversation between husband and wife is one of the most moving scenes in Wells's later fiction. Throughout their conversation they are talking at cross-purposes: Tewler can think about nothing but the presentation at the Palace, his wife has thoughts only for her son. Even at the last they misunderstand one another. Soon her life draws to its end:

For a few seconds she stared at her husband's evident self-satisfaction as though it was something strange to her, and then as steadfastly at the cross in his hand. She made no further effort to speak. Slowly her interest faded. She closed her eyes like a tired child. . . . Presently the sister put a hand on his arm.

This little scene, like so many in *You Can't Be Too Careful*, is presented with the utmost economy and yet a simple dignity which compels attention. The prolixity of Wells's Edwardian novels would be quite out of place here. In its place is this simple, unemotional passage: Tewler, overcome with grief, mentally at odds with his wife even at her death. The scene is none the less moving despite the spareness of its language.

The dominant motif of the novel is that of metamorphosis. Edward Albert's metamorphoses from gawky child to adolescent, from adolescent to credulous adult, from errant lover to suburban husband, from spectator to war hero, are recounted with candour and compassion. Wells continually places Tewler in a biological frame of reference, as a microcosm of humanity caught at a precise moment in time. 'Nature is a sloven', he adds, 'she never cleans up completely after her advances, and so we abound in vestigial structures, and our beings are haunted by the ghosts of rhythms that served her in the past' (III, 2). This vision of man as a vestigial creature, as a being haunted by the rhythms of the past, links the novel with the Swiftian romances of the 1890s and with his sense of man's plasticity.

Fifty years separate the writing of *You Can't Be Too Careful* and the first drafts of *The Time Machine*. Both novels are dominated by a sense of man's evolutionary past, by a vision of humanity as a species with a precarious foothold in the time-scale of history. The tendency of both is to displace man from his central position, to emphasise 'the extreme primitiveness of the *Hominidae* in the scale of being' (II, 3). Gillian Beer has drawn attention to the fact that evolutionary theory 'has persistently been recast to make it seem that all the past has been yearning towards the present moment and is satisfied now'.[92] Wells's first and last novels counterbalance this trend: *The Time Machine* by positing a bifurcation of humanity into degenerate species; *You Can't Be Too Careful* by demonstrating man's immaturity and the superficiality of the civilising process.

Both novels are concerned with time and change, with the thesis that man is transitory and provisional. Wells's choice of 'Tewler' as the surname of his hero, his microcosm, can surely be no accident (he insists that 'every word in this conscientious narrative is written with deliberation'). Tewler suggests Thule, the extreme limit. The thesis is that *Homo sapiens* has not yet been attained, that he exists 'as yet only in the dreamlands of aspiration' (III, 1). Man is not *Homo sapiens* but *Homo Tewler*, the extreme limit of his development which could prove to be his final phase. The novel's opening sentence highlights the parallel between Tewler's individual life and the life of the species: 'It took Mrs Richard Tewler, his mother, three and twenty hours to bring her only son into the world.' On the time-scale of evolution, man is in the 23rd hour of his existence, a species teetering on the brink of extinction. The novel was written before the advent of nuclear weapons but Wells was fully aware that there was 'no limit apparent to the destructive power of a bomb, which again must increase to world-destroying dimensions' (V, 2).

As in *The Time Machine* there is a continual attempt to place the narrative in relation to space and time, to fix the story and characters in a locus of history and cosmology:

I am telling the simple life story of one individual Londoner, and I am pledged not to stray from a plain objective narrative; neverthe-less it has already been necessary to supplement this record of acts and deeds by statements of a more general nature, to place the story definitely in its historical perspective. Just as if you are making a deposition about murder on the high seas you have, if possible, to indicate the latitude and longitude of the ship. It has been necessary, for instance, to indicate the role of the feudal and Christian traditions, if the story is to be read understandingly by an enlightened American or Russian or Chinese reader, or to have any value for that posterity to which, under the restrictions of the present paper shortage, it is mainly addressed. And now furth-ermore in one brief but concentrated section we must broaden our reference wider still and show not merely Tewler in terms of terrestrial latitude and longitude but Tewler in relation to the starry universe, to space and time and ideals.   (III, 1)

It is as if the novel is being stretched to demonstrate its utmost possibilities, a technique Joyce had adopted in a very different manner in *Ulysses*. As Sterne widens the scope of his narrative from the narrow range of Shandy Hall to Europe and ultimately the universe, so Wells expands the parameters of his fiction to embrace a discussion of man's place in the evolution of species. The chapter titles – 'Metamorphosis of Man', 'Species *Homo Tewler*', 'And After *Sapiens*?' – continually return the reader to the novel's central question: whether man is a species at the end of its tether or whether he is capable of regeneration. Is Edward Albert Tewler typical of his time and background, or is he exceptional, an irrelevance? In contrast to the sombre pessimism of *The Time Machine* Wells's last novel ends on a note of stoical agnosticism:

> Yet a vista of innumerable happy generations, an abundance of life at present inconceivable, and at the end, not extinction necessarily, not immortality, but complete uncertainty, is surely sufficient prospect for the present. . . . They will see far and wide in an ever-growing light while we see as in a glass darkly. Things yet unimaginable. (VI, 5)

The extinction of man had been a recurring theme in his work since his earliest essays. But in his final novel it is uncertainty rather than extinction which is the ultimate speculation. Characteristically we are left with a question mark. 'Why should they not be in the nature of our good and much more than our good – "beyond good and evil"?'

In an illuminating aside Wells described *You Can't Be Too Careful* as 'a sustained attempt to render life, and particularly one specimen life and group of lives as starkly as possible' (III, 13). He prefaced this remark with the admission that 'The last thing a speaker or writer can perceive is his own limitation, and with that the critical hearer and reader must deal.' He was 75 when the novel was written and in ill health for much of the time. The marks of old age and illness are evident in its unevenness, the hectoring quality of some of the homiletic passages – particularly in the final section 'God, Satan and *Homo Tewler*' – and the bitterness of its satire. But these limitations apart, the abiding impression left in the mind is one of astringent energy, of a novel rich in humour and acute observation of human foibles. If it was merely a recapitulation of his early work it would be of comparatively minor importance. Its significance lies in the way in which Wells renders the 'insoluble dualism' of his narrative, the interplay between the Tewlers as individuals and the forces that have shaped them. It has been said of Sterne that his great aim 'was to give as true a picture as possible of real human beings as they are in themselves, not as they imagine themselves to be, nor as others judge them to be by their actions and outward behaviour alone.'[93] In focusing on the emotional development of a sample human being and showing how other lives impinge on that of his hero Wells was treading on familiar ground, for he might easily have done so in a conventional novel in the manner of *Clayhanger*. Instead he chose a decidely unorthodox perspective, a hybrid of novel and dissertation. It is one which permits the most intimate observation of human behaviour coupled with a stoical detachment, an ability to view his characters from the standpoint of universal history.

Perhaps the most remarkable passage in the novel is a paragraph towards the end in which Wells looks back on his hero and offers a dispassionate appraisal of Edward Albert as a microcosm of humanity:

Edward Albert Tewler is still alive. I am afraid he at least is lost to the revolution. I have told his poor sordid story and that of the people whose lives he helped to spoil; I have mocked at his absurdities and misfortunes and invincible conceit; but all the way along as I wrote it something has protested, 'This is not fair. Given a broader education, given air, light and opportunity, would he have been anything like this?'

He is what our civilisation made of him, and this is all it made of him. I have told the complete truth about a contemporary specimen man. This brings me into conflict with my most intimate and trusted critic and with my loyal but anxious publishers. Your hero is detestable, they protest, and there is not really a nice human being in the book. Couldn't you put in some flash of real nobility in him, and can't you redeem the spectacle by one or two *good* people, essentially good people, behaving in an exemplary manner, people your readers would like and with whom they could identify themselves and so hold themselves aloof from the harsh veracity of your story? That is exactly what I refuse to do for them. My case is that Edward Albert is not so much detestable as pitiful, and that for the rest I like nearly all my characters as they are – except Mr Chamble Pewter, whom manifestly I loathe. To love without illusions is to be secure against surprise. It is the quintessence of love. I follow in the tradition of Hogarth and Tom Jones and not in the footsteps of Richardson, and I shall count myself wholly damned if I let my friendly advisers induce me to pander to these people for whom reading is nothing better than material for Grandisonian reverie. (VI, 3)

There is a similar moment of appraisal at the conclusion of *The History of Mr Polly*, a point at which Wells begs the reader to understand that Polly is the innocent victim of forces outside his control. But the narrative voice in *You Can't Be Too Careful* is merciless in its candour, in its freedom from illusions. Wells says of Tewler: 'I have mocked at his absurdities and misfortunes and invincible conceit. . . . My case is that Edward Albert is not so much detestable as pitiful.' This treatment of his central character as a homunculus, a specimen under a microscope, is relentless in its scrutiny, yet Wells has more than passing affection for him. Behind the folly and ineptitude of Tewler and Evangeline Birkenhead can be discerned the warm humanitarianism of their creator, a novelist who both pities and understands. There can also be discerned the hand of a writer experimenting with his medium, one whose work from first to last has been an experiment in statement.

'I follow in the tradition of Hogarth and Tom Jones and not in the footsteps of Richardson', he proclaims. Not for him the reading which is 'nothing better than material for Grandisonian reverie'. The contrast between *Tom Jones* and Richardson's novel *Sir Charles Grandison* brings into critical focus an apposition which was central to Wells's concerns throughout his writing life – that between the discursive and the formal, between the novel in which one was free to 'sprawl and flounder, comment and theorise'[94] and one bound by conventions of aesthetic perfection. *You Can't Be Too Careful* belongs firmly in the discursive tradition of Sterne, Fielding and Dickens. Whilst owing much to this tradition Wells builds creatively upon it and by placing his characters in a cosmological framework adds a new dimension. The novel is not simply the story of Edward Albert Tewler. It is the story of a generation. Beyond this it is the story of a complex of forces which shape man's evolution and determine his response to his environment.

Wells sensed that it was not only man who was subject to metamorphosis, it was his institutions, his art, and the novel itself. In parodying the conventions of the realist novel and presenting it within a framework of evolutionary time he was widening its scope in an innovative way and looking ahead to the experimental fictions of the century's final decades.

Appendix

1. Wells at Work

A detailed examination of Wells's methods of composition is beyond the scope of the present study. The reader interested in this aspect of his work is referred to *H. G. Wells à l'oeuvre* by Bernard Loing (Didier Erudition, 1984) and to *The Wealth of Mr Waddy*, ed. Harris Wilson (Southern Illinois University Press, 1969).

To give an indication of Wells's methods of revision I reproduce below two early drafts of the opening paragraphs of *Love and Mr Lewisham* followed by the final text. A comparison of these reveals the process of accretion through which his manuscripts passed before he was satisfied – a process entirely characteristic of his methods of work.

FIRST DRAFT

Mr Lewisham at his Studies

The reason why the world lost a great man, one probably of the first magnitude, and gained – the present Mr Lewisham, should surely interest it. And apart from the particular loss is the general application. There have been other cases, there may even be cases in progress, sympathetically analogous. For we begin with Mr Lewisham at seventeen setting out for the conquest of God's universe, and we end with him at seven and twenty humming cheerfully and putting up a garden shed. And the world beyond the reach of the hammering as serenely unconscious of its loss as it is possible to imagine. Surely the world should hear of it.

At seventeen Mr Lewisham was driving headlong at greatness as anyone who entered his little study-bedroom would have seen at a glance. For example, over the head of the bed, these truths, not to be forgotten for a moment written in a clear bold hand – youthfully florid – ; "Knowledge is Power" and "What man has done man can do." Mr Lewisham sees these afresh every morning as his head comes through his shirt.

SECOND DRAFT
Mr Lewisham at his Studies

How it came about that the world lost a great man, one possibly even of the first magnitude, and gained in exchange [word indecipherable] – the present Mr Lewisham, should surely interest it. There have been other cases, there may be cases in progress even, sympathetically analogous. We begin with Mr Lewisham at seventeen setting out for the conquest of God's universe, and we end with him at seven and twenty humming cheerfully in the sunset and putting up a summer house in a Turnham Green back garden. And the world beyond the reach of the hammering as serenely, as beautifully, unconscious of its loss as it is possible to imagine. That evening tranquillity behind the smart whack, whack, whack – two inch nails and the household hammer – is in itself an ample excuse for this novel.

At seventeen Mr Lewisham was driving headlong at greatness – headlong is the only word for it. Anyone who entered his little study–bedroom would have seen that at a glance. For example, over the head of the bed, where good folks hang texts, these truths, not to be forgotten for a moment, written in a clear bold hand – youthfully florid – ; "Knowledge is Power" and "What man has done man can do." Man in the second instance referring to Mr Lewisham. Mr Lewisham could see these afresh every morning as his head came through his shirt.

FINAL TEXT
Introduces Mr Lewisham

The opening chapter does not concern itself with Love – indeed that antagonist does not certainly appear until the third – and Mr Lewisham is seen at his studies. It was ten years ago, and in those days he was assistant master in the Whortley Proprietary School, Whortley, Sussex, and his wages were forty pounds a year, out of which he had to afford fifteen shillings a week during term time to lodge with Mrs Munday, at the little shop in the West Street. He was called "Mr" to distinguish him from the bigger boys, whose duty it was to learn, and it was a matter of stringent regulation that he should be addressed as "Sir."

He wore ready-made clothes, his black jacket of rigid line was dusted about the front and sleeves with scholastic chalk, and his face was downy and his moustache incipient. He was a passable-looking youngster of eighteen, fair-haired, indifferently barbered and with a quite unnecessary pair of glasses on his fairly prominent nose – he wore these to make himself look older, that discipline might be maintained. At the particular moment when this story begins he was in his bedroom. An attic it was, with lead-framed dormer windows, a slanting ceiling and a bulging wall, covered, as a number of torn places witnessed, with innumerable strata of florid old-fashioned paper.

To judge by the room Mr Lewisham thought little of Love but much on Greatness. Over the head of the bed, for example, where good folks hang texts, these truths asserted themselves, written in a clear, bold, youthfully florid hand: – "Knowledge is Power," and "What man has done man can do," – man in the second instance referring to Mr Lewisham. Never for a moment were these things to be forgotten. Mr Lewisham could see them afresh every morning as his head came through his shirt.

2. A Checklist of Wells's Fiction

The Time Machine, 1895
The Stolen Bacillus, 1895 (short stories)
The Wonderful Visit, 1895
The Island of Doctor Moreau, 1896
The Wheels of Chance, 1896
The Invisible Man, 1897
The Plattner Story, 1897 (short stories)
The War of the Worlds, 1898
Tales of Space and Time, 1899 (short stories)
When the Sleeper Wakes, 1899 (revised edn, *The Sleeper Awakes*, 1910)
Love and Mr Lewisham, 1900
The First Men in the Moon, 1901
The Sea Lady, 1902
Twelve Stories and a Dream, 1903 (short stories)
The Food of the Gods, 1904
A Modern Utopia, 1905
Kipps, 1905
In the Days of the Comet, 1906
The War in the Air, 1908
Tono-Bungay, 1909

Ann Veronica, 1909
The History of Mr Polly, 1910
The New Machiavelli, 1911
The Country of the Blind, 1911 (short stories)
The Door in the Wall, 1911 (short stories)
Marriage, 1912
The Passionate Friends, 1913
The World Set Free, 1914
The Wife of Sir Isaac Harman, 1914
Boon, 1915
Bealby, 1915
The Research Magnificent, 1915
Mr Britling Sees it Through, 1916
The Soul of a Bishop, 1917
Joan and Peter, 1918
The Undying Fire, 1919
The Secret Places of the Heart, 1922
Men Like Gods, 1923
The Dream, 1924
Christina Alberta's Father, 1925
The World of William Clissold, 1926
Meanwhile, 1927
Mr Blettsworthy on Rampole Island, 1928
The King who was a King, 1929 (film scenario)
The Autocracy of Mr Parham, 1930
The Bulpington of Blup, 1932
The Shape of Things to Come, 1933
Things to Come, 1935 (film scenario)
The Croquet Player, 1936
Man Who Could Work Miracles, 1936 (film scenario)
Star Begotten, 1937
Brynhild, 1937
The Camford Visitation, 1937
The Brothers, 1938
Apropos of Dolores, 1938
The Holy Terror, 1939
Babes in the Darkling Wood, 1940
All Aboard for Ararat, 1940
You Can't Be Too Careful, 1941

Posthumously Published

The Desert Daisy, 1957 (juvenilia)
Hoopdriver's Holiday, 1964
The Wealth of Mr Waddy, 1969
The Man with a Nose, 1984 (short stories)

Notes

(Quotations from novels are identified by chapter and section number.)

Part One: Overview
1. Mark Schorer, 'Technique as Discovery', *Critiques and Essays on Modern Fiction 1920–1951*, ed. J. W. Aldridge (New York, 1952) p. 72.
2. Introduction to Geoffrey West, *H. G. Wells: A Sketch for a Portrait* (Howe, 1930) p. 13.
3. 'The Betterave Papers', *Cornhill Magazine*, July 1945, p. 363.
4. *Henry James and H. G. Wells*, ed. Leon Edel and Gordon N. Ray (Rupert Hart-Davis, 1959) pp. 122–3.
5. Robert Bloom, *Anatomies of Egotism: A Reading of the Last Novels of H. G. Wells* (University of Nebraska Press, 1977) p. 8.
6. *Experiment in Autobiography* (Gollancz, 1934) p. 499.
7. Letter to Elizabeth Healey, quoted in West, *H. G. Wells: A Sketch for a Portrait*, pp. 137–8.
8. Edel and Ray (eds), *Henry James and H. G. Wells*, p. 264.
9. Quoted in Norman and Jeanne Mackenzie, *The Time Traveller: The Life of H. G. Wells* (Weidenfeld and Nicolson, 1977) p. 110.
10. Malcolm Bradbury and James McFarlane, *Modernism 1890–1930* (Harvester Press, 1978) p. 27.
11. 'The Rediscovery of the Unique', *Fortnightly Review*, July 1891, p. 110.
12. 'Scepticism of the Instrument' (1903), reprinted as an appendix to *A Modern Utopia*.
13. Jeremy Hawthorn, *Studying the Novel* (Edward Arnold, 1985) p. 29.
14. Introduction to *The Country of the Blind and Other Stories* (1911).
15. 'Scepticism of the Instrument', appendix to *A Modern Utopia*.
16. *A Modern Utopia*, p. viii.
17. Bennett to Wells, 27 October 1926.
18. James W. Gargano, 'The Question of Poe's Narrators', *College English*, xxv (December 1963) pp. 177–81.
19. E. M. Forster, *Aspects of the Novel* (Edward Arnold, 1927) ch. 4.
20. Preface, *The Scientific Romances of H. G. Wells* (Gollancz, 1933).
21. 'The Novel of Ideas', Introduction to *Babes in the Darkling Wood* (Secker and Warburg, 1940).
22. *The World of William Clissold*, I, 2
23. 'Scepticism of the Instrument', appendix to *A Modern Utopia*.
24. A bibliography of his book reviews is contained in Robert M. Philmus, 'H. G. Wells as Literary Critic for the *Saturday Review*', *Science-Fiction Studies*, July 1977, pp. 166–93.
25. 'The Making of Men at Cambridge', *Saturday Review*, LXXXIII (13 February 1897).
26. Introduction to West, *H. G. Wells: A Sketch for a Portrait*.

27. West, *H. G. Wells: A Sketch for a Portrait*, p. 141.
28. *Experiment in Autobiography*, p. 493.
29. 'The Contemporary Novel', reprinted as ch. 9 of *An Englishman Looks at the World* and in Edel and Ray, *Henry James and H. G. Wells*, pp. 131–56.
30. West, *H. G. Wells: A Sketch for a Portrait*, p. 114.
31. 'The Contemporary Novel', in Edel and Ray, *Henry James and H. G. Wells*.
32. Edel and Ray, *Henry James and H. G. Wells*, p. 128.
33. *Experiment in Autobiography*, p. 499.
34. Gilbert Phelps, *A Survey of English Literature* (Pan, 1965) pp. 349–50.
35. *The Happy Turning: A Dream of Life*, pp. 48–9.
36. Malcolm Bradbury, *The Social Context of Modern English Literature* (Blackwell, 1971) p. xxxii.
37. David Lodge, *Language of Fiction* (Routledge and Kegan Paul, 1966) p. 218.
38. Introduction to *Babes in the Darkling Wood*.
39. Originally entitled 'At a Window', *Black and White*, 25 August 1894; included in *The Stolen Bacillus*.
40. *The Research Magnificent*, I, 15.
41. Raymond Williams, 'Realism and the Contemporary Novel', *The Long Revolution* (Chatto and Windus, 1961).
42. *Joan and Peter*, V, 1.
43. Frank Swinnerton, *The Bookman's London* (Allan Wingate, 1951) p. 30.
44. George Orwell, 'Charles Dickens', *Inside the Whale*.
45. *Textbook of Biology*, Part I, 'The Theory of Evolution', para. 54.
46. 'Under the Knife', *New Review*, January 1896; reprinted in *The Plattner Story and Others*. Cf. John Fowles, *The Magus*, ch. 36 and also H. W. Fawkner, *The Timescapes of John Fowles* (Associated University Presses, 1984) ch. 9.
47. *Apropos of Dolores*, II, 3.
48. Introduction, Atlantic Edition, vol. 1.

Part Two: Case Studies

1. Contemporary reviews of *The Time Machine* are reprinted in P. Parrinder (ed.), *H. G. Wells: The Critical Heritage* (Routledge and Kegan Paul, 1972).
2. Bernard Bergonzi, *The Early H. G. Wells* (Manchester University Press, 1961) p. 61.
3. Lodge, *Language of Fiction*, p. 223.
4. 'The Extinction of Man', *Pall Mall Gazette*, 59 (September 25 1894); reprinted in *Certain Personal Matters*.
5. Cf. *Experiment in Autobiography*, ch. 2 and *This Misery of Boots*, pp. 5–6.
6. Anthony West, 'My Father's Unpaid Debts of Love', *Observer*, 11 January 1976.

7. Anthony West, *Principles and Persuasions* (Eyre and Spottiswoode, 1958) pp. 4–20.
8. *The Fate of Homo Sapiens*, p. 311.
9. See, for example, Max Byrd, *Tristram Shandy* (George Allen and Unwin, 1985) *passim*, and Patricia Waugh, *Metafiction: The Theory and Practice of Self-Conscious Fiction* (Methuen, 1984) pp. 69–71.
10. Preface to the 1931 edition of *The Time Machine* (Random House).
11. Preface to the Atlantic edition of *Tono-Bungay*.
12. *Experiment in Autobiography*, pp. 503, 639.
13. *Tono-Bungay*, III, 2, 10.
14. Ibid., IV, 3, 1.
15. Bradbury, *The Social Context of Modern English Literature*, p. xxxii.
16. Malcolm Bradbury, *Possibilities: Essays on the State of the Novel* (Oxford University Press, 1973) pp. 81–2.
17. *Tono-Bungay*, III, 4, 3.
18. 'Pollock and the Porrah Man', *New Budget*, 23 May 1895. Reprinted in *The Plattner Story and Others*.
19. The manuscript of *Tono-Bungay* is preserved at the University of Illinois at Urbana-Champaign.
20. *Tono-Bungay*, I, 1, 3.
21. J. E. Cirlot, *A Dictionary of Symbols* (Routledge and Kegan Paul, 1962).
22. 'The Door in the Wall' was published in 1906. Wells was at work on *Tono-Bungay* throughout that year, completing the novel in the spring of 1908.
23. See, for example, *D. H. Lawrence: A Personal Record* by E. T. [Jessie Chambers] (Jonathan Cape, 1935) p. 121: 'I remember his telling me how Wells's *Tono-Bungay* made him feel in despair about himself.'
24. Parrinder, *H. G. Wells: The Critical Heritage*, p. 20.
25. *The World of William Clissold*, I, 12.
26. *The Passionate Friends*, II, 1; *The World of William Clissold*, II, 1; *Experiment in Autobiography*, pp. 132–8.
27. *Tono-Bungay*, II, 1, 1.
28. Ibid., II, 2, 3.
29. Ibid., III, 3, 5.
30. Lodge, *Language of Fiction*, p. 223.
31. *Tono-Bungay*, I, 1, 1.
32. West, *H. G. Wells: A Sketch for a Portrait*, p. 181.
33. *The History of Mr Polly*, ch. 7.
34. Introduction to *Rasselas* (Penguin English Library, 1976) p. 11.
35. John Fletcher, *Novel and Reader* (Marion Boyars, 1980) p. 182.
36. *Experiment in Autobiography*, pp. 114–15.
37. University of Chicago Press, 1980, pp. 4, 17.
38. N. and J. Mackenzie, *The Time Traveller*, p. 291; W. W. Wagar, *H. G. Wells and the World State* (Yale University Press) p. 110; J. Batchelor, *H. G. Wells* (Cambridge University Press, 1985) p. 122.
39. Preface to *Babes in the Darkling Wood* (1940).
40. Preface to Atlantic edition of *Boon*.
41. *Boon*, 2, 3.

42. Ibid., 7, 3.
43. West, *Principles and Persuasions*, p. 19.
44. Wells, 'The Contemporary Novel', in Edel and Ray, *Henry James and H. G. Wells.*
45. *Boon*, 7, 2.
46. Batchelor, *H. G. Wells*, p. 138.
47. *Experiment in Autobiography*, p. 501.
48. Cf. also *The Soul of a Bishop*, 5, 6. At the commencement of the bishop's vision 'something snapped – like the snapping of a lute string – in his brain'.
49. Introduction to *The Food of the Gods* (Atlantic Edition) vol. 5, p. ix.
50. Cf. Gordon N. Ray, *H. G. Wells and Rebecca West* (Macmillan, 1974) *passim.*
51. 'The Apple', *Idler*, October 1896; included in *The Plattner Story and Others.*
52. The Nazi Party was founded in Germany in January 1919.
53. Cf. Bennett, *Things That Have Interested Me* (1921–6) p. 191: 'I read *A Portrait of the Artist as a Young Man* under the hypnotic influence of H. G. Wells. Indeed, he commanded me to read it and to admire it extremely.'
54. *Experiment in Autobiography*, pp. 737–8, 739.
55. 'The Betterave Papers', *Cornhill Magazine*, July 1945.
56. *The World of William Clissold*, VI, 8.
57. *Experiment in Autobiography*, p. 740.
58. *Mr Blettsworthy on Rampole Island*, I, 1.
59. *Experiment in Autobiography*, p. 131.
60. *The World of William Clissold*, I, 15.
61. *Mr Blettsworthy on Rampole Island*, I, 2.
62. Wells to Julian Huxley, 12 February 1928.
63. Preface to *The Scientific Romances of H. G. Wells* (Gollancz, 1933).
64. *Mr Blettsworthy on Rampole Island*, IV, 7.
65. Ibid., I, 2.
66. Ibid., IV, 5.
67. Ibid., IV, 10.
68. Ibid., II, 10.
69. Ibid., I, 4.
70. *Experiment in Autobiography*, p. 503.
71. See Cedric Watts, *Conrad's 'Heart of Darkness': A Critical and Contextual Discussion* (Mursia International, 1977) pp. 55–6.
72. David J. Lake in 'The Whiteness of Griffin and H. G. Wells's Images of Death', *Science Fiction Studies*, vol. 8, no. 23 (March 1981) pp. 12–18, points out that 'Wells's names are often carefully symbolic'.
73. Cf. *The Island of Doctor Moreau*, 7: 'On the day of its publication a wretched dog, flayed and otherwise mutilated, escaped from Moreau's house.' For a comparison of allegorical texture see *Moreau*, 22, and *Mr Blettsworthy*, IV, 13.
74. Odette Keun, 'H. G. Wells: The Player', *Time and Tide*, 15 (1934) pp. 1249–51, 1307–9, 1346–48.
75. 'Scepticism of the Instrument', appendix to *A Modern Utopia*.

76. Preface to *The Scientific Romances of H. G. Wells* (1933).
77. Chapter IX of *The Way the World is Going* (1928).
78. Wells discusses the dialogue novel as a genre in 'The Novel of Ideas', the preface to *Babes in the Darkling Wood* (1940).
79. Cf. John Fowles's *The Ebony Tower* (1974), a novella which also explores the theme of divergent approaches to life and art.
80. J. Laplanche and J. B. Pontalis, *The Language of Psychoanalysis* (1973) p. 349.
81. *Experiment in Autobiography*, p. 499.
82. Introduction to West, *H. G. Wells: A Sketch for a Portrait*.
83. *Principles and Persuasions*, p. 20.
84. *Experiment in Autobiography*, p. 493.
85. 'The Betterave Papers', *Cornhill Magazine*, July 1945. Joyce died in January 1941, Virginia Woolf died in March 1941. Wells completed *You Can't Be Too Careful* in August of that year.
86. *H. G. Wells in Love*, ed. G. P. Wells (Faber and Faber, 1984) p. 225.
87. Peter Quennell, *Four Portraits* (Collins, 1945) p. 140.
88. 'The Contemporary Novel', in Edel and Ray, *Henry James and H. G. Wells*.
89. *The War of the Worlds*, I, 1.
90. *The Wheels of Chance*, XXVI.
91. Max Byrd, *Tristram Shandy* (George Allen and Unwin, 1985) p. 10.
92. Gillian Beer, *Darwin's Plots* (Ark, 1985) p. 13.
93. A. A. Medilow, 'The Revolt of Sterne', *Time and the Novel* (Peter Nevill, 1952) p. 158.
94. *Tono-Bungay*, I, 1, 2.

Bibliography

General

Robert Bloom, *Anatomies of Egotism: A Reading of the Last Novels of H. G. Wells* (University of Nebraska Press, 1977).

Malcolm Bradbury, *The Social Context of Modern English Literature* (Basil Blackwell, 1971).

Leon Edel and Gordon N. Ray (eds), *Henry James and H. G. Wells: A Record of their Friendship, their Debate on the Art of Fiction and their Quarrel* (Rupert Hart-Davis, 1958).

Royal A. Gettman (ed.), *George Gissing & H. G. Wells: A Record of their Friendship and Correspondence* (Rupert Hart-Davis, 1961).

J. R. Hammond, *An H. G. Wells Companion* (Macmillan, 1979).

J. R. Hammond, *H. G. Wells: An Annotated Bibliography of his Works* (Garland, 1977).

David Lodge, *The Novelist at the Crossroads* (Routledge and Kegan Paul, 1971).

Bernard Loing, *H. G. Wells à l'oeuvre* (Didier, 1984).

Norman and Jeanne Mackenzie, *The Time Traveller: The Life of H. G. Wells* (Weidenfeld and Nicolson, 1973).

Patrick Parrinder, *H. G. Wells* (Oliver and Boyd, 1970).

Patrick Parrinder (ed.), *H. G. Wells: The Critical Heritage* (Routledge and Kegan Paul, 1972).

Patrick Parrinder and Robert Philmus (eds), *H. G. Wells's Literary Criticism* (Harvester Press, 1980).

W. W. Robson, *Modern English Literature* (Oxford University Press, 1970).

W. Warren Wagar, *H. G. Wells and the World State* (Yale University Press, 1961).

H. G. Wells, 'The Betterave Papers', *Cornhill Magazine*, no. 965 (July 1945) pp. 349–63.

H. G. Wells, *Early Writings in Science and Science Fiction*, ed. Robert Philmus and David Y. Hughes (University of California Press, 1975).

H. G. Wells, *Experiment in Autobiography* (Gollancz and The Cresset Press, 1934).

H. G. Wells, *The Wealth of Mr Waddy* (Southern Illinois University Press, 1969).

Anthony West, *H. G. Wells: Aspects of a Life* (Hutchinson, 1984).

Geoffrey West, *H. G. Wells: A Sketch for a Portrait* (Howe, 1930).

Harris Wilson (ed.), *Arnold Bennett and H. G. Wells: A Record of a Personal and a Literary Friendship* (Rupert Hart-Davis, 1960).

Individual Works

The Time Machine
Text: *The Time Machine: An Invention* (London: Heinemann, 1895). It should be noted that there are significant differences in the text between the first American edition of *The Time Machine* (Henry Holt, New York, 1895) and the Heinemann edition. The Heinemann edition is directly ancestral to the present standard text, that of the Atlantic Edition of 1924, which differs from it in some minor emendations and a rearrangement of the chapter divisions. An episode omitted from all previous book editions and featuring kangaroo creatures and giant insects is published in *Three Prophetic Novels of H. G. Wells*, ed. E. F. Bleiler (Dover, New York, 1960).

Criticism:
Bernard Bergonzi, 'The Publication of *The Time Machine*, 1894–5', *Review of English Studies*, n.s., vol. XI, no. 41 (February 1960) pp. 42–51.
Bernard Bergonzi, 'The Time Machine: an Ironic Myth', *The Critical Quarterly*, Winter 1960, pp. 293–305.
Bernard Bergonzi, *The Early H. G. Wells* (Manchester University Press, 1961).
David J. Lake, 'The Drafts of *The Time Machine*, 1894', *The Wellsian*, n.s. no. 3 (Spring 1980) pp. 6–13.
Patrick Parrinder, 'The Time Machine: H. G. Wells's Journey through Death', *The Wellsian*, n.s. no. 4 (1981) pp. 15–23.
Robert M. Philmus, 'The Time Machine; or, the Fourth Dimension as Prophecy', *PMLA*, 84 (1969).
H. G. Wells, Preface to *The Time Machine* (Random House, 1931).

Tono-Bungay
Text: *Tono-Bungay* (London: Macmillan, 1909; New York: Duffield, 1909). A critical edition with an introduction and notes by A. C. Ward was published by Longmans, Green (Heritage of Literature series) in 1961.

Criticism:
Jerome Hamilton Buckley, 'H. G. Wells, The Hero as Scientist', in *Season of Youth: The Bildungsroman from Dickens to Golding* (Harvard University Press, 1974).
Lucille Herbert, 'Tono-Bungay: Tradition and Experiment', *Modern Language Quarterly*, vol. 33 (1972). Reprinted in Bergonzi (ed.), *H. G. Wells: A Collection of Critical Essays* (Prentice-Hall, 1976) pp. 140–56.
David Lodge, 'Tono-Bungay and the Condition of England', in *Language of Fiction* (Routledge and Kegan Paul, 1966).
Kenneth B. Newell, 'The Structure of H. G. Wells's Tono-Bungay', *English Fiction in Transition*, vol. IV (1961) 1–8.
Max A. Webb, 'The Missing Father and the Theme of Alienation in H. G. Wells's Tono-Bungay', *English Literature in Transition*, vol. 18, no. 4 (1975) pp. 243–7.

The History of Mr Polly
Text: *The History of Mr Polly* (London: Nelson, 1910; New York: Duffield, 1910). A critical edition with an introduction by Gordon N. Ray was published by Houghton Mifflin, Boston, in 1960. The edition includes an appendix containing two successive versions of the final page and a cancelled passage from ch. IV.

Criticism:
Gordon N. Ray, 'H. G. Wells Tries to be a Novelist', *English Institute Essays* (1959) pp. 106–59.
Christopher Rolfe, 'A Blaze and New Beginnings: the Ironic Use of Myth in *The History of Mr Polly*', *The Wellsian*, n.s. no. 4 (1981) pp. 24–35.

Boon
Text: *Boon, The Mind of the Race, The Wild Asses of the Devil, and The Last Trump*: Prepared for publication by Reginald Bliss, with an ambiguous introduction by H. G. Wells (London: Fisher Unwin, 1915; New York: Doran, 1915).

Criticism:
John Batchelor, *H. G. Wells* (Cambridge University Press, 1985).
Lovat Dickson, *H. G. Wells: His Turbulent Life and Times* (Macmillan, 1969).

Men Like Gods
Text: *Men Like Gods* (London: Cassell, 1923; New York: Macmillan, 1923).

Criticism:
John Batchelor, *H. G. Wells* (Cambridge University Press, 1985).
Geoffrey Leeper, 'The Happy Utopias of Aldous Huxley and H. G. Wells', *Meanjin* (1965) 24.

The World of William Clissold
Text: *The World of William Clissold: A Novel at a New Angle* (London: Ernest Benn, 1926; New York: Doran, 1926).

Criticism:
Patrick Parrinder (ed.), *H. G. Wells: The Critical Heritage* (Routledge and Kegan Paul, 1972).

Mr Blettsworthy on Rampole Island
Text: *Mr Blettsworthy on Rampole Island* (London: Ernest Benn, 1928; New York: Doubleday, Doran, 1928).

Criticism:
John Batchelor, *H. G. Wells* (Cambridge University Press, 1985).

Alfred Borrello, *H. G. Wells: Author in Agony* (Southern Illinois University Press, 1972).
Roger Bowen, '*Mr Blettsworthy on Rampole Island*: The Story of a Gentleman of Culture and Refinement', *The Wellsian*, n.s. no. 2 (1978) pp. 6–21.
J. R. Hammond, 'Three Satirical Novels', *The Wellsian*, vol. II, no. 3 (1968) pp. 16–19.

The Croquet Player
Text: *The Croquet Player: A Story* (London: Chatto and Windus, 1936; New York: Viking, 1937).

Criticism:
J. R. Hammond, 'Three Satirical Novels', *The Wellsian*, vol. II, no. 3 (1968) pp. 16–19.
William J. Scheick, 'Exorcising the Ghost Story': Wells's *The Croquet Player* and *The Camford Visitation*', *Cahiers Victoriens et Edouardiens*, vol. 17 (April 1983).

The Brothers
Text: *The Brothers: A Story* (London, Chatto and Windus, 1938; New York: Viking).

Criticism:
Gloria Glikin Fromm, 'Through the Novelist's Looking-Glass', *Kenyon Review*, vol. 31 (1969). Reprinted in Bergonzi (ed.), *H. G. Wells: A Collection of Critical Essays* (Englewood Cliffs, N. J., Prentice-Hall, 1976), pp. 157–77.

You Can't Be Too Careful
Text: *You Can't Be Too Careful: A Sample of Life, 1901–1951* (London: Secker and Warburg, 1941; New York: Putnam, 1942).

Index

221